LADIES AND GENTLEMEN

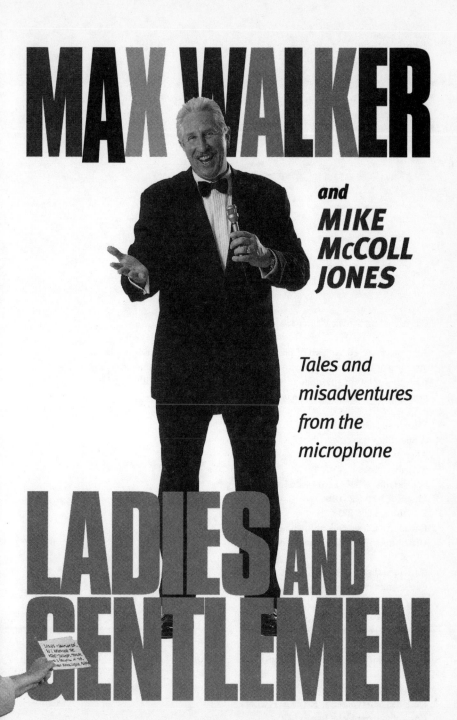

MAX WALKER

and
MIKE
McCOLL
JONES

Tales and
misadventures
from the
microphone

LADIES AND GENTLEMEN

A Sue Hines Book
Allen & Unwin

First published in 1999
A Sue Hines Book
Allen & Unwin Pty Ltd
9 Atchison Street
St Leonards, NSW 1590, Australia
Phone: (61 2) 8425 0100
Fax: (61 2) 9906 2218
E-mail: frontdesk@allen-unwin.com.au
URL: http://www.allen-unwin.com.au

National Library of Australia
Cataloguing-in-Publication entry:

Walker, Max, 1948–.
Ladies and gentlemen.
ISBN 186508 080 2.
1. Australian wit and humor. I. McColl Jones, Mike. II. Title.
A828.302

Designed and typeset by P.A.G.E. Pty Ltd
Cover photography by Barrie Bell
Printed by Griffin Press

10 9 8 7 6 5 4 3 2 1

*To my father Big Max . . . how lucky I am to have a
mate like him. He encouraged me to laugh through
many of life's examinations . . . he helped me
understand why and showed me how—a genuine
lover of people.*

Dad, this book is a tribute to you.

Max Jr

To my mum.

*Apart from being there, like all mothers, my mum
was a never-ending source of encouragement,
especially in those early years. She never lost faith
in me, nor did I in her.*

*At some stage of every day, I unconsciously say
'Gee, I must ring Mum to tell her that . . .'
and suddenly realise that not even Telstra can
help me with the number.*

*I dedicate this book to her and the rich memory
that she has left behind on earth.*

Mother dear . . . thank you!

Mike

Contents

Foreword

In 354 Aristotle wrote, 'Public Speaking is an Art'. I am sure that he could not have imagined the breadth and depth of the importance of the spoken word as a communication tool in today's society. Public speaking is the foundation of the corporate conference, the essence of the social function and the fabric of the media. Almost everyone is faced, at some time or other, with the challenge of speaking in public—be it the 21st birthday toast, the presentation of a product or the full-scale after-dinner speech. It is universally accepted that the prospect of having to deliver a speech turns all the but the rarest of individuals into something varying from nervous to a shivering mass of jelly.

Ladies and Gentlemen examines the phenomenon of speaking in public and looks at some of the most remarkable examples of the best and the worst of those very special occasions where one is called upon to say a few words.

I first became aware of the industry (and it is now very much so) in 1989. I was fortunate to meet the doyen of the speaking industry, Joan Saxton, who founded the first public speakers' bureau in Australia in 1965. Shortly thereafter, my partner Nanette and I purchased her business and Joan became a very close friend.

It seemed a fairly straightforward business: get the speaker right; the timing right; the introductions right; the travel; pitch it at the right level for the audience—and there was much more. To be successful it is necessary to mesh together a myriad of factors. A failure of any one of them could lead to disaster.

Over the last ten years we are proud to say that Saxton has become one of the leading bureaux in the world. This is unquestionably due to not only the Saxton team but also to some of the very special speakers who we represent.

In the early days, one of those who particularly stood out from the rest was Max Walker. I remembered him well as a cricketer, even as an England supporter. He was the man who landed on the wrong foot, had the uncanny knack of being able to destroy an innings and who could develop a rapport, even without a microphone, with the multitudes in Bay 13. Max has become a speaking phenomenon, having been described early in his speaking career as being able to speak under water with a mouthful of marbles. He has established himself as a legend in the speaking arena. Today he remains one of the most sought-after speakers in Australia and, increasingly, internationally—be it for his motivational addresses or for his characteristic brand of wit and entertainment.

In this work, Max teams up with a different kind of wordsmith in Mike McColl Jones, known for many years for his comedy writing and television production.

Ladies and Gentlemen has something for everyone. It is readable, gives an insight into the remarkable world of the speaking professional, and has a host of helpful hints showing how almost anyone can improve their public speaking skills. I'm delighted to be able to recommend it.

Winston Broadbent
Managing Director
Saxton Speakers' Bureau
www.saxton.com.au

Acknowledgements

My father Big Max told me many years ago that 'anything you are good at will contribute to your happiness'. Great advice.

The success of this tome would not have been possible without the support of many people. People are like elastic when asked for help: the more work they have to do, the more they stretch. And stretch they did.

Our ability to communicate with one another will always be proportionate to the sort of success we can achieve.

Mike and I would like to say thank you to everyone who contributed their creative energies to make *Ladies and Gentlemen* a reality, not merely just a good idea.

Firstly, our respective wives, Kerry and Val, who sanctioned the intrusive writing process that stole so much precious family time.

To all those people who, for decades, have been enthused by what we've said and written.

A lifetime cast of characters who have been impossible to forget . . . many of whom have enriched our experiences and eventually wandered into the pages of this book.

Our mentors young and old.

A special thank you to Joan Saxton for crank-starting the speaking profession in Australia . . . and her legacy.

Winston Broadbent and Nanette Moulton and the dedicated team at the Saxton Speakers' Bureau for creating so many opportunities to talk.

Bert Newton, Dr Don Jeffreys, Steve Vizard and Dr John Tickell for their generous advice and contribution.

To the masters of the thin and thick black line—Bill (Weg) Green,

George Haddon and Mark Knight for allowing us to feature their collective talents.

To Barrie Bell, Bruce Magilton and the other men and women who captured the photographic moments that enhance the message of this book.

AFL coaches Ron Barassi, David Parkin and Kevin Sheedy who were so open in sharing their passion for imparting the spoken word to their troops.

To all of our colleagues and friends in television, radio and the print media.

To my little mate Lou Richards and Stephen Phillips for research into those early sportsnights . . . and their friendship.

Fellow speakers and performers who have shared a microphone and stage . . . so much to learn from.

To Sue Hines, Foong Ling Kong and the entire Allen & Unwin gang . . . for their amazing transformation of a patchwork, often handwritten, manuscript into this very professional book. To Neil Conning for his editor's scalpel—sharp and clean!

Sara Kennedy and staff at the Rydges Riverwalk Hotel in Melbourne. They now know for sure it was a book we were nurturing!

The exercise has been a huge challenge . . . words do not seem a sufficient way to say thanks. But thank you all from the bottom of our hearts. Your generosity is the mortar between the building blocks.

Fear is the darkroom where negatives are developed. We trust this book will switch on the darkroom light, forever leaving the fear of public speaking in public untenable.

Max Walker

To Speak or Not to Speak

The three most difficult things in life: number one,
kissing a woman when she's leaning backwards;
number two, climbing a wall that's leaning forward;
number three, speaking in public.

ATTRIBUTED TO WINSTON CHURCHILL

All the great speakers were bad speakers at first.

RALPH WALDO EMERSON, 1803–82

The beads of perspiration were as large as 20-cent pieces . . .
multiplying rapidly until eventually a trickle began to run down
his rather prominent nose. His throat became parched . . . as dry as
the Nullarbor. His heart was trying to leap through his rib-cage. His
eyes were open, but not seeing, and he was almost choking in a
failed attempt to breathe normally. The audience totally understood the speaker's predicament (they always do).

He was using the lectern as a crutch . . . still yet to utter those
familiar opening words, 'Ladies and Gentlemen'. A mild sort of

panic set in. His head was spinning from the reams of foolscap jottings he agonised over until 3 a.m. The words are on the sheets of paper stacked neatly on the lectern, yet he cannot see them, and even worse, he can't say them! The paralysis of fear had set in.

This unfortunately is such a common occurrence—a man or woman, boy or girl forced into the terrifying role of standing up and attempting to speak to a crowded room. Even the description above does not convey adequately the sheer terror involved for some people confronting a jury-like gathering of people.

To a great majority of the western world, the examination is looked upon as a fate worse than death. For my part, I was only twelve years of age when I was cajoled into experiencing that very same fear. It all began with my best mate's dad reckoning I was gutless—and he was right! I'd refused to enter the school lecturette competition.

Now being a young man of principle, to be tagged 'gutless' was totally unacceptable, and in terms of an old sporting cliché, for the first time in my life I had to dig deeper than I ever had dug before. Right on the 'death', I relented and agreed to participate. (At least then I wasn't an outcast.) Mind you, it may have been better being a gutless outcast.

This was to be a decision which shaped my life beyond the indelible classrooms of the Friends' School, Hobart, Tasmania.

The first big question to answer was—what could this son of a Master builder and hotel proprietor talk about that would keep an audience spellbound for five minutes? My mate John had confided in me that his topic would be: 'The Impact of the Presidency of J.F.K. on the People of the United States of America'.

I don't have to tell you that John was one hell of a smart guy, and predictably went on to become a school Prefect. I suppose I took the easy way out, as so many people often do—they attempt to regurgitate words or facts that were given birth to by someone else.

Back in 1961, the best source of reference was undoubtedly the Encyclopaedia Britannica. (The reference library cost about $1500, and was sold to your parents, usually your dad late on a Friday night, by a door-to-door salesman. Nowadays, you can buy it complete on a CD-ROM for under two hundred dollars.)

Not wanting to get too highbrow, I chose for my topic 'The Tiger', probably because it was an animal I was fascinated by, and the big book had plenty of info that I could lift almost completely.

On the day, John spoke before me, which made my task even tougher. The bulging Middle School hall, full of parents and friends, loved what he had to say. In other words, he was extremely good.

A clear fact. It's always very difficult to follow a speaker who has absolutely 'brained' them.

MAX AT TWELVE . . . MORE SHOTS THAN STORIES.

I knew I was in trouble the moment the headmaster mentioned my name. At the time, the walk down the aisle, up the polished timber stairs to the lectern on stage took on the dimensions of the long, lonely trek from the players' dressing room to the middle of the Melbourne Cricket Ground in front of a crowd of 50,000.

All those symptoms mentioned at the start of this chapter took a vice-like grip over my body. I'd never experienced fear like it! The crazy thing was that I couldn't pinpoint what I was actually frightened of—failure, embarrassment, peer rejection, stupidity? Would I become a quadrangle joke?

Whatever it was, one thing was for certain. There was an urgent and extra pressure for my bowels to open.The tension in my neck and throat muscles was suffocating. Nobody had suggested how important relaxed and correct breathing was to performance.

I'd carefully prepared five pages of word-perfect prose, direct from the encyclopaedia. At precisely the same moment as I began to speak, someone opened the back stage door, and as if in a wind tunnel, my five beautiful pages fluttered and floated from the elevated stage into the stunned audience.

They just hung in the air like my pause. A large neon sign appeared in my head WHERE TO NOW? I could just make out another one—HELP! At that stage I made a commitment to myself. I would never put myself into such a terrible predicament again.

What followed was THE GET OUT OF HERE STAKES. I came out with a rather disjointed series of thoughts describing a large four-legged animal with bright eyes, large paws and big teeth, easily distinguishable by its black and yellow markings. Fortunately I'd remembered its name—but that was about all I could remember.

I'm sure I didn't speak for five minutes, and it felt like an eternity before my rubbery legs could carry me back to the safety and anonymity of my seat. John was assessed with an 'A' mark, while yours truly was given a pathetic 'C minus'.

Pathetic it may have been—but how often do we learn more from our failures than our successes. That experience was a huge lesson about the value of homework, preparation, confidence and performance.

What a different scenario it was when entertaining seven or eight mates with the retelling of an anecdotal yarn in the comfort and security of the playground's familiar territory. Charged with enthusiasm and a captive audience, it all seems so easy. Change the surroundings and the audience, and it all seems so hard.

Maybe my ability to spin a yarn stems from this beginning. Or perhaps it was from being a seriously interested witness to a police apprehension on the first floor of my old man's pub, the Empire in Elizabeth Street, North Hobart.

My sister Lexie and I had just lobbed home after a torrid day of classroom captivity. Hardly unusual, but the arrival of a police car and the serious looking constables was something that instantly grabbed my interest. It was shortly to be revealed where my sister's missing piggy bank and Beatles and Rolling Stones record collection had disappeared to.

The suspect's name was Frances Anne Sullivan, a hard-faced lady, who to me had always seemed very friendly. Maybe my dad knew differently. Anyway, she was now a prime suspect in the Great Piggy Bank Heist.

The plan of attack was to raid her room with police authority and catch her by surprise. The plan couldn't have worked better from this 12-year-old boy's point-of-view. As the police crashed through the door of Room 2, I claimed the particularly fantastic vantage point beside the crack between the door and door jamb.

I couldn't believe what I saw! Up until then I'd been led to believe that taking a peek at Lady Godiva riding bareback could send a young man blind. I don't know what Lady Godiva looked like, but Frances Anne Sullivan, a flaming and natural redhead, was certainly taken by surprise. Imagine the two boys in blue, expecting to find a piggy bank full of coins, but instead being confronted by a naked and outraged lady of the night, who had just completed a daytime matinee.

The 'client' was a lonely looking Japanese fisherman, seated on a chair at the end of the bed attempting to suppress a nervous smile, while tying the bows in his bootlaces. Within seconds, the fair-skinned Frances Anne occupied centre-stage on the double bed. Like a caged tiger, she held a high-heeled shoe in each hand with the intention to decapitate, or seriously maim her old foe— the coppers. What an eyeful I was copping from my vantage point. I'd never seen a naked woman in the flesh, so to speak—and oh so animated! To this day I'll never forget the sheer fury of that spirited woman venting her anger.

It took a tackle round the ankles from one of them to bring her crashing down. The second constable literally fell on top of her, pinning her arms and white shoes to the bed with his sheer bulk.

At this stage, Exhibit A, the piggy-bank, hadn't even been sighted. The Japanese client took advantage of the confusion to bolt down the stairs and into a taxi. I know it's thirty years later, but I've got a feeling that the runner hasn't yet recovered from that fright, and he's still on the run—but no doubt still smiling.

The incident took five minutes from entry to capture, to charge, but like slow motion, in retelling it, I was able to milk it for ten minutes, and on one occasion I think the story commandeered the entire recess break.

A week later the adventure was reaping a cult-like following. Can you believe it—kids were offering to buy me anything up to a coffee-scroll if I'd tell the story. And with each retelling, the yarn grew bigger, bolder and better.

In captivating an audience, subject matter is all important. So is the language of telling the story—a little bit of creative licence in the crusade to bring to life your story.

It's a blending of harnessing that fear and feeling relaxed with a group of people whom you regard as your friends. If you can keep them happy, chances are you're doing it right.

It's a good idea to try out new material on your friends, because honest to the back teeth, your friends will only laugh or listen if what you have to say is good.

In captivating an audience, subject matter is all important.

I am not on my own when it comes to having a terrifying experience. Back in the early 1970s, the 'King' of daytime TV, Mike Walsh and Mike McColl Jones used to 'do lunch' on a

Common situations invoking social phobias

Performance situations

- public speaking
- eating in front of others
- writing in front of others
- speaking in a group
- drinking in front of others
- entering a room where others are seated
- using public toilets

Interaction situations

- interacting with others
- conversing on the telephone
- speaking with strangers
- dating
- interacting with the opposite sex
- attending social gatherings
- dealing with authority figures
- negotiating with others

Common somatic symptoms

- palpitations (79%)
- trembling (75%)
- sweating (74%)
- tense muscles (64%)
- sinking feeling in the stomach (63%)
- dry throat (61%)
- hot and cold feelings including blushing (57%)
- pressure in the head (46%)

Symptoms of a panic attack

- palpitations, pounding heart or accelerated heart beat
- sweating
- trembling or shaking
- dyspnoea
- feeling of choking
- chest pain or discomfort
- nausea or abdominal distress
- feeling dizzy, unsteady, light headed or faint
- derealisation or depersonalisation
- feelings of losing control or going crazy
- fear of dying
- paraesthesia
- chills or hot flushes

Dr Don Jeffreys
PhD, BA, BEd,
MACE, MAPS

regular basis. In fact, the two Mikes had such a good time that many hotels and restaurants used to try to bid to gain their business. On one of these days, Mike Walsh suggested they get an early start.

I'll let Mike McColl Jones tell the story.

On this particular day, neither of us had a show to worry about, so the combination was a bit lethal. We met at Mike Walsh's parents' pub, the Royal Oak in North Fitzroy, at about 10 a.m. We had a nice chat (and several drinks) with his dad Mick. Mike remembered there was a fashion parade and luncheon at the Southern Cross Hotel, so of course we went there.

About 3 p.m. we were really enjoying ourselves. We'd already solved the problems of TV worldwide, politics, foreign affairs, and we were heading into familiar territory, solving all the problems of the Catholic church. By this time we really needed a drink, so we adjourned to Lou Richards' famous Press Bar at the Phoenix Hotel.

We propped there for a while, and explained our views on practically anything to practically anybody who was bored enough to listen. After this we had to go to dinner, and it was during the main course that Mike said, 'You really should forget your fear of going on TV, and come on my *Midday Show* and talk about practical jokes.'

The next morning my throat felt like it had been massaged with steel wool. I vaguely remembered the conversation with Mike the night before. 'He'll forget,' I said to myself, knowing he wouldn't. Mike didn't forget a thing, let alone something like

9

me appearing on his show. Soon afterwards, his personal assistant rang and told me she had my flight details.

I knew I'd been caught, but I had a major problem. Now I was sober! There was nowhere to go. I couldn't say, 'Buy me another drink, ho ho, of course I'll appear on your TV show. Me, nervous? Naaahh—it'll be a breeze.'

Flying to Sydney I was almost ill with fear. I remember saying, almost out loud, 'Please dear God, I know it's rough on the other passengers, but please let us crash.' (If any of you were flying on that plane, I do apologise for such a terrible thought.)

I was soon in a car heading towards Channel 10. Once I was in a Sydney cab, I didn't have to pray for a crash. It was likely to happen anyway.

A while later in makeup, Mike popped in to say hello. He wondered why I'd been in the chair for 35 minutes. One of the girls explained that as soon as they put the Max Factor on my face, it flowed off—with the sweat being generated by fear. Mike went back to his dressing room with an odd look on his face.

Somehow or other, the makeup girls worked their magic and managed to coat enough pan-stick on my face, by mixing it with Clag.

I was finally ready to go on. As I was waiting for Mike to introduce me I remember saying in my mind: 'Dear God—I know the plane crash was out of the question, but how about an earthquake?'

'. . . Please welcome my first guest, Mike McColl Jones.'

I walked out. The lights were bright, the audience was

clapping. I didn't know why—I knew there wasn't much chance of entertainment for them here.

Mike went to shake my hand and I think this was the moment when he realised that all was not going to be apples and cream. I looked into his eyes and saw genuine concern. He looked into mine and saw abject fear.

I looked at the coffee table, and the small cards that I'd printed for cues to stories, jokes, etc.—but I actually saw nothing. Several members of the production crew were frantically running around looking for tissues and towels to try to stem the Niagara-type flow that was coming from my body.

The good news is that as far as I can find out there is no copy of that interview on tape or film anywhere. The bad news is that I can still remember the occasion as if it were yesterday!

Mike Walsh, by the way, had a great method by which he assessed the 'interest level' of his studio audience during an interview. He called it the Mike Walsh 'cough count'. If, during an interview, he heard more than just the usual few coughs coming from the audience, he knew it was time to wind up the chat and get rid of the guest as soon as possible.

Yes . . . it always gets back to knowing your audience and maintaining their level of interest. There are many parallels between speaking and sport. Old and new injuries are difficult to totally recover from. Intensive rehabilitation is required. The best way, of course, is to be so well prepared physically and emotionally that injury . . . or humiliation and fear are prevented from occurring.

None the less, every now and then one feels the phantom described as 'remembered' pain—a combination of self-doubt and the mind playing tricks. That's why initially a fitness test is necessary to suss out where the body and mind are at.

Well, almost thirty years after leaving the Friends' School, I was invited back to address the assembly. Weeks before I crossed Bass Strait, I started to wonder what it was going to be like, how much had changed.

Visiting the school again was part of the promotional tour for a book I had just completed with my dad, appropriately titled *A Chip Off the Old Block.*

We would return to the Empire Hotel where I grew up in Big Max's shadow. We also paid a nostalgic visit to the TCA ground above the Derwent River where we both played cricket for North Hobart.

Each location, once revisited, unlocked a filing cabinet of dusty memories and emotions. Yet it was going back to school that brought to the surface an immediate sense of trepidation. The extraordinary mix of learning the academic curriculum and learning to overcome the constant fear of failure. Peer-group pressure was a powerful engine . . . so many wrong turns.

Officially within the walls of the classrooms the fear of letting both parents and self down was extremely motivating for those who could harness it.

In the presence of the headmaster or deputy head, a kind of short-term mental and physical paralysis overcame me. So imagine how I felt standing in front of the current generation of students! In 1997, Stephanie Oates and her husband were the joint heads of the school. Three decades before, Mr Bill Oates, Stephanie's father, was the boss.

I could sense her gaze . . . it made me feel the same as I used to as a teenager. Surely I had improved in my time away from this place of learning?

The audience was complex, even though they were students. The ages varied by six or seven years . . . you

> **In the presence of the headmaster or deputy head, a kind of short-term mental and physical paralysis overcame me**

don't need me to explain the difference between the mind of an eleven or twelve-year-old versus that of a seventeen or an eighteen-year-old. My brief was to entertain and inspire all of them, and my learned friends. It felt like an assignment that would be marked!

I never did get my official mark, but the incident proved to me that I could overcome collected and dormant fear with practice and experience. It made me appreciate how young my mind is, how much capacity it has to be stretched.

You, too, can improve your presentation and communication skills with time and practice. Want to improve, and provide the creative energy to make it happen.

By merely opening this book, you are already on your way. As Seeker Bruce Woodley says, 'Carry your dreams in your pocket'.

Make memories . . . and your fears will dissolve.

BACK TO SCHOOL FOR BIG MAX AND LITTLE MAX—AFTER 30 YEARS ONLY THEIR SIZE HAD CHANGED!

2

A Funny Thing Happened
on the Way to . . .

There is no security in this life, only opportunity.

DOUGLAS MACARTHUR

Never knock back a chance to speak.

MAX WALKER

It took most of puberty for the mental scars earned on that stage at school to heal. Then in my Matriculation year I was confronted once again with the same dilemma: how do I overcome my fear of speaking in assembly?

Peer group pressure and elementary lessons in communications grasped in the quadrangle helped. Let's call that environment a more relaxed audience. But not always cooperative.

Over a time spanning the following 2000 days or so I gained much self-confidence in my various learned skills and abilities. Respect earned accompanied me on the journey. By final year I had been named as a Prefect and Captain of the school football team and the first XI. As a consequence, I had to stand in front of the entire school every Monday morning to present a sports update.

Even then I was being judged. At the conclusion of one assembly, I was summoned to a rendezvous with Miss Yeates, our legendary English mistress. Over the years I had stood outside her office many times due to my defective use of the English language, and the inability to recite poetry or Shakespeare.

'With less than 60 seconds remaining, Scotty Grant grabbed the ball, balked, weaved and hammered home the final nail in the Hutchins coffin for an unforgettable three-point victory.'

It was revealed to me eyeball-to-eyeball that there was definitely no place for this manner of colourful sports reporting at the Friends' School.

> *For a while this tête-à-tête with the most feared woman at school diminished or stunted the growth of a unique turn of phrase.*

For a while this tête-à-tête with the most feared woman at school diminished or stunted the growth of a unique turn of phrase. Almost thirty years later, with much experience, I was invited home to a 100-year school reunion, held at the Wrest Point casino. When I think back, my headmaster in the 1960s, Mr Bill Oates, may have had a serious problem with the casino as a venue because Friends' was a Quaker school. I guess a compromise was reached.

During formal recollections of a time three decades past, I just had to mention Miss Yeates. Earlier that evening, I kissed her on the cheek for the first time. I now realise how lucky I had been to be under her watchful eye in the back row of my English classes. She was a perfectionist and strong disciplinarian. Her pupils' academic results were outstanding over time.

So, I couldn't let the opportunity pass by without publicly thanking her for a huge contribution to my literary efforts. At first she blushed with genuine embarrassment. But it was difficult to detect what she was really feeling and thinking as I listed on one hand several of my literary triumphs: *How to Hypnotise a Chook*, *How to Tame a Lion*, *How to Kiss a Crocodile*, and *How to Puzzle a Python*.

Afterwards we engaged in some mutual admiration and an honest chat—a conversation I'll treasure till my meter expires. We spoke about creativity, spontaneity and finding your own voice—the same stuff she had attempted to communicate to her classes all those years ago.

To be a great communicator, or to be heard, firstly you have to be understood. I can't thank my most unlikely mentor enough for helping me to understand the English language and how it works. But sometimes I still let her down!

It has been suggested that the moment somebody opens their mouth to speak, they reveal the level of education they have undertaken. How true. We witness it every day.

I would never have imagined during those formative adolescent years of study and games that there would be a career for me in the ability to construct interesting sentences, both scripted and ad-lib.

I could kick a football, bowl a cricket ball, and draw a line, but never imagined a professional life in close proximity to a microphone.

The next half dozen years whirred by in fast ambitious FORWARD mode. 'Home' was the Melbourne Cricket Ground. During RMIT holidays I worked at the historic ground painting the rows of thousands of seats that run the circumference of the hallowed turf. At first a sanding-back to remove splinters and dead paint, and next the red-lead undercoat, followed by a further two coats of green all-weather paint. By this stage my back would be crying out to be straightened from the human question mark it had become.

My two partners in this never-ending task were Dave and a wonderful guy named Joe Kinnear. You could say I was their apprentice or 'gofer'. Both loved a laugh, and if I could provide one it would get me a seat ahead, albeit under threat of painting well into 'overtime' if my attempts at humour were duds.

My incentive to collect new material on a daily basis became No. 1 priority. This ritual of attempting to make two ageing lads in overalls laugh while seated alone in the area near Bay 13, at the base of the old Southern Stand, under a fierce summer sun, became invaluable as the years rolled on. Practice will not make you perfect but believe me, it does make you a whole lot better, even when you're painting seats and telling yarns.

Take the night of my first big gig—a businessmen's dinner at the Courthouse Hotel in Brunswick, Victoria. I was there only because former Australian captain and pigeon lover, Bill Lawry, had pulled out the night before. Maybe he received a better offer.

As the night unfolded, I found myself in the very difficult position of speaking last. Kevin Sheedy, the evergreen Essendon football coach, was then a cheeky back-pocket player for Richmond. He claimed that his coach, the teetotalling Tom Hafey, wanted him out of the hotel early. And Dr Rudi Webster, the West Indian fast bowler, reckoned he was still on medical duty and would have to leave as soon as he finished speaking— which left yours truly to bring home the night through a gathering of half-filled beer jugs and glasses.

> *To be a great communicator, or to be heard, firstly you have to be understood.*

One speaker had peppered his contribution with several big-noting football names and anecdotes. The giant 'quick' from the Caribbean talked about the great Sir Gary Sobers, legend Wesley Hall, the notorious Charlie Griffiths and the 'run machine', Rohan Kanhai.

With a sporting career in its embryonic stages what could I possibly offer to top them? Maybe why I preferred Dulux to Taubmans on the MCG seats? Did Bill Lawry specialise in pidgin English? Nothing! I thought to myself. My predicament was serious—how could I get out of there without making a fool of myself?

I decided NOT to try name-dropping but used the tried and true material that moved Dave and Joe to laugh. Incredibly, my offering worked. And yes, I enjoyed the applause that closed the night.

From this lone night came a slow trickle of invitations to Lions, Rotary and Apex clubs. These institutions became for me a wonderful vehicle for practising my craft, and honing my skills in front of a real audience. No pay but invaluable experience. I also ended up with a great collection of silver spoons, biros and logoed pewter goblets.

> **Don't tell your audience you will not speak for long. They won't believe you.**

On my return from the Australian cricket tour of the West Indies in 1973 I was invited to attend the Carbine Club cricket luncheon. The manager and captain of the team were special guests Bill Jacobs and Ian Chappell (who had to accept wearing a tie for the occasion).

Today the Carbine Club, named after the mighty thoroughbred, Carbine, is one of the most respected luncheon clubs in Australia. It has sister clubs in New Zealand, Hong Kong, Papua New Guinea, London and South Africa. Speakers are not offered a fee. An amazing collection of people including prime ministers, Prince Charles, Sir Edmund Hillary and many sporting legends, have all addressed the club.

Way back then, as is the case today, lunch is held in camera. In other words, what is uttered in the confines of the gathering is a privilege to hear and is not to be leaked to the press.

Both Bill and the skipper were questioned on the highlights and various trying aspects of touring overseas. We had won the series 2–0, which gave everyone a reason to be positive and smile. The answers flowed from both men like well-timed cover drives.

In the 1970s, players were asked to sign a clause in their Australian Cricket Board contracts which meant they were not allowed to comment on any tours until three months after the Test series was completed. Only the captain and manager were allowed their voice. How times have changed. (Every player in the Australian test team which contested the 1998–99 Ashes series had either written a book or was in the process of having a tome published, and many have magazine and newspaper columns.)

That bleak day in May 1973, behind closed doors at the old Australia Hotel in Melbourne, gave me an opportunity to have a say. Before long, attention moved away from the two outspoken leaders to the player.

'Can Max answer a question or two?' one club member asked the President. Little did I know at the time, but what transpired turned out to be the formative stage of a career in public speaking.

Unlike Bill and Ian, I started talking about barbed wire fences, Jamaicans 'necking' bottles of rum in the freedom stands (trees); alsatian dogs with rolled up upper lips revealing sharp menacing teeth; policemen with truncheons, machine guns, and perspex shields; and marijuana smoke wafting into my very large nostrils at deep fine leg from the rasta boys seated in the back row of the bamboo grandstands.

There were to be many more experiences of touring to talk about and mould into captivating yarns. The microphone had become less intimidating. I joined the ranks of sportsnight trail blazers: 'Have Tongue and Tale—Will Travel!'

About four decades back my little mate, Lou Richards (ex-Collingwood captain and 'Kiss of Death'), Channel 7's Ron Casey, Doug Ring (leg spinner extraordinaire and member of Don Bradman's 'Invincibles'), Bill Collins (horse racing legend and 'The Accurate One') and Colin Long (former Davis Cup player), set the guidelines for an amazing trend which is still very much alive and kicking. Jack Dyer, the infamous 'Captain Blood', also became part of the touring panel—adding his unique brand of football language and humour.

It began as a concept to get radio station 3DB more exposure throughout Victoria. Every week the lads would spin their yarns to adoring audiences in townships everywhere. In the beginning, they travelled hundreds of miles for free. 3DB became more popular and the clubs made a profit on the side. Everyone was a winner.

Before long, the team members were paid for their troubles, on top of the free beer and petrol money. Each personality was an integral part of Channel 7's *World of Sport* program, which, when the curtain finally closed, was the longest running television program in its original format, on the planet. Not bad for a collection of mischievous old sporting types in Melbourne. In fact, the Sunday morning Slobs of Sport became part of the school curriculum—a must-watch if a kid was to keep up with the schoolyard conversations at recess and lunchtime.

The life of *World of Sport*, spanning an amazing 28 years, was a classic case of—'If it ain't broke, why fix it?' Television programmers of the 1990s would get the yips merely trying to comprehend that sort of life on the screen.

Max and Lou Richards: Inseparable . . . only their mother could tell them apart!

Within months of an achilles tendon injury forcing my retirement from the gentleman's game of cricket in 1981, I was fortunate to be recruited into the gang for the final three years of its 'on-air' life—a period I'll deal with later in the book.

Bob Davis, the 'Geelong Flyer', and other players also became regulars on the sports night circuit. These fundraising functions became part of the culture of sporting clubs across this beautiful brown land we know as Australia—north, south, east and west— and they are still happening.

Let me share a handful of those wonderful early days and late nights with you. When I look back, they resemble a sandpapering effect on my raw talent to tell a story. I needed to clock up all of those thousands of miles, and the journey has shaped my career in the most delightful manner.

One way or another, the irascible Louie the Lip has been the focus of incredible media attention for six decades—from the days of home-and-away matches for Collingwood when he was wearing long baggy shorts and metal-toe-capped football boots, to the in-your-face humour of his *Herald Sun* football columns, to the wise-cracking little chimp on television. The mould hasn't changed— he's still the same little fella today. Mind you, the majority of his opinions are the first vacant thoughts that enter the empty parking lot above his bushy eyebrows.

Radio was no different. He always beat his gums before thinking. I got to match my wits with the ex-Collingwood captain on the air-waves on Saturday mornings early in the 1980s. Peter Landy, a very experienced talking head, and myself would huddle around an old-fashioned microphone in a very tight studio below street level in Flinders Lane, Melbourne.

We revelled in the interaction with random callers—Sri Lankan bus drivers, gentlemen suffering from speech impediments, drunks, anti-Collingwood fans and racegoers—they all used their index finger to have a say.

The Saturday morning to top all Saturday mornings unfolded live-to-air on Louie's 60th birthday. The management at 3DB agreed to help him celebrate by inviting a Fat-O-Gram to be delivered while we were solving the week's many sports controversies. I'll never forget the reaction on the craggy-faced rover's dial. Gob-smacked would be a pretty realistic description.

Peter and I began to give a move-by-move call of the action. At precisely the moment her first and outer layer of clothing slid slowly from her woodchopper's shoulders to a crumpled heap on

> **I'll never forget the reaction on the craggy-faced rover's dial.**

the floor, Lou's bottom jaw rebounded off the table top. The big girl then wanted to complete her preamble on the Laminex tabletop.

By now the silver-haired grandfather had copped enough. Peter and I were having difficulty describing the proceedings without breaking up.

Rrrrrip! I swear I heard a seam tear in the bloomers, and by now our visitor was barefooted. Only a crimson ruffled garter remained around mid-thigh before the lady's well-painted face almost cracked while uttering those immortal words 'Happy Birthday'. She then settled on the Lip's knee, draining all colour from his face, and produced the telegram from inside her black silk ballooning knickers.

In situations of extreme danger it is possible to perform incredible feats of strength, like lifting the weight of a car to save the life of another. With his back pressed hard to the chair against the soundproof wall, the little bloke had nowhere to go! Incredibly, he burst from the pack, upending the woman into an ungainly position with legs pointing to the ceiling (some years since that had happened I reckoned).

Louie fled without hearing his singing telegram. It was still early in the program, with at least an hour to run. But that's the way Louie operates—never quite knowing what might happen next.

In between all of his media commitments Lou was the proprietor of a notorious watering hole in the shadows of the Herald and Weekly Times building in Flinders Street, Melbourne for eighteen years—a source of much material.

> *In situations of extreme danger it is possible to perform incredible feats of strength . . .*

'We've just finished renovating the Phoenix. It's the smallest hotel in Melbourne—so small, in fact, that we had to paint the furniture on the walls. We did up the men's and ladies' toilets. Fresh phone books in the men's room, and went posh with the girls'—we put the yellow pages in there.'

It certainly was an experience to buy a drink at the Phoenix. Lou behind the bar encouraging the bulldust to continue—more rings on the cash register. The walls were covered with yellowing old newspapers—cheap way to cover 'em, eh?

During the early 1970s Lou and his wife Edna went way upmarket and settled into life across town in the posh suburb of Toorak. Jack Dyer used to love to slip the boot in by

proclaiming that property values fell
50 per cent overnight.

'You can take the Richards out of
Collingwood, but you can't take the
Collingwood out of Richards,' Jack
Dyer stated at every sports night.

That was always the perfect
chance—a great opening to get stuck
into the famed 'Captain Blood'.

'You know Jack was at school for the

JACK DYER

best seventeen years of his life?' Lou would tell
audiences from Bordertown to Bendigo. 'He was in grade three the
whole time. He couldn't go up to grade four because his dad
was there.'

Jack looked daggers—always did. He'd sit there at the head
table kneading his massive, gnarled fists, which resembled a couple
of mallee roots that had been out in the weather too long. 'Every
time he gets into a cab, the driver leaves the vacant sign on.' Jack
would seethe.

Louie would grin. 'When *Lawrence of Arabia* was first shown
in Melbourne, Jack bought two tickets—asked for them in the
shade. He was so dumb as a kid he didn't know the difference
between arson and incest, so he went home and set fire to
his sister.'

My favourite Jack Dyer story, and one that got an airing
wherever we appeared together, is about the time Jack went on
holidays to Lorne. The old-timers reckon it's true.

Jack came out of the Lorne hotel one night and looked very

much the worse for wear. His eyes looked glazed and those massive ears were flapping around, pretty much like a cab with its doors open. He jumped into his car and was off along the Great Ocean Road. Somehow he hit the kerb and the car flipped, did three somersaults, tumbled down the cliff and landed flat—bang—on all four wheels on the beach.

A police officer appeared at the door. 'Sir,' he said to Jack, who was still sitting in the driver's seat, 'I believe you're drunk.'

'Of course I'm drunk, you fool. What do you think I am—a bloody stunt driver!'

The sportsnight formula still works well, even today in this age of computers and technology. A trestle for the head table, as many sheets of white butcher's paper as is possible to lay your hands on, some pies, sandwiches and saveloys to fill 'em up, and beer to quench the thirst. Offer a list of speakers—say, two or three tried sporting identities, and a stand-up comic—and it cannot fail.

One piece of advice for organisers of nights like these is never to use a speaker whom you have never heard before, or who doesn't come with several recommendations.

Unfortunately there is a contemporary trend among today's heroes and sporting stars on huge wages to ask for too much money before their speaking ability is of a professional quality. This is the major reason for panels being smaller in numbers than in Lou and Jack's time.

The stand-up comedians are brilliant to work with, but never try to out-do them at humour—you'll die on stage.

Three decades back we would drive anywhere to go to a function. Ron Blaskett sometimes drove members of the panel to the venue. In the boot, safely locked away would be his outrageously 'blue' and engaging dolls, Gerry Gee and Adolfus Querk. Ron would barely say 'boo' over 200 kilometres, but when he thrust his hand up the large external orifice of either doll, he was dynamite, and took absolutely no prisoners. Nothing and no person was safe. A patron going for a 'nervous one', on returning to the hall, would be grilled and humiliated by a talking doll.

At a hotel in Sydney Road, Brunswick, in Melbourne, a short tram ride from Optus Oval, the proprietor gambled on a large crowd turning up to hear the gang, but lost. No promotion was done—merely a hope that the 'names' would pull a crowd. They alone never do—you have to promote as well. It's the old familiar awareness factor. If they don't know what is on offer, how can they be expected to turn up?

> The stand-up comedians are brilliant to work with, but never try to out-do them at humour—you'll die on stage.

The takings across the bar were meagre, and not enough to pay the panel of Kevin Sheedy, Peter Bakos (the four foot seven and one eighth jockey), the ventriloquist and myself. The general feeling of the panel was: 'Walk away now and we'll never see the colour of this man's money.' We waited and waited. Midnight passed, and Gerry Gee was out of his suitcase, tired, angry and unpaid.

I'll admit that back in the 1970s we looked forward to the brown paper bag containing 'folded' quality printed paper. Shane

Warne and Mark Waugh have since made the biscuit tin and brown paper bag notorious. We didn't receive as much cash, but then again I guess we were not giving weather reports.

Only thirty-five patrons had attended; nevertheless it was an extremely funny evening. The 'talent', like a line-up in a game of British Bulldog, were not going to let the owner get to the door without reaching into the drawer or pocket, or both if necessary. Through the articulate, R-rated Gerry Gee, we pressed home the point with four, sometimes five colourful adjectives of dissent per sentence, straight for the pressure points.

The reality of conversation was a sight to behold. You'd reckon the doll and his offsider Adolfus were the ones being short-changed. Blinking eyes and flapping tongues made the artificial head come to life, with the defendant answering 'badly' all of his cutting questions. The language seared my eyebrows—it was red hot!

In the end, the only way the hotelier was going to get any peace was to surrender. The scenario could have been a pub holdup. The only item missing was a weapon (that's if you don't count Gerry Gee's tongue). A magnum would not have hit its target as consistently as the caustic-tongued puppet. Come to think of it, none of us had to ask for our money, and Ron Blaskett barely moved his lips. What a night!

One of the first comedians I shared a stage with was the unforgettable Mel Meikel—an original. He had an elastic face and a rapid-fire delivery which traversed the range of subject matter as if on a switch-back railway. You had to concentrate hard, but it was difficult not to notice the black or brown shirt which took on the role of sight screen for the white or pale ties. Long before Richie Benaud made the white, beige and powder-blue sports jacket popular, Mel was giving them a huge run, always set off with white patent leather slip-on shoes.

The great thing about working with Mel was his happy disposition and desire to help young guns like Tanglefoot succeed. But as he stressed, not without working hard at the craft of making people laugh.

In remote places like Jabiru, Groote Eylandt, Tennant Creek, Coober Pedy and Leigh Creek, and megacities such as New York, London, Bangkok, Rio de Janeiro and Hong Kong, one of my privileges has been to meet many of the very best entertainers in this caper. In Australia, we loved people like Ugly Dave Gray, Richard Stubbs, Paul Martell, Jimeoin and Billy Connelly. How difficult must it be to create new material when it's obvious many of the audience will retell the best of the night's offerings to their mates the next day.

It's different with music. If you're a composer, performer or musician you get royalties every time your music is played or performed. If you write comedy, the instant it's delivered it belongs to anyone smart enough to copy it down. One famous Australian comedian once said when he was asked why he didn't do sportsmen's nights, 'I'd prefer to sit home with a can of beer and pass five hundred bucks from one hand to the other.' Johnny Garfield would often begin a routine by saying, 'Got your pen and paper ready Sam and Neil'—and they were always ready!

In the case of my mate Brian Doyle, we simply put all of our jokes and stories together in book form, called it *Sports Jokes*, and sold 'em. Brian has a sense of timing, mischief and drama second to none. He is sad sack Irish at its very best. He comes on stage looking devastated, leans against the microphone stand and grabs his furrowed brow. 'I've had shocking bad luck,' he'd moan, and we'd all feel for him. 'I lost my wife last night in a poker game— I had to throw in four aces.'

> *One thing I have learnt from working with these blokes is to sit back and enjoy—never compete, because you can be made to look very ordinary.*

One thing I have learnt from working with these blokes is to sit back and enjoy—never compete, because you can be made to look very ordinary.

Let me share just this one from *Sports Jokes* about the terrifying duo, D. K. Lillee and Jeff Thomson. Dennis Lillee and Jeff Thomson were a fearsome combination, both on and off the ground. A young woman interviewer at Lords in England once said to Lillee, 'Tell me, Dennis, what would you do if you discovered you only had 30 minutes to live?'

Dennis said, 'I'd make love to the first thing that moved.'

'And what would you do, Mr Thomson?'

Tommo said, 'I'd stand very bloody still for half an hour.'

While a speaker might only be up on his or her feet for 45 minutes regaling the masses, the journeys to and from the venue occasionally turn out to be unforgettable, especially in a light aircraft.

'We all ought to be certified for getting back into this bastard of a plane!' shouted Sam Newman from the rear of our temporary prison. For surely, we were doing time the hard way—trapped in a tiny flying machine.

Sam, the former Geelong footballer and now a multimedia megastar, was sharing the second, or back row, of a four-seater, twin-engine Cessna next to notorious Melbourne television and radio character, Peter 'Crackers' Keenan, a veteran of more than 250 games with Melbourne, North Melbourne and Essendon.

Yours truly was in the cramped cockpit—in the seat reserved for the co-pilot. From the beginning, I had been almost hypnotised by the glaring mass of illuminated green and yellow gauges before my eyes.

Graeme, our young pilot, was responsible for safely transporting Sam, Crackers and myself to and from a speaking engagement in the small town of Cohuna, in the north of Victoria.

The aircraft was being buffeted continually, like a lost balloon, in strong wind gusts. The plane had just fallen abruptly—about 300 metres—when Crackers said, 'Gee, I feel close to God, but I don't want to meet him just yet!'

I've got it on pretty good authority that there was some good money within the four of us to suggest that we would not make it back to ground in one piece! And I'm not telling any lies when I say we were very frightened. Maybe it was the bad beginning to our epic journey.

What a way to start! As we calmly taxied down the black bitumen tarmac, there was very little discussion, other than the preceding week's events. At near top speed, our wheels left the tarmac of Essendon airport.

A perfect takeoff, I thought. Sammy and Crackers didn't really care as they dissected footballers' recent performances. Whatever the game, old players never die, they just become experts in their sport.

'Bloody hell!' Sam screamed, as we were barely 100 metres above the ground, and still climbing. The pilot's door flew open. Wind at about 160 km gushed into the cockpit. My heart began pounding very loudly—I was terrified! And I know I wasn't an orphan in feeling like that!

I flung my left arm across the pilot's back, like any great slips fieldsman might, to grab the flapping door. Simultaneously, both hands from the 6-foot-4 ruckman from Geelong appeared from the other direction, desperately trying to pull the door shut.

Crackers was issuing the obvious instruction at the top of his voice: 'Shut the bloody door, quick shut it, c'mon Sam shut it!'

The door would not close, despite superhuman efforts by Sam and myself.

Through all this, the pilot was hunched grim-faced over the aeroplane's controls to give us a better chance to slam the door.

The lights of Essendon were all too bright below us—barely 200 metres off the ground. For some reason, the door still would not slam shut after several more vigorous attempts. Graeme struggled with the joystick as we banked steeply around the control tower.

At one stage, I reckon we must have been flying sideways at ninety degrees to Earth and hanging on for grim death. I felt the long legs of Peter Pius Paul Keenan almost push through the back of my seat as he fought the forces of gravity.

My heart began pounding very loudly—I was terrified!

A unanimous decision was made to land the plane and find out what was wrong—who said footballers had no brains? On this occasion, common sense prevailed!

I had visions of someone—hopefully not me—being sucked out the open door into the cold dark night air, never to be seen again!

The very large lump in my throat had moved and lodged somewhere near the back of my ears as we levelled out over the Tullamarine freeway—if only we can land this plane safely?

I should not have doubted Graeme's ability, for the Cessna came in for a smooth landing. The 'team' was right back where we had started five minutes earlier.

Nerves frayed, but confidence restored, we powered down the runway for the second time. Crackers suggested that the air traffic controller in the tower probably thought he was drunk, seeing the same plane take off twice in seven minutes. But it didn't last long as we struggled into very strong headwinds. We should have been travelling at 160 knots, instead we were averaging only 105.

Long before we reached Bendigo, we agreed that it was the

worst flight we had ever been on, except for Graeme, who was showing a brave face.

Then the small charter plane pressed forward relentlessly into the face of a very nasty storm. Visibility was barely 10 metres—we truly were flying blind.

Graeme would not dare let his hands leave the controls as we continually dropped out of the sky with devastating effects on my stomach, which had become horribly knotted.

We were told that sick bags were in the seat pockets. I was too scared to be sick. Crackers said that if he was going to be sick, then it was only right the pilot should wear it. From where I sat, it was odds on that I'd be the one wearing it.

I should mention too that Crackers had been out to lunch; and garlic prawns had been on the menu. Every time he opened his mouth it suggested an Indian flame thrower at work, and the plane's interior was beginning to smell like yesterday's garlic bread.

My palms were very sweaty, and I'm certain that the giant ruckmen behind were holding hands as we plummeted through the clouds.

The rain on the wings now looked like huge sparks illuminated by the flashing wing lights—heavy drops were pounding on the windscreen.

I never have felt so insecure for such a long period of time! The two lads in the back were joking nervously about the possible news stories if we went down.

Something along the line of: 'Football will miss Peter Keenan and Sam Newman, the two VFL champion footballers tragically killed with their friend, former Test cricketer Max Walker, when their light aircraft crashed north of Bendigo last night on its way to a speaking engagement at Cohuna.'

I don't think our pilot was impressed. But I'm sure he realised our grave situation. As Crackers said, 'Don't worry Maxie, he's a mature twenty-one-year-old.'

I thought, here we are, our lives in the hands of a fragile, metal machine with two props and a twenty-one-year-old pilot. Unreal, and for what? A few hundred dollars for the night.

Sam said, 'How far is it to Cohuna, one and a half hours? We've been going for one and a half hours and haven't looked like sighting bloody Cohuna!'

'Yeah,' Crackers said impatiently, 'we should've driven up— could have saved a few bob and a lot of heartache!'

Finally, almost two hours after our original take-off, we were in the vicinity of our flight destination, Kerang. We were flying at about 1500 metres, give or take a few hundred metres, depending on the clouds and rain. All we had to do was find the airstrip.

I watched the altimeter spin from 1600 metres to well below 300 metres—still no sign of the strip. My ears popped and I hung on tight, hoping there was no radio tower or mountain tucked away secretly in the darkness below us.

Then, from nowhere, the two parallel blue lines appeared to our right—I didn't think that two blue lines could ever look so good. We did one arbitrary lap of honour before we made our final approach to land.

The nervous tension had got to us—we all started laughing as Graeme again put us on deck with a beautiful landing in pouring rain.

While the propellers unwound, and our aeroplane came to a standstill, I thought: no way am I getting back into this kite, unless we've got clear skies. Judging by the amount of water bouncing off the wings it looked like overnight at Cohuna.

You are not going to believe me when I tell you this, but about 12.30 a.m. we left Kerang in clear skies. But around Bendigo we hit the storms again and sat through the same fear for another hour.

We could not get Graeme to admit that it was the worst flying conditions he had flown in. But he did describe them 'as a long way from the best'.

I can understand why people hate small aircraft—you feel so helpless! Never again!

Noted doctor and motivationalist Dr John Tickell remembers flying to Istanbul for a speaking engagement. The airline, Olympic Airways, managed to send his luggage to Cairo.

Make it law that if an airline loses your baggage, they have to award 'frequent flyer points' for all the miles the lost baggage accumulates.

Tick reckoned, that was funny, but the unfunny bit came as he was dreaming about all the new clothes he was going to buy with the insurance money. Then after a week his clothes turned up.

Mike McColl Jones' theory on how to get airlines to take more care of your luggage is really quite simple. Make it law that if an airline loses your baggage, they have to award 'frequent flyer points' for all the miles the lost baggage accumulates. If the airlines start losing points, *they'll* find a way to look after our bags.

Seat allocation on a plane can be very much a gamble, especially when travelling alone. The random manner in which the airline computer spits out the all-important seat number is a lottery. You can never tell until you've actually planted your bum on the seat, whether you're a winner or loser, whether you've got the window or the aisle, and who's next door or in front.

How about if you draw a 'Black & Decker drill' as a partner—someone who doesn't draw breath from the moment the pointy end tilts to the sky for fear of losing 'airspace', or should I say conversation space. The only way to deal with this sort of bad luck is to bite your tongue, close the eyes, incline the head to one side and force yourself to go to sleep. Then, when you feel the undercarriage make contact with the runway below, awaken to the screech of burning rubber, as the tyres tear up the tarmac, you sheepishly look across the armrest to your frustrated companion in travel, and apologise for having gone to sleep halfway through a sentence.

Believe me, it's really easy to do, especially if the person has had a big night out on the garlic! Even looking straight ahead at the seat back—which by the way is very rude when the person on your left is trying to speak to you—the stench of a dead prawn drowned in a garlic bath hits your sensitive nasal passage. There is no escape.

Then of course there's the drunk, or should I say, the over-indulged traveller. There's not a lot either you or the flight attendant can do with this sort of character. Generally his attitude will be one of having paid for his trip like everyone else, and he's going to enjoy it by participating in a few extra sips to ease the nerves.

My wife Kerry and I were returning to Melbourne, on the 6.45 a.m. earlybird special, following a speaking engagement in Launceston. This is always a bad time of the morning to travel, as it's possible to crack it for customers on their way home from the casino. We hit the jackpot—not one but two.

> *You can never tell until you've actually planted your bum on the seat, whether you're a winner or loser, whether you've got the window or the aisle, and who's next door or in front.*

Both men had bulging pockets and obviously had enjoyed a truckload of bourbon and coke before the sun rose above the horizon. Initially we thought how lucky we were to be upgraded by the friendly officer at the check-in counter of Qantas to seats up-front. A comfortable roomy flight and hearty breakfast to look forward to. Well, that was until our two would-be wobbly friends climbed the staircase at the rear end of the aircraft.

Against the general flow and wishes of the passengers, they pushed, shoved and jostled their way loudly to their seats in the front. Our not-so-well-slept flight attendant was unimpressed by the impatient waving of their boarding passes under her nose.

She couldn't believe her misfortune in copping this terrible twosome. It was quite funny—until she extended her right arm stiffly, gesturing the pair into seats directly in front of us! The crotchety attendant in the dark blue uniform could walk away. But we were going to be stuck with 'em.

The younger man of the ill-mannered double was rapt to get the window seat. His partner was a lean 'n' hungry bearded man with darting eyes.

While he searched for the seatbelt, his unshaven apprentice did a doubletake—he spotted my ugly dial above the headrest. He couldn't believe his eyes.

'Maxie Bloody Walker! Jesus Christ! What are you doing here?'

'Just grabbing a ride back to Melbourne like you,' I explained.

'Wow, what a buzz. I used to watch you when you played for the mighty Demons.'

Obviously a Melbourne supporter since he was weaned off his mother's milk. Words just kept flowing from the heart.

'I never thought I'd see the day. Bloody hell, Colin. Do you realise who's sitting behind us?'

'No, who?' questioned the senior partner.

'Don't you recognise 'im? Maxie Walker.'

With a blank look of nobody's home. 'Naaah,' he whined mischievously. 'What's he do? I'll bet he never played for Collingwood.'

'You can say that again.' I bellowed back, and I meant it!

As I said that, it reminded me of a question I was once asked by a Collingwood detractor: What's the difference between a Collingwood supporter lying dead on the road and a dead pig? And you're not going to believe the reply: obviously the skid marks are in front of the pig.

We hadn't even taxied along the runway and the trip looked doomed. There we were, Kerry, no great Aussie Rules lover, and myself, on a hiding to nothing, sharing a back seat with two inebriated winners—one of whom couldn't see past his nose or Collingwood. At least one was a Demon through and through, and for only that reason could the trip have been bearable.

In a complex volley of slurred words, he attempted to explain to his slippery mate who I was. 'You know, the bloke on television. He used to spray that little kid in the face with a can of Aerogard every time he went out to play cricket. You remember, Lillee and Thomson, when they blitzed the Poms?'

'Yeah, but I can't remember him,' his mate barked with a sarcastic sting to it. It was now obvious we didn't like one another and the chances were that the temperature wouldn't get any warmer.

'What did he do? Bat or bowl? Or just hang around in the field while Lillee stuffed 'em?' he teased.

At this stage, the ball bearing in each man's neck was working overtime. Mind you, if they continued to unleash much more verbal diarrhoea, then my intentions were to stretch the ugly Magpie supporter's Adam's apple to about a foot above his shoulder blades!

The signs were now illuminated: NO SMOKING, FASTEN SEAT-BELTS. The focus of attention moved back towards the blonde, complete with the yellow inflatable lifejacket and red toggles. She was standing in front of the toilet sign which must have caught the eye of Colin in front. As he leant across into the aisle for a better squiz at the young woman's legs, the call of nature urgently registered somewhere upstairs above his bushy eyebrows.

Like a schoolboy, up went the hand in question to the hostie. 'Lady, I need to go to the dunny.' This broke up the occupants in the front of the aircraft, which only served to encourage him.

'You'll have to wait sir, until we level out. And do up your seat belt for takeoff!'

She continued her well-rehearsed routine, 'Pull this, blow that, don't inflate your lifejacket until you're outside the aircraft!'

It was all too much for our gambler. 'I'll never make it till 10,000 metres! I'll explode!' He painfully pleaded. 'Well, you'll just have to keep your legs crossed and mouth closed!' she snapped.

'What's your caper, lady? I'm telling ya, I've got to go to the bloody toilet!'

The exchange was very funny for everyone except our intrepid gent. For him the pain was very real as he waited impatiently.

Not much happening out the window, only grey concrete and grass rushing by, so my Demon mate suggested: 'Let me buy you and your lady a drink Maxie!'

Just as well the NO SMOKING sign was on because I'm sure if anyone struck a match, the plane would be up in flames—his breath was ninety per cent alcohol.

I was conscious of trying not to offend the odd couple, because drinking, and drinking heaps, was a subject very dear to both of them. As we angled towards the clouds I declined the offer, 'It's a bit early yet!'

'C'mon, Tangles, I thought you'd be a real drinking man like us. You know, Dougie and you, you're always drinking on them ads!'

I didn't have the heart to tell him they basically were the same commercials played over and over again. Then again, it would be very fair to say that my former cricketing mate and co-star of the Toohey's 2.2 commercials did take the opportunity to 'sink' quite a number more cans than was necessary to complete the thirty-second commercials. Dougie was never one to pass up the opportunity to have a beer, especially a free one!

As we levelled out, the OCCUPIED sign was illuminated by our impatient drinker. Now with one seat vacant, it was easier for the Demon fan to turn right around to face us. He ran his eyes quickly over Kerry from the top of her head of dark brown hair all the way down to the carpet supporting her shoes, and I'm sure he approved.

'You must do a lot of walking to have calves like that!' he remarked. Kerry continued reading.

His mate, who resembled a prawn fisherman back from a haul, returned with a real wildcard comment: 'You know, listening to golf on radio is as boring as listening to you!'

What could I say? One of 'em loved Kerry's legs and the other hated my commentating!

He went on, 'McEnroe's my idol. He's got so much aggro in him!'

'Yeah, and he's got a lotta beaver in him too!' his mate replied.

'I like champions—they're great 'cause they always win!'

I thought, He doesn't kick with the breeze much this bloke, does he? They wouldn't be bloody champions if they kept on losing! I bit my tongue and kept quiet. No need to keep the fire burning and what's more, I understood that no amount of discussion was going to alter the way they thought about anything.

Tomorrow they would be nursing a nasty hangover and amnesia.

Kerry thought about a sleep but gave up—too many loudmouthed interruptions. Next thing, up went the arm in front, like a Heil Hitler salute. Bang, flush on the service button. This time a more matronly hostie arrived and I decided to take a few notes on proceedings while they ordered.

The elder statesman couldn't help himself. The hostess had an open-necked shirt on and from where he was sitting, she looked great. So out of the pocket came a wad of bank notes the size of a large tin of peaches. The body language was very much c'mon—wink, wink—nudge, nudge—what do ya reckon! Our senior hostie wasn't impressed.

'Ya want a drink, love? You name it, you've got it!' followed by a big, beaming grin. Tiredness must have set in because he couldn't hold the smile, or maybe he recognised his offer was just not on!

'We don't drink on the job,' was the cool reply.

'Aw, c'mon, just one won't hurt ya!'

Not to be outdone, our Demon supporter stood up. He too had a bundle of notes larger than his fist could hold. 'Do you reckon we haven't had a good night!' he bragged. 'We blitzed 'em on the tables, didn't we?'

'Sure did!' Then the bearded one turned around and in a more pleasant manner said, 'He loves you, Maxie!'

> *Tomorrow they would be nursing a nasty hangover and amnesia.*

'Anyone who plays for Melbourne is all right by me!' his mate declared.

'Na—Collingwood forever!'

'Up the Demons!'

'Go on, prove you love him, you miserable bastard. Give him half your winnings! See, now he doesn't love you. He's only saying he does!'

At this stage I thought we were set for a right old barney, but the hostie did her bit.

'What did you ring the button for?'

'What do ya reckon. A drink, of course!'

'You'll have to wait until we serve breakfast.'

'Breakfast?' Colin exclaimed. 'It's a bit early for breakfast. We haven't been to sleep yet!'

Commonsense prevailed, and they soon got their bourbon and cokes, before breakfast!

But far from keeping them quiet, this was merely another reason to argue about whose shout it was and the splitting of the taxi fare.

Kerry and I couldn't help but laugh. It was spontaneous slapstick entertainment.

> *Commonsense prevailed, and they soon got their bourbon and cokes, before breakfast!*

As a good gambler always out of luck, the obvious thing to do was to ask if they worked to a system, or if in fact they did play the roulette table. So I tapped my tired Melbourne supporter on the shoulder and popped the thought-provoking question.

His reply was wonderfully simple. 'Nope! We just sit and think, and watch a bit.'

Soon, with all the twisting and turning in their seats, it was bound to happen. Off the tray table and into the lap slid the plastic cup. Nothing like the cold shower treatment with the bonus of a few ice cubes. And a nice wet telltale patch on the front of the trousers to go with it. Not that they cared. The remains of the bourbon and coke were brushed off the tray and onto the floor. The problem was easily solved with the hasty order of drink number two. Neither was feeling any pain or discomfort at this stage.

Nevertheless, one must give them full credit for having enough sense to stop when they were well in front—breakfast was coming!

The food silenced the entertainers for a short while. Still, I kept jotting down some classic one-liners like these:

'How do me eyes look!' Colin quizzed.

'Dreadful! Road maps everywhere!'

'Gee!' he said, 'you ought to climb inside my head and take a look at 'em from this side!'

I was beginning to warm to the Collingwood guy. At least he was loyal—even the hoops on his T-shirt were black and white.

The pair confided to us that about once a month they made the pilgrimage to Tassie to watch the little ball roll and clatter its way around the coloured edge of the roulette wheel. But as is the case with anyone who is unfortunate enough to be a victim of the gambling disease, they never lose, or you never hear about the losses.

I became the subject of conversation again as they noticed the pad beneath my hand. They didn't miss a trick.

'Don't make out you're intelligent.'

Then in popped the other. 'Trying to make out your $5 shopping list?'

The interrogation in stereo continued. 'What's it like living with a spendthrift?'

'Gee I thought celebs looked after their women. He won't even let you have a drink! What a tight bastard he is!'

They broke into a teasing banter again and began discussing their other halves.

'Will the missus be there to meet ya?'

'Yeah, she'll be there.'

'No she won't! She doesn't finish at the parlour till 8 o'clock!'

A loud gravelly guffaw accompanied that little gem. The girl across the aisle jumped in fright. She thought she was having a bad dream, only to discover it was real! It was two gorillas having an early morning romp about the clouds.

'That's where we should go!' the bearded one suggested, realising they were about to arrive back in Melbourne on a Saturday morning. 'The races!'

'No, let's go to the pub and have a drink!' Obviously the grog was doing a fair bit of talking.

'Where are the races today?'

'What about the greyhounds? They're easier!'

Their discussion was interrupted by a thud as Tullamarine airport rushed past the windows. We were back on deck. The journey seemed to take no time at all. You know, time flies when you're having fun. We had no alternative.

As for Kerry and I, the return flight was more entertaining than the function.

'A funny thing happened to me on the way here today.' A very old line, but how true. The Australian continent spans more than 3000 kilometres. If speaking is your profession, be prepared for many memorable flights.

Destination: Brisbane. My brief was to both motivate and entertain. The client, the auditors of Queensland.

The consistent question on my mental screen as I planned the presentation was: 'What will make a bunch of computer-literate number-crunchers laugh?'

> *If speaking is your profession, be prepared for many memorable flights.*

The gentleman across the aisle, ruddy faced and clad in a very expensive pin-striped suit was preoccupied in interesting yours truly about the strengths and weaknesses of Australia's latest Test captain Steve Waugh. He must have been a lawyer, given his machine-gun manner of speaking, probing like a dentist's drill—never ending, and painful.

On touchdown I noticed a concerned look in my direction from the flight attendant in the jumpseat. What had I done to deserve this? Before the giant metallic cigar came to a halt, she was on one knee and speaking softly into my left ear. 'Are you all right?'

I didn't feel sick. In fact I felt in A1 condition, ready to do lunch with the auditors in Brisbane.

'Yes, sure!' I replied.

Obviously not convincing enough, because she tried again.

'Are you sure you're okay?'

'Absolutely!'

Just let me get my jacket on and I'm out of here was my strategy.

Then she really stuns me. 'I hope you don't think I couldn't see. You're obviously in great pain!'

'What!' I said. 'How come?'

'The blood,' she said. 'You're bleeding quite profusely!'

'Where?' I said.

The clot of dark red just below my left nipple and above the lowest rib must have looked really bad—like the outpouring of a bullet wound.

I cast my eyes below the chin to the offending area. It was my worst nightmare. In shaping the skeleton for my talk, I love to use coloured felt pens and pink markers. I had unknowingly placed the red felt pen into my shirt pocket with the cap on the wrong end. Capillary action, I think, is the term—where moisture is sucked from wet to dry absorbent material.

I offered to send her the bullet I'd stopped, once the doc had plucked it out.

As I overcame the 'My goodness, what am I going to look like at lunch?' flush, I grabbed the opportunity to milk the moment. I jokingly or mischievously suggested I had been involved in a bank hold up, and took the lead pellet on the scramble to the getaway car. A blank, bewildered, even scared reaction gave way to a 'Maxie-Walker-in-a-bank-holdup, you've-got-to-be-having-a-lend-of-me' face.

The colour of her pretty face went from skin colour to red, almost a match for the stained pocket.

I offered to send her the bullet I'd stopped, once the doc had plucked it out.

Observing myself in the mirror of the gents' toilets, I thought, A bad look, Maxie! The gag might work to open the proceedings, but not for the entire speech should I be wearing the purple heart. Lucky I had a spare shirt. I would be saying 'Ladies and Gentlemen' inside two hours, so there was no time for another catastrophe.

While we are discussing travelling from one end of this wonderful island continent to the other, let me describe another experience.

The day was 13 March 1985, not a Friday. I'm not superstitious, but I woke up with a start as my head bounced off the passenger window. Charging straight at our car at 120 km was a yellow and black, diamond-shaped signpost saying FLOODWAY. In that split second of opening my eyes it was terrifyingly obvious that the car in which I was a passenger was not on the black bitumen stuff where it ought to be!

There was no question and no escape—we were definitely going to crash into the post. In fact we hit it dead centre and it buckled like a toothpick. The next few seconds were horrific.

The metal sign crashed into the windscreen right in front of my eyes. Splinters of glass flew everywhere as the window crazed like a spider's web. My door began to open, but I pulled against it. The potentially lethal sign somehow didn't get through the window, but ricocheted over the bonnet as the car began to spin. I momentarily felt like Steve McQueen filming the stunts in *Bullitt*, but what a waste—there were no cameras.

Finally, the car came to a standstill after completing about eight loop-the-loops across the red dust and short-tufted scrub grass. My arm was aching from holding the door shut against the force of gravity. At this stage, I had stopped screaming expletives!

Lionel, the driver, looked ashen. His colour returned, except for the knuckles of his fingers tightly gripping the steering wheel. A deadly silence prevailed. Yes, we were very lucky to be alive after leaving the road at such a speed and not rolling the vehicle.

We were on our way to a speaking engagement at Leigh Creek football and cricket clubs, some five hours' drive north of Adelaide. As I looked back to the road, I could see the mangled signpost pointing to the sky like a scorpion's tale. I also noticed a 2-metre-wide concrete culvert or waterway 10 metres away from where the car had stopped spinning. I thought of all the possibilities. We certainly were lucky!

Within minutes, a sparkling metallic-blue Range Rover came to an abrupt halt in a cloud of dust and two guys, Dave and Leon, rushed over to see what had happened. As I found out later, it wasn't the first time these two blokes had stopped to lend a helping hand. 'Anyone hurt?' they shouted, scampering quickly towards Lionel and myself.

All four of us did a complete lap of honour, inspecting the white, late-model Ford Falcon. By the time we had completed the enlightening walk, I noticed Leon staring at me. He thought he'd seen me somewhere before, but the penny didn't drop quickly for him. Then again, I guess he thought, 'What's Dennis Lillee or maybe Max Walker doing in the region of the Iron Triangle? No it couldn't be him!' After all, it was a long way from the turf at the MCG.

I felt some pain in my left hand. Blood was dripping from my fingertips. Lionel said, 'Max, are you all right?' then Leon, the short yet enormously wide man, smiled with recognition. He must have been 23 stone (convert that to metric if you can), and was dressed for the trip in blue singlet and shorts, topped off with an unbuttoned and unpressed khaki shirt.

His thin mate Dave's trousers told the story of his trade, such was the amount of grease on them. In many ways together they appeared like Laurel and Hardy—Leon providing the laughs while Dave was the straight man.

Gee, were we glad to see them as we stood in front of the crumpled bonnet and watched a jet of steam escaping from a damaged radiator. All our efforts to prise open the bonnet failed until a crowbar was produced. Any hope of the car being driveable was quickly diminishing. Then, the sound of serious air brakes punctuated the air. We looked up and saw a magnificent road train pull up, its chrome trim shining. It is moments like these that you reflect on the world and realise there really are some tremendous people around. The first two vehicles to come our way had stopped and couldn't do enough for us.

The two-way radio inside the cabin was of great assistance in calling the local Ford dealer. Lionel stayed with his car on the roadside and waited, and it was agreed that I should continue on to Leigh Creek. As luck would have it, Dave and Leon were going to Leigh Creek to put some heavy earthmoving equipment on the train to Port Augusta.

When we arrived at our destination, words didn't seem to be

enough, so grateful was I for Dave and Leon's help. Maybe one day I will be able to reciprocate.

After a quick shower, the canteen soon became the venue for swapping cricket stories. This time I was mainly listening, fascinated by real red dust Australian tales of bat and ball.

The match was an annual event played for the fourth time between Wilpoorinna, a team provided by wealthy station owners, the Litchfield family, and the Leigh Creek boys, selected from those still standing and available. I hadn't heard of the Wilpoorinna Sporting Complex before—this was where the game was played.

An early disappointment was the fact that 'Two-Step Terry', the president of LCFC would be unavailable due to poisoning—it's not known what sort, but I doubt if you'd need a medical degree to guess.

The wicket itself was a 1.2-metre wide concrete test strip laid by an inexperienced local concreter. From end to end there was no less than a 15-cm fall—talk about the slope at Lords!

A boundary line was achieved by dragging around a fallen log behind a horse about 65 metres from the concrete pitch, forming a groove. The outfield itself consisted of Leigh Creek mulch or basically a lot of rocks and no grass—no curator needed at this ground.

The main pavilion was two horse drays and a canvas secured only by logs. This provided limited shade, considering temperatures regularly hit 45°C in this part of Australia. In the outer, I'm told, were just a couple of EH Holdens with their own tent outhouses and well-stocked coolers.

The stumps fascinated me, firmly set in concrete and made from one piece of flat metal— and the metal bails were welded on! This had been a contentious point because in one game a wicket-keeper had broken his hand trying to remove the bails. There was some talk of removing the bails with a hacksaw blade!

Beside each of the fieldsmen's feet it is not unusual to spot a stubby marking his position. The general idea with these is to break your mate's stubby with a rock before he can drink it.

Three cork cricket balls are used per innings because of wear and tear caused by the rocky surroundings. Fieldsmen don't dive for the ball in these games. The possibility of the ball ricocheting into your face from the rock is very real. As they say in Leigh Creek, you can either be a dead hero or a squib.

> *The stumps fascinated me, firmly set in concrete and made from one piece of flat metal— and the metal bails were welded on!*

Because of the type of balls used, the bats are covered with black Polypipe melted by oxy torches and shrunk around the face of the bat. You'd need forearms like a weightlifter to wield one.

Casualties are a common occurrence, the worst being Kempie, who had only just returned to Wilpoorinna. He had scored ten, looking for a second run after a particularly fast single, when he ran smack-bang into George Menangitus, a new school teacher in town. The final outcome was ten painful stitches in the chin. And he'd just driven 600 km from Mt Barker to play. Then he had to drive 80 km to hospital. All fixed, he desperately drove back to the club only to find the beer off and the club shut! You can't beat bad luck.

One interesting dismissal entered into the score sheet on the back of a piece of cardboard was: 'Tommo' caught Tort (wicket-keeper) bowled Bouncie (swing bowler). Score—not many.

I should mention that Leigh Creek won this 1985 encounter for the first time in four years after scoring 124 in 20 overs. The event raised $1500 for the Isolated Children's and Parents' Association, and a memorable day was had by all. That's what I call real cricket—no coloured gear, no flash million-dollar lighting poles, no electronic scoreboards, no run rates or third umpires. Only the game.

> As they say in Leigh Creek, you can either be a dead hero or a squib.

We have fallen into the trap of taking it for granted that Australia's airline system is as good as anywhere else in the world. Like a lot of good things about Australia, it used to be. Nowadays, all you have to do is mention Sydney Airport and air travellers shake with fear or rage! Many business people around the country and also tourists have been giving Sydney a wide berth, and who could blame them?

The flashpoint occurred when those eagle-eyed folk up in the control tower—the air traffic controllers—spat the dummy over the crazy congestion. Sydney airport was as busy as a beehive. It was bumper-to-bumper traffic on the tarmac and in the air. With that number of planes darting across the sky like angry bees searching for a place to land, it was the last place on earth you'd want to be if you'd figured on leaving on time! I should say though that it's better to be late than sorry. The Olympic games 2000 will be interesting to monitor.

Well, Sydney Airport netted me. I gambled and lost. I knew I shouldn't have stayed the extra night in Sydney, but the opportunity to get extra work got the better of me. I decided to earn a few extra dollars at a speaking engagement.

Now, you would have thought a 7.30 a.m. flight out of Sydney would give me quite sufficient time to get to work on time—that being 11 a.m. when the *Wide World of Sports* Sunday Edition used to go to air. My co-host was Lou Richards. How wrong a man can be!

The alarm went off at around 6.15 a.m. It sounded like a guy inside my head with a pneumatic sledge-hammer trying to blast out—a horrific noise! I jumped to attention and unconsciously answered the phone. Like a wet rat, I scrambled out of the shower, towelled myself down, quick lick of the razor, bit of aftershave, deodorant, pull the tie up around the throat, look forward to another day at the office. Red lights, tight underpants and make-up.

Then things started to go wrong. The taxi was late. The part-time driver wasn't sure which way the airport was. Then it took him forever to scribble three words on the receipt. I don't know what they meant. All I know is that the ride cost a lot more to get to the airport than I expected.

Well, let's kick the day off with a heart-starter. Why not use the VIP lounge. Put the feet up—yeah—have a croissant, bit of apricot jam, black coffee. Check out the monitor—correct—

Melbourne–Sydney flight, 7.30 a.m., board at 7.10. On time, you little beauty, the gamble's paid off. The croissant certainly tasted good because I had another one! A couple of cups of coffee later I was all about like a tin of worms. Couldn't wait to board the plane. I was fortunate to get upgraded to first class. Looking good!

It was simply marvellous sitting up there in the front row—1A—gazing out the window, thinking about how I'd start off the day's show: 'Good morning, welcome to another edition of *Wide World of Sports*. Big weekend of sport . . .' No. Perhaps something else—all the different permutations were there.

I read the sports section of the Sunday paper, a bit more, then a bit more. Most of it! It occurred to me that we had been stationary for a long time. This has become a pretty regular occurrence in Sydney, especially when you have two four-seater Cessnas waiting in line to take off and behind them are six jumbo jets with hundreds of passengers on each! Seems a bit rich for a couple of crop-dusters to be given priority, but that's the way it happened. For half an hour we parked on the tarmac waiting, waiting and waiting. My heart wasn't beating quickly yet! There was no problem really, it was just a matter of taking off. We'd pick it up in the air, no worries. Then the captain spoke: 'Unfortunately, we've discovered—just in time—this aircraft is unserviceable. We'll have to go back to bay No. 9, where you'll disembark. All

> Seems a bit rich for a couple of crop-dusters to be given priority, but that's the way it happened.

passengers will be able to catch the next flight to Melbourne—the 9 a.m.'

At hearing this, the blood started to surge through the veins at a million miles per hour, and the heart started to beat rapidly. On my reckoning the 9 a.m. flight arrived at about 10.15 a.m.—that's if we're on time—and even Mick Doohan wouldn't get from Tullamarine to Richmond in 40 minutes!

So rather sheepishly I rang Melbourne, hoping there'd be some sensitive soul at GTV9 who could save the day. Jo Hall, then one of the news reporters, was on the control desk. I asked her nervously about the possibility of being able to use the chopper! Now this is really going first class—to chopper in from Tullamarine into GTV Channel 9. I would arrive with a few minutes to spare.

I sounded fairly anxious. She knew I was fair dinkum. 'Well,' she replied, 'maybe, just maybe . . . but if a news story breaks, that'll have priority.' That's all I needed. Another sensational story, a shooting in town, maybe a bank robbery, or even a superstar arriving in town.

I then rang Annie at *Wide World of Sports* to alert her to

the new arrangement. She seemed to be the only one who wasn't worried!

Finally at 9 a.m. the flight takes off. Well, it seemed like an eternity before Tullamarine loomed up. I waited for a sign of the GTV chopper. It's now 10.20—still no chopper.

The pilot of my flight had suggested the chopper would be

> **I climb aboard the vibrating egg beater, up into the air we go.**

waiting near the terminal. But still no sign of it. Mild panic. So I went back to the lounge and phoned in. 'Where's the chopper?' 'Sorry, we can't get it going.' Twenty minutes later they finally succeed in getting the blades to spin around. This will be close.

A very windy journey scampering across the tarmac, hair vertical, I climb aboard the vibrating egg beater, up into the air we go. It was 20 minutes to 11 at this stage and we were a long way from the Richmond studio of Channel 9! All sorts of eventualities were crossing my mind. The trouble I would be in! Nevertheless, it was a very quick trip. We arrived with eight minutes to spare.

A car was waiting on the ground—straight to security and into makeup. I was sitting down in the host chair, ready for action with only 60 seconds to on-air time.

Meanwhile, Lou Richards had been pacing up and down the corridor, like an expectant dad, repeating, 'Good morning and welcome, welcome and good morning, er, to Wide Sunday Edition, um . . .' Louie couldn't spit it out correctly without the script!

Everyone was making plans in case I didn't arrive on time. But, as so often happens, in the nick of time, everything rolled on cue and away we went. What a relief!

When you look at what might have happened, you've gotta think to yourself, 'Would I trust the airline system in Australia, if it meant my job? It could've cost me my job that day!'

Now after more than 3000 hours of 'live' television behind me, I put it down to experience—creating memories. It never happened a second time. With 'live' television there are no second chances. Leave nothing to chance—especially the transport.

3

The Institute of Experience

Don't give the public what they want. Give them something better.

SAMUEL LIONEL BUTTERFIELD (OWNER OF RADIO CITY MUSIC HALL)

The difference between a successful person and others is not a lack of strength, not a lack of knowledge, but rather in a lack of will.

VINCE LOMBARDI

It takes courage to stand up in front of a crowd of people and successfully entertain them by either speaking or singing. I've never attempted to sing for my supper, but have been fortunate enough to visit most of Australia through various speaking engagements. They have ranged from the opal fields of Coober Pedy in central Australia to the tiny manganese mining settlement on Groote Eylandt in the Gulf of Carpentaria and Gove.

In many ways the first two or three minutes of a talk is a bit like bowling the first over of a Test match in front of a big crowd—it can really be a test of nerves! You never quite know whether or not the new ball is going to swing; how the wicket will react; or whether the batsman is in a positive or negative frame of mind.

Audiences are no different. You've got to sum them up in the first two or three minutes. It's nice to know whether they like you or not early on, whether or not they want to laugh, or whether they're interested in the information you are giving them.

> **'tell 'em what you're gonna tell 'em, tell 'em, and tell 'em what you've told 'em!'**

The great American comedian Red Skelton once said, 'The hardest spot to do in any show is opening remarks, but until such time as someone comes up with something that's better, I'll continue to do them.'

Speaking is a bit like having guests to your home. And on opening the front door, you usher them through to the dining room without a word of welcome. One way to break the ice is to get a laugh in the first couple of minutes, usually at your own expense. It's not hard to verbally abuse ourselves, is it?

As a basic philosophy and guide to public speaking, I was told a long time ago to 'tell 'em what you're gonna tell 'em, tell 'em, and tell 'em what you've told 'em!' The formula works pretty well too! In over two decades I've presented almost 3000 talks, with no two the same. In three decades, Mike has written opening remarks for about 5000 television shows for people such as Graham Kennedy, Bert Newton, Don Lane, Steve Vizard and Richard Stubbs, as well as creating approximately 750,000 jokes. That's a lot of experience.

Always be prepared for unexpected situations. A few years back I was asked to speak at a dinner in the MCC members' dining room at the Melbourne Cricket Ground. I understood the function was to celebrate 100 years of competition between English and Australian blind cricketers. Much to my amazement, on arrival at the historic cricket venue, ready for the evening's formalities, I was informed I was speaking to an audience of mainly deaf cricketers. How do you think I felt? Uncomfortable and edgy to say the least! Up the degree of difficulty—real pressure.

The night consisted of a very excitable gathering of no less than 160 deaf players, plus wives and friends. A small contingent had travelled all the way from England to watch their own special centenary Test match. Apart from the catering staff, only three other people the audience were able to hear 100 per cent. Some could lip read, but many could not!

How was I going to make this work? The manager of the English team was able to communicate verbally and I had been given an interpreter to help me communicate with the audience.

My first mistake was to pick up the microphone: 'Ladies and Gentlemen . . .' Amid a very loud and spontaneous roar of laughter I realised what I'd done—the microphone was absolutely useless.

Standing on a chair behind me was the interpreter translating everything I said through his hypnotic magic fingers. At first, the scenario was very off-putting because everyone's eye line was focused on the interpreter's lightning fingers and not my face. Also, the response to the punchlines of my anecdotes was rebounding about 45 seconds later.

I would be well and truly into a new story and the crowd would only just be reacting to the previous one. I got used to it, but there was an enormous amount of nervous energy expended by both the interpreter and myself. It was a hot night and before long, perspiration was trickling down the side of my face.

Through the agency of my interpreter and a piece of paper, one of our English guests had the audacity to suggest that my accent was a bit off. Cheeky bugger. There is a rumour that Bill Clinton and Saddam Hussein actually get on very well—it's just that their interpreters hate each other's guts.

Full points to the wonderfully talented man standing on the chair—my speech was only ever going to be as good as his fingers. Public speaking is not only the choice of words, but also timing and inflection. He did all of these things with the movement and shape of his hands. He even created humour. Clever.

Some time later, I spoke to a group of blind cricketers at the Victorian Blind Cricket Association presentation night. Cricket is a difficult enough game with full use of both eyes, but to tackle the game of white flannelled gentlemen with less than 15 per cent sight available is a tribute to these courageous players. I still treasure the 'blind cricket ball'—a wicker woven ball with a bell in it—presented to me at that function.

Many years before, I did play in a blind cricket match at Mornington Peninsula. It was a fundraising game including several Test cricketers— Doug Walters and Gary Gilmour were two of them. The outsiders were allowed to bat through the first over without the blinkers on—that was okay. But during our second over—talk about the blind leading the blind—I don't know whether my hearing is poor or not, but I didn't have a clue where the hollow ball was coming from. Gary Gilmour wasn't much better. The local underarm quick bowler soon wrapped up 'Gus' with a bouncer that clanged against the metal stumps. A bouncer is a cunning delivery when bowled underarm . . . and requires much skill.

The game works this way. One of five players points the bowler in the direction of the batsman. The bowler then shouts 'Ready John' or whatever the batter's name is, and away the ball goes rolling down the wicket. The trick is to get the ball to jump or bounce awkwardly over the horizontal bat, which is used with a scraping technique. You'd be amazed how regularly a good bowler can achieve this.

At the presentation night, I was proud to be among such wonderful people totally committed to playing the game. Those with exceptional performances were rewarded with trophies. The only problem for me

> *There is a rumour that Bill Clinton and Saddam Hussein actually get on very well—it's just that their interpreters hate each other's guts.*

was handing them over. It was easy to get the trophy in a player's searching, outstretched hand, but it was the other hand which was a worry. Every second bloke 'king hit' me between the legs trying to shake hands with the free one. They were still ringing twenty-four hours later. I managed a lot of laughs, and a few claps at the end, so it made my night memorable as well.

When you are talking to a live audience, compared to television and radio, it's easy to know how you're going because of the feedback. Whatever we do in life, we need feedback, either positive or negative.

In sport that feedback is spontaneous—hit a boundary or kick a goal and the spectators will roar with delight. Drop a catch or get hit for six, miss a goal or drop a mark, and you'll be able to judge by the noise of the boos how badly you've performed.

It's exactly the same with a microphone in hand or lectern in front of you. Relate to the people you're talking to. Remember, talk to your audience—not at them—and their reaction to you will come back like a mirror image. Treat them all as very important people.

There are some who reckon that standing up and talking to groups of people, mostly strangers, in various parts of the country is a pretty easy life. You'll get no argument about that from me when the subject of sportsmen's nights is discussed. They are generally a ball of fun for everyone concerned. On the sportsnight circuit hecklers are looming in every corner of the room. During a speech you cannot let them get out of hand and you must not lose your cool. Be prepared. The sample toe-cutters on the facing page may at first glance appear a little aggressive but I speak from experience. They are necessary and they work, especially at rowdy sportsnights.

Under normal speaking conditions—well-behaved interested crowd—there are three ways of coping with the odd heckler.

- ignore the heckling if possible
- be courteous and polite in reply or use a verbal toe-cutter
- the heckler wins and you lose your temper—and the audience.

I would be telling lies if I said that there weren't a few occasions

THE INSTITUTE OF EXPERIENCE

VERBAL TOE-CUTTERS

Would you please move that man/woman closer to the wall. That's plastered as well . . . Thank you!

It just goes to show the effects of drinking alcohol on an empty head.

Somebody please pour that bloke back into the bottle.

- Now here's a guy who was born on 2nd April—a day too late!

- I'm currently designing an idiot and gee, I'd love a blueprint of your brain.

- Have a look at this fellow, Ladies and Gentlemen—absolute living proof that brain transplants never work.

- I seem to remember you. You're the same bloke I saw fifteen years ago when I spoke here. How could I forget that suit?

- OK, let's make a deal: if I want your opinion I'll rattle your cage. Now shut the door and be quiet.

- What did you say? Is that really your own mouth or are you breaking it in for an idiot?

- Many of you may not realise it but this guy (gestures to heckler) actually started off in movies thirty years ago. He had a small part in The Hunchback of Notre Dame. He played the hump.

- Round of applause for our friend here . . . tonight is the first night he's been allowed out without a leash.

- Only ducks, snakes and fools make that hissing sort of sound. Sir, please join me on stage and identify yourself.

where the happenings of the night were different and did create a seed or two of doubt in my mind about what the hell I was doing there. The best way to explain this is with a few examples.

In the early days of my 'Have Tongue, Will Travel' life there was a lot of driving involved, and in other books I've described what it's like to spend the night under the Milky Way, in the middle of a Victorian winter, precariously parked in an up-country culvert, at 45 degrees, suffering from sore ribs, all because I'd fallen asleep at the wheel. I was lucky to be alive.

> *Whatever we do in life, we need feedback, either positive or negative.*

So as an insurance policy of sorts, I used to invite a business friend of mine, Garry Sparke, along for the ride. Not that he took much dragging. Garry is the guy I thank for getting me started in the writing business—together we produced eight books.

'Gaz' has never knocked back a 'free' meal in his life. He also loves to beat his gums (have a chat). So what better way to do what he enjoys doing—a three-hour drive was ample opportunity to solve the problems of the world, indulge in a few rumours and discover a new way to make a dollar!

There was one evening when neither Garry nor myself needed to drive all the way to the function. Our directions were to get to the post office in Kilmore, north of Melbourne, where we were to be met by our contact. He said he would recognise me—no need to worry.

We turned up on time. It was 6.30 p.m. in mid-July, visibility about 20 metres and temperature about 1 degree. Garry had his diabolical Castrol bomber jacket on—he wasn't going to get dressed up for the occasion, as usual. It was hardly Christian Dior fashion, but to give you an idea of how much he thought of the jacket, we had been to more than a hundred 'sportsnights', and about 90 per cent of them saw Gaz and his faithful jacket as an inseparable twosome—a real item.

No flies on Garry that night. The former Williamstown boy was correctly attired for the night ahead. He was warm and I was cold. He was rugged up, and I had a suit and tie on. I was dressed for the occasion, not the weather.

Our lift arrived in an old blue Falcon and we piled into the back seat. As befitted a well-travelled after-dinner speaker and his guest, they then blindfolded us! There we were proceeding to a professional appointment like a couple of guys who had just been kidnapped! God only knows why they would want to kidnap us. Nevertheless, we found ourselves sitting uncomfortably in the back seat of this old banger, not knowing where we were being taken.

After about half an hour of blindness over a winding, bumpy road, my eyes started to ache. We could hear the trees rustling in the wind, water, even cows mooing. The sound of horses galloping was unmistakable. Maybe there were some sheep present as well. It was pretty obvious we weren't visiting a five-star hotel.

Gaz had plenty to say along the way. Eventually he blurted, 'We've been kidnapped. This is for bloody real!'

When the engine stopped both of us were speechless, unusual as this may seem. Out we stumbled into the freezing cold.

Blindfolds off, we still couldn't see anything. Not a star in the heavens above. We followed our guide 50 metres up the drive, squelching up to our ankles in the mud. Before us stood a huge barn. The structure consisted of rusty old corrugated iron roofing supported on several ageing telegraph poles. The warm orange glow from inside was inviting. We were shivering—at least I was!

The first thing that captured my eye was the Persian rug. Yes, a beautifully patterned black and maroon carpet. There was no shortage of ripples and bumps where it had been laid directly on the dirt floor. Who knows how much the carpet was worth. Yes, we certainly had been taken for an interesting ride.

We looked around and there were guys sitting up on haybales, seated among picks and shovels, they were even hanging out of rafters. Obviously the idea of the night was to raise a few dollars for the club.

Gaz organised himself pretty quickly as usual and latched on to the food. The savs were getting cold. They also had meat pies and the compulsory plates of sandwiches. The sandwiches had been hanging around for a while and were like models of the Sydney Opera House, with curved white walls on them. The tomatoes were standing limply next to the cheese, which was stale, browned on the edges and beginning to buckle. It was nowhere near the best feed Gaz had tackled while on duty with me. In fact he would generally rate a night on the food available rather than the speakers.

It was a relief to know we were in good company, which is always the case in country towns. They gave us a very warm welcome. There was a crackling bonfire in the middle of the barn to keep us all cosy. I had to take a position right in front of it to speak to the gathering. Minutes into my talk, I'd just about burnt the bum out of my trousers. The hotter it got, the closer to the audience I shuffled, until I was treading close to the front row.

That was helpful as we didn't have a microphone. And by the time I had entertained for an hour, I had almost lost my voice. I was stuffed, and ready for a rest and a drink. No way, because as soon as my speech had finished, all sorts of furniture was whipped out from nowhere. Suddenly there was a bush casino in the barn! That explained the blindfolds. Card tables were set up. One table needed a few folded up cigarette boxes pushed under each leg to make the top horizontal. That supported the popular roulette wheel! It was a gamble to have a gamble on that setup! Still, they all huddled around with fists full of notes.

There was the obligatory two-up school. They even gave me $100 to join in. That was never going to last long, because the minimum in the two-up school was $50! They were producing $50 notes like they were going out of fashion. I had about three slices at the school and quickly lost my $100—a good player, out of luck!

> They even gave me $100 to join in. That was never going to last long, because the minimum in the two-up school was $50!

Incredible as it was, we discovered a local policeman was running the show, so I don't know what the secrecy was all about. It was one of those bizarre nights. The club raised $15,000—not a bad effort considering the dirt floor and rusty corrugated iron roof.

Then gambling was against the law. We knew that, but we heard no evil and saw no evil, as we got back into the car, blindfolded again for our return journey. What a contrast to the Crown Casino extravaganza on the banks of the Yarra River today.

Our driver had had a truckload. He had definitely not been drinking light, and seemed to be operating on a full tank of the real stuff. That was a worry! But we eventually made it back to the post office safely.

Gaz and I wound our way back to Melbourne a pretty happy duo. This was one of the better ones—things turned out pretty well, everyone was happy, they made money and it was a different, interesting format.

But there was also another night . . .

Garry picked me up from my place, but he refused to get back in the car until he had his caffeine fix. And just as well he did hold out for a drink. The other good news in hindsight was a phonecall which prevented our departure.

I remember chatting for about 5 minutes, and thinking to myself my head was blowing up like the inner-tube of a football—it couldn't possibly get any bigger without bursting and I didn't have a leather casing around the outside to keep it in.

I inspected my hands. They appeared to be getting longer, fatter and redder! I checked out my stomach. It, too, was very inflamed. My arms felt puffed up like Popeye's. My feet tingled as if they were blowing up inside my shoes. My toes were jamming up the ends and the circulation was being cut off.

I put down the telephone and said to Gaz, 'I don't feel too well. I'm crook.'

'Ah! Come on. There's nothing wrong with you,' he replied.

'Have a look at my hands! How big's my head now!' I was losing control of my body.

Garry made a rude comment. 'Do ya want me to burst it? Your head's big enough at the best of times,' he laughed.

I had never felt quite like this in my life. He still wouldn't believe me. Then finally he did after he had a closer inspection. My fingers were swollen badly and the circulation was going crazy. I had a very, very puffy face—ruddy in colour, skin taut!

What happened was I'd taken an antibiotic earlier in the afternoon as treatment for an inflamed larynx. No good for an after-dinner speaker to have tender tonsils or a sore throat. It is not unusual for media guys and gals to smoke heavily in order to achieve a gravelly voice. Mad!

At some stage in a busy schedule you can get a bit run down and vulnerable. I had picked up a touch of tonsillitis. For unknown reasons the antibiotic was doing me more harm than good. Or I was sicker than I first thought. I was getting

Under extreme duress and some pain, it was time to find out what I was made of.

worse by the minute and continued to puff up like a balloon. This really was an emergency. I was certain my head was going to explode.

My cheeky mate wasn't too worried. He felt just fine after his coffee. There he was—hyperactive, mischievous eyes dancing across his face, showing absolutely no sympathy for my condition, full of rude, crude and unattractive one-liners and ready to go.

I called for an urgent crisis meeting between the two of us. Our conclusion was to get me to the outpatient department of the nearest hospital, which was the Austin in Heidelberg. We wasted no time getting there and explained my condition. The staff were extremely helpful, and after a jab in the bum and a munch on a couple of sulphur tablets, my body began returning to normal again.

Nevertheless, the show must always go on. Under extreme duress and some pain, it was time to find out what I was made of. I was prepared to keep my commitment to speak, providing Garry would drive me. We were expected in Echuca, a two-and-a-half-hour drive from Melbourne.

Garry was actually pretty dirty on my recuperation. A two-and-a-half-hour sleep all the way to Echuca. Actually, I had a sneaking suspicion he may have slipped in a couple of cigarettes while we were in transit, but I was too tired to care.

I arrived at the venue feeling pretty shabby. How was I going to stand up and entertain 250 people and make them laugh, when I felt as crook as a dog? Somehow they laughed, and genuinely appreciated the effort I made to get there.

It would have been so easy to use my condition as an excuse to not turn up. Don't let your audience down by not showing up. You'll do irreparable damage to your standing as a speaker.

This had been my second trip to Echuca in a year. The year before

I spoke at an open-air sportsnight under an enormous gum tree beneath the Milky Way. The Murray River flowing by in the background. An old paddle-steamer was choofing up the river, the savs were out, the steaks were on the barbie and we had a huge speaker system hanging off the gum trees ready to blast. Ninety per cent of the sound, like a balloon, straight to heaven. After 45 minutes of shouting into a lame microphone system and swatting mosquitoes I had lost my voice and had had enough. Time for a drink and a mingle.

The bottom line is still people.

While we might live in a high-technology society of information shufflers via networks of computers, the bottom line is still people. Our ability to communicate with each other will be directly proportional to the amount of success we have in life. People are what make it all worthwhile. In sport, success and failure is very spontaneous, particularly at an elite level. Kick a goal on the siren to win a football match and the crowd roar applause. Miss it and they'll boo. Become a hero in the space of seconds.

The feedback from a live speaking performance has for me replaced the intoxicating cheer from an MCG grandstand. And the wonderful aspect of being able to talk with people across this vast continent of ours is it gives me the opportunity to get a feel for their thoughts—what they want to hear about. Question time can be a very testing and stimulating time, with an infinite subject range to test the brain. But very rewarding.

Person-to-person verbal debate has been helpful to my career in television. Basically, if it works live it will work on television.

The difficulty for a television presenter is that there is no spontaneous reaction, no comment, from a camera lens. Sitting in a television studio with only a camera operator, floor manager and autocue operator can be very barren in terms of energy. Yet television is all about energy. And feedback from whatever source is still necessary. A good floor manager is invaluable.

I love the nervous energy in television and I love my sport! In 1987 there was a memorable occasion caused by a combination of travel, television, sport and a speaking engagement, and resulting in one of the more forgettable nights at the microphone. Then *Wide World of Sports* on a Saturday afternoon kept me occupied in Melbourne until 6 p.m. On the night in question it was a mad scramble to catch a 7 p.m. flight to Sydney to speak to an association of agriculturalists who were in town for a convention.

I was aware of makeup marks on the shirt collar. I didn't have time to change the shirt; I quickly took the blazer off and put the suit coat on. I was expecting to walk straight in, maybe have a little to eat, then stand up and perform. Not much time for a breather.

I had already had a pretty hard day, and of course they sat me next to the President's wife. It always seems you have to sit next to either the president or chairman or his wife, or both! I reckon over the years I have sat next to more presidents' wives than Juan Antonio Samaranch of the

> I reckon over the years I have sat next to more presidents' wives than Juan Antonio Samaranch of the International Olympic Committee.

International Olympic Committee. Fortunately she was terrific, and memorable. She wore a tailored jacket, sparklers adorning each ear, full bright red lips and sipped a medicinal glass of scotch. Right away she said, 'Can I get you a drink my dear?' A friend.

I'd been sitting only five minutes and I could feel myself sweating—perspiration building on my forehead. I was thinking, 'Gee, I must look pretty average to this woman . . . because I feel terrible.'

Then I experienced an excruciating pain in the pit of my stomach. Lightning. My head started to spin and I felt woozy. She was offering me a glass of white wine. As she was about to say cheers, I had to interrupt, 'Excuse me, I'd better sneak out for a nervous one! I always get nervous before I speak. I'll be back in a moment.'

I staggered through the crowd as quickly as I could, trying to ignore questions on the way past the tables—they wanted to have a chat, they were a very friendly lot. Finally I dragged myself through the toilet door and into the nearest cubicle. I thought I was going to faint.

Without being rude, crude and unattractive, I was going at both ends. I was in a lot of trouble, I really was. The head was spinning and the shirt at this stage was wringing wet. I had undone my tie.

I wondered what would happen if I fainted, if I keeled over in a heap in there, locked in one of these little cubicles? Someone's going to think, 'Hello, there's another drunk on the floor. He has had a big day out . . . here at the club!'

So in a rather ungainly fashion I wedged one foot against the door. A few moments later, a couple of locals came in to check out the purple lollies in the urinal. One of them turned over his shoulder and caught a glimpse of my crumpled form. The door was ajar, courtesy of a size 11 shoe.

'Hey, that's Maxie Walker! G'day Maxie. How are you, Tangles? All right mate?' They were so excited about saying hello, they didn't notice my jaw down around my kneecaps. I must have resembled a mean and hungry dog—the old cheeks had gone shallow, and my complexion was pale green to grey. I managed to get out a groan. 'Can you help, mate?'

'Anything for a pal. What do ya want me to do?' he enthused. We'd known each other at this stage the best part of 15 seconds.

'For God's sake. Just get me some help. I'm in a lot of trouble.'

'Yeah, you're not wrong. We're all in a lot of trouble, Maxie,' he laughed. 'Gee are we going to get into some trouble tonight,' he went on to speculate mischievously.

It took me ages to convince this guy that I wasn't perched in there because I had had too much to drink, but I was in fact attending the function in the adjoining room. I really did need his assistance.

Finally he acknowledged my problem. I had arrived wearing a tie, and looking spick and span. Now I was absolutely dishevelled wet, coat crumpled on the floor, belt buckle half undone and shirt soaked with perspiration, open to the navel. It crossed my mind, 'Even if I do recover, I can't go back to speak looking like this.'

It was soon spotlight on sport—me seated in the dunny with several onlookers, including the President, all crowding the doorway. I pleaded, 'Have you got somewhere where I can lie down for about ten minutes? Then I'll be right. I'll bounce back.'

With the help of a couple of human crutches, I hobbled downstairs and into an empty office. There I was, draped across somebody's designer office furniture, half undressed, rumpled with bare feet elevated onto an expensive antique desk. I slipped into a nice slumber and was just starting to feel like I was getting it back together again, when the club manager came back with more help. He had found

> **They kept asking silly little questions. I scored 10 out of 10 too.**

a doctor on the premises. In fact, two: a husband and wife team. It was obvious both had had a big sip too—they'd been sailing on Sydney Harbour all afternoon.

'What's your name?' the husband slurred, checking that I had my faculties. Even at that stage I knew he didn't have his!

'Max Walker.'

'What time is it?'

'Twenty-five to nine.'

'Where are you?'

'Middle Harbour Yacht Club.'

'How old are you?'

'Thirty-nine.'

They kept asking silly little questions. I scored 10 out of 10 too.

'He's not too with it,' the husband whispered to the Manager. 'Not too with it at all! Better check his heart beat.'

He took my pulse and appeared vaguely concerned. 'I reckon we'd better be sure and send him off to hospital. He may have had a heart attack,' he mumbled.

By this time, I reckoned I was in a fitter state than they were.

I was on the receiving end of a smelly blast of breath from both medicos as they swayed over me. They must have been on pure vodka, the truth serum, as my old man called it. One match and the whole office would have gone up in smoke! True lies, eh?

There was nothing I could do. They diagnosed a heart attack. All the supposed symptoms were there. I was sure I hadn't, but they were not prepared to take the risk. So they rang an ambulance and went back to the bar. Sorry I interrupted their drinks!

Half an hour later, I was stretched out on a stainless steel trolley, white sheet draped over me and bare feet sticking out the end. My damp suit coat and folded trousers accompanied me.

To get to the ambulance, the two attendants had to wheel their patient through the heart of the function room. People were calling out, 'See ya later Maxie!' They all waved on the way out. I hadn't had a drink, I hadn't had entrée, I hadn't even had main course, and they hadn't had my speech! Yet, they didn't seem too worried.

My hair was matted from the hairspray, the stale makeup was smudged, there was a line of makeup around my collar, shirt half open, tie a long way off centre and the jacket was crumpled. I must have resembled a zombie.

Off we headed to North Shore Hospital. That place was an education in itself. I won a biggish matron on arrival. She was great — checked me in quickly. After check-in, proceedings became pretty rough, I went through the whole gamut, from a cardiograph to blood test—everything possible. I was feeling the worse for wear because the longer I stayed there, the busier the hospital became. More and more car accident and fight victims. I still felt mighty crook. All I wanted to do was escape. The pain was still doubling me up and I had absolutely no chance of presenting my talk. Angry and disappointed.

Finally, after three hours, I said. 'Look. This is it! What's my situation? Am I going to die or not?'

'You've got a 24-hour virus,' the doctor said. They suggested I stay for observation. I couldn't handle it any longer and booked myself out. No one from the function had travelled to hospital with the ambulance. No one was worried whether I was going to be all right or not.

I can still vividly remember ambling into the foyer of the Hilton Hotel in Sydney at 3 a.m. My hair was matted from the hairspray, the stale makeup was smudged, there was a line of makeup around my collar, shirt half open, tie a long way off centre and the jacket was crumpled. I must have resembled a zombie.

The receptionist couldn't stop gaping at me as she checked my booking. I read her mind. She couldn't resist, 'Well, haven't we had a good night, Mr Walker?'

I said 'You wouldn't believe me if I told you what sort of day I've had.' She raised her eyes at me and said, 'Oh yes I would! Well, you're a bit late,' she replied, looking at the clock.

'Yeah I guess I am a bit late. I was going to check in at midnight . . . but well . . . you know, things got a little out of hand! I couldn't get away.'

I turned the key in the door and flaked as soon as I put my head down. The next thing I knew, it was 9.30 in the morning.

Unbelievably, two weeks later, I got a letter from the president on behalf of his association asking for a refund of airfare and accommodation. Obviously as there was no talk—no fee! That's a pretty tough call considering that on the night, from the moment I'd left the venue, there wasn't even a phone call of concern to the hospital from my let-down audience.

So it is pretty clear to see a profitable career in speaking is not just a matter of standing up, chewing a microphone, with a view to grabbing a bulging envelope and then shooting through—thank you very much for dinner. Definitely not!

Before you can both justify and collect a fee, many elements of the jigsaw puzzle need to fall into place.

As Joan Saxton, founder of the successful speaking agency, pointed out to potential speakers, 'Just because you've spoken regularly for free, doesn't mean you will automatically be able to command a payment.'

Ever arrived at the airport and found that your plans have fallen apart dramatically? In my case it was a walk up to the counter, smile and ask, 'Ticket for Mr Walker. The flight to Auckland.'

'Oh, that left three hours ago. Didn't you get a phonecall to say that the departure time had been changed?'

'No,' I challenged.

'Well, you should have.'

Then began one of life's big problem-solving adventures. The problem: how to get from Melbourne to Auckland in time for lunch the next day. It was 5.30 p.m. If I left immediately, I would arrive late evening. A good night's sleep, late brekky, a leisurely stroll around town and roll up at the venue in plenty of time. Thank goodness the airline had employed an 'eagle' at the desk instead of a 'duck'. With not too much consideration for cost equivalents and who was going to pay, the 'eagle' came up with a successful plan of travel. Air New Zealand arriving Wellington about midnight. Check into James Cook Hotel about 1 a.m. (not looking like a great night's sleep but at least I'm in New Zealand). The only flight from Wellington to Auckland leaves around 10 a.m.

To cut the story short, I arrived at the Sheraton in Auckland with barely 45 minutes to spare, then I find out—what else can go wrong—that it's a black-tie function. Try to find Maxwell Henry Normal Walker an XXXL dinner suit in downtown Auckland inside an hour—good luck!

> *Try to find Maxwell Henry Normal Walker an XXXL dinner suit in downtown Auckland inside an hour— good luck!*

Things were so bad, I thought of ringing the guy from Air New Zealand back in Tullamarine to help out. The trousers were a bit short, the waist was a bit big, but the performance was a winner.

Jetlag was a by-product of this successful mission.

It's so important to dot the i's and cross the t's, especially with interstate and overseas travel. You can't afford a mistake. Check, check and check.

On the odd occasion I have referred to myself as a good player out of luck. Bad luck is one matter but bad planning is very different. Take my invitation to speak at Port Pirie in South Australia—yes, just a little way off the beaten track—truck drivers and hitchhikers know it well but how many people living on the Eastern seaboard have been to Port Pirie, Port Augusta or visited the Left-Handers club in Whyalla. (I was stupid enough to drink my first beer with my right hand—had to shout the bar. Costly mistake.)

In my capacity as a Qantas sports liaison officer I was scheduled to speak to a group of travellers and friends. Peter Meade, a former SANFL umpire, was my contact—the man who would organise the detail and make things happen. We met at Adelaide airport and talked football and cricket before catching a light plane to our destination, arriving late in the afternoon.

I was still playing first-class cricket, and Peter was a super-fit whistle-blower. A five-kilometre run was on our agenda before dinner. Peter headed off to make contact with the Mayor while I changed into shorts and runners.

> *It's so important to dot the i's and cross the t's, especially with interstate and overseas travel. You can't afford a mistake.*

When he returned quickly with a look of bemusement I sensed something was out of the ordinary. 'Would you like the good news or the bad news? The good news is that we don't necessarily have to go for a jog. The bad news is that we are a week early!'

'What,' I said in disbelief. 'Melbourne to Port Pirie a week early—unbelievable!'

We could have stayed overnight, but I opted to catch the plane home. Around 8.30 p.m. I knocked on the door back home in Melbourne. My wife opened the door. 'What are you doing home?'

'Just checking,' with a big grin.

Amazing but true—and it gets worse.

I once picked up my ticket at the airport to travel to Sydney for an awards night at Sutherland RSL. I checked in quickly at the hotel and took a taxi to the venue.

I was greeted at the entrance to the function room—filled with smiling parents and boys. The President got me a drink and very enthusiastically introduced me to everyone within arm's length— what a happy and friendly group of people.

Several awards were presented early. Still the President hadn't briefed me on exactly how he wanted to use me. So I asked, and got an instant reply. 'Why don't you present this next award!' It was the Under-14 Goal Kicking Award.

A little light flashed inside my head as I presented the award to a ginger-haired freckle-faced kid who obviously knew how to boot a goal. He was chuffed to shake hands and triumphantly held the silver football above his head.

The problem was I thought I was to talk at a hockey function that night. I unfolded my booking sheet and sure enough the Sutherland Hockey Association was the name on the paper.

When quizzed, the happy President knew nothing of such an evening—he just assumed I was part of his night and tried to make me feel at home with his boys—footballers.

Downstairs I checked the bookings for that evening—they came up with a blank. We rang the Hockey Association president's number—answerphone. As it unfolded, he was at hockey practice.

A long way from home and nowhere to go. I must have looked

lonely because the manager of the RSL Club invited me to stay for dinner in their Chinese restaurant. I'm sure the offer to eat with the football club still stood, but I opted for the restaurant.

During the meal it was discovered that yes, in fact there was a booking for the hockey dinner—but next month.

This was incredible—ticket at airport was valid, hotel booking in place, all a month in advance of when I was supposed to speak.

Later in the night the hockey president and I spoke. We had a chuckle and exactly one month later I did it all again—flew to Sydney, booked into my hotel—but this time I had a function to speak at. Take two!

It was another memorable sports night at Heidelberg, featuring Sam Newman, a pretty average comedian, and yours truly. Heidelberg, despite being the Olympic Village for the 1956 Games, is one of the toughest areas you'll ever find yourself in. (In one area, the school paper has an obituary column . . . only joking.)

> *I never touched the subject of football—concentrated solely on cricket. I read my audience like a Melways—didn't take a wrong turn!*

Scanning the audience, there was an overabundance of tattoos and a scarcity of ties. There was hardly a vowel that hadn't been dropped in this room. This night was the closest I've ever been to seeing a comedian actually dying on stage. Before the comic could deliver his old clichéd punchlines, the back half of the full house delivered them for him.

Batting No. 2 was Sam Newman, the 53-year-old teenager with runaway girlfriends and a penchant for walking the pavement in white football boots. He's the only guy I know who has an interchange bench in his bedroom. Predictably, Sam began to hammer the Collingwood Football Club and anyone even remotely associated with it, but his biggest mistake was to ask a simple long-winded question of the audience: 'How many of you mongrels barrack for Collingwood?' Eighty per cent of the audience either stood up, shouted 'we do' or simply glared back!

The curtain almost dropped on the now familiar Sam Newman glazed stare as a large round man with a carrot-top crewcut, blue singlet, tatts on arm, a couple of teeth missing, asked Sam: 'Does that red Falcon with the mag wheels belong to you Sam?'

'Yes,' said Sam.

'Well, if you continue to shitcan our beloved Pies, I guarantee all four tyres will be slashed before the night's over.'

Sam continued, 'Well in my opinion, the Collingwood football club is the most wonderful . . .'

I batted last. I never touched the subject of football—concentrated solely on cricket. I read my audience like a Melways —didn't take a wrong turn!

Then there was a gig in big Methodist town—actually it wasn't that big. It only had a population of 300. Everyone but the babysitter turned up that night in Airlie.

As invariably happens when you're introduced, there are usually two or three interjections from the floor. I replied with something like, 'It doesn't matter where you are in the world, there's always one in the crowd, and tonight, he's here . . . over there!'

We had a short exchange, which threw the skeleton of my speech out the window, but I continued to feel the energy of the room, and I went with it. Within the first 10 minutes, I'd told the Mop Bucket Story:

There was one unforgettable night in the north of England in 1975 when a couple of Test heroes were having a quiet one. The local watering hole had a nice, intimate atmosphere—low ceilings, dim lighting, great for a social night out.

Those terrors of the 1975 Ashes tour, Western Australians Dennis Lillee and Rodney Marsh, were there having a quiet sip from their Whitbread pint mugs in between bets.

I should tell you that in England back then, you were in no danger at all of getting a cold beer. They didn't even store the beer close to the fridge, let alone inside it. So there they were—Rodney and Dennis, bristling moustaches, pints in hand, and iceblocks melting as quickly as they could get them into the warm beer.

Down with the pints—one, two, three, four, five. About half an hour later, nature took its course. That fabled drinker, Rodney Marsh, was the first to signal to the little Pommie barman, 'Hey pal, whereabouts is the gents?' he demanded. Bacchus chuckled at the directions shouted across the bar: 'Down the corridor, over the dirt track, come to the green sawtooth door, and that's it!'

'Bloody beauty, we're away,' Rodney says, as he sways to his feet. Five steps forward and three back, the little fat fella waddled out of the bar, bounced off the walls of the corridor and across the dirt track until he spied a green sawtooth door.

'Aaaaaaaaaah!' Very few sensations in the world even go close to that when you're under pressure do they?

About fifteen minutes and a few more pints later, Lillee realised his drinking partner still hadn't returned. 'Must have fallen in,' the fast bowler chuckled. So across the bar, down the corridor, over the dirt track marched Dennis—not much quicker or straighter than Marshie had managed. He came to the same green sawtooth door and barked his arrival: 'Hey, Bacchus! Bacchus, what's happened? You fallen in or something?'

A pained reply came under the door: 'No, but every time I go to stand up, some bugger grabs me by the Niagaras.'

Fearing his little mate was in real trouble, Lillee kicked the door open.

One look at the scene inside and Dennis doubled up in laughter. 'You silly bugger, you're sitting on the mop bucket!'

> *I charged on, one liner after one liner, laugh after laugh—getting a great reaction from the minister's wife who became the cue for the minister and their guests to throw off any inhibitions and go with the energy.*

At the end of the night, I agreed that I'd never seen a minister of religion laugh so much. What I didn't realise at the start was that the minister, his wife and eight friends were seated in the middle table, right in front of the lectern (it was a case of 'ignorance is bliss').

I charged on, one liner after one liner, laugh after laugh—getting a great reaction from the minister's wife who became the cue for the minister and their guests to throw off any inhibitions and go with the energy. Just as well I didn't know who I was working to. I'm certain I would have been less cavalier.

Apart from the fundraising side of non-corporate public speaking engagements, which is always near the top of the priority list, there is always the menu to struggle through before being given control of the microphone. Some nights are better organised than others. This is generally reflected in the choice of food—a quick and easy solution is often the good old chook!

Yes, in the industry the nightly vigil is called the 'chicken circuit'. How do you feel about eating chicken (hot or cold, it doesn't really matter) on average nine out of every ten nights on the road? Well, I'm not a huge chicken fan. In fact, I haven't been since my three-month-long diet of rubberised waterfowl in the West Indies, way back in 1973 and again in 1979. Gee, they were tough old birds!

The mere thought of eating chook these days is fairly unpalatable, even with a bottle or two of champagne. Not that you get to sip bubbly too often at a sports night. Although a while ago, while on a working adventure to North Queensland, I was lucky enough to sample one or two glasses of the real bubbly, but that was well before heading off to the venue. I should have known it was too good to be true when the receptionist handed me the key to room No. 13. 'The one with a great view,' she stated.

Sure enough, the night rolled on through a comedy of errors. If Australia is going to show the world what a marvellous country we live in, then our attitude to serving tourists definitely needs a kick in the pants. First impressions are lasting!

I knew we were operating on Queensland time, hoping for an 8 p.m. 'sit-down'. But ten minutes past nine is running a bit behind schedule even in tropical balmy night air. And especially so when the caterer expects to finish by 10 p.m. to avoid paying his indifferent staff for an extra hour's toil. A 10 o'clock finish on Saturday night anywhere in the world is optimistic! And the way this bunch were travelling, there was no hope!

The eating format for the evening was Coles cafeteria style for the entrée and smorgasbord for the main course. Now, I don't mind queuing up for a meal—I've been doing that all my life. But the special invited guests' table was the last one to join what turned out to be a long and restless line of hungry people.

Before any of our table members got near the hot lamps shining on the servery area, the word was out—there was no beef stroganoff left! We must have been standing patiently for almost 15 minutes before that bad news. (Actually, from reports I received later, 'no beef stroganoff' was also the good news.)

Wait for the excuse served up by the empty-handed chef: 'Gee, they never usually eat an entrée, so we didn't make much!'

Nevertheless, there just happened to be plenty of rice. But let's be honest, plain white rice tastes pretty bland on its own without gravy or sauce. Even the gravy leftovers were wiped clean.

So an alternative was offered—one very skinny slice of ham topped with a circular piece of pineapple. By the time this appetising little number was ready, the rice was stone motherless cold. As hungry as I was, somehow the dish lacked quite a deal of appeal. I thought, It can only get better from here. I just kept on grinning and pressed on down the line for main course.

Again we were last to fill our plates with the remnants of what might have been an appetising spread. I knocked over three blokes getting to the last half dozen prawns. All the chicken breasts and drumsticks had been sifted through. Only the bones remained.

By now I was getting nervous about my talk. I had lost my appetite. Meanwhile, the quick and the hungry locals managed to keep downing the odd glass or dozen of cold beer, and had loosened up considerably compared with the quiet group of people that started out the evening.

Yes, the time was ripe to launch into a few stories to entertain the gathering. A belly full of food and plenty of liquid refreshment had certainly put the crowd in the right frame of mind.

> *I knocked over three blokes getting to the last half dozen prawns. All the chicken breasts and drumsticks had been sifted through. Only the bones remained.*

Their response was fantastic, but my task was made more difficult by the heavy-handed waitresses collecting the plates and cutlery as I spoke. The amplification of shuffling cups, saucers and plates, knives and forks was very loud as it bounced off the shiny surfaces in the room. Never agree to speak while clean-up is in progress. You will do yourself a huge disservice. This is a no-win environment . . . only for the kitchen.

Forty-five minutes later I finished. So too the eager catering staff, who were very keen to be off the premises. Several people moved to the rear of the room in search of sweets, but they too had disappeared into thin air. This time the explanation was: 'No one seemed to want any, so we cleared them away thinking we might use them at tomorrow night's function.'

After some very stern words to the head caterer, the apple slices and cream reappeared. Our next problem was how we were going to eat them. The plate removers had been instructed to pick up the dessert spoons!

At the top table I ate my sweets with the tiny spoon out of the sugar bowl. When I had finished scraping the bottom of the bowl, I handed it on to the gentleman sitting next to me.

At this stage the thought of a nice coffee and port took my fancy. You will not believe this—they ran out of hot water for the tea and coffee! I'm glad there were only 125 people present— imagine the problems 250 people would have created.

One young lady, who was lucky enough to have her cup filled with coffee, then suffered the disappointment of seeing it whisked away from under her nose before she could finish it!

A couple of beers later and a chat with several stayers brought the night to a satisfactory end, or so I thought.

It was 1.30 a.m. and my room key—No. 13—was still at reception. This was shaping up as a major problem because the lobby area of the hotel was dark, locked and deserted. I remembered looking out of my window earlier in the night and thinking, what a magnificent view across the ocean. I didn't bother to lock the sliding doors because my room was on the second floor.

Now try to visualise a 17-stone man, with several drinks under the belt, attempting to scale the balconied façade of the hotel. I was within metres of my destination when a security guard appeared and scared the living daylights out of me. He also had a companion who was breathing very heavily—a German shepherd watchdog!

The adventure ended on a tired, yet happy note, when the guard shoved me over the balcony of No. 13 with both hands. Perhaps I would wake up with a start to find the events only a nightmare. No such luck—it really happened!

> *Life is all about creating memories, whether at home, play or work!*

A colleague recently suggested: 'Life is all about creating memories, whether at home, play or work!' How true. The wonderful memories of people, events and places have stacked up like a metal filing cabinet above my eyebrows—the bio-computer—just waiting to be recalled and retold to an appropriate audience.

Be a student of people and places, and you will discover the investment of time and a genuine curiosity will provide an endless source of material. Make notes, not just mental notes—write them down—and use a camera wherever you travel. I love my small-format 35 mm fixed lens camera. It is so easy to carry—it lives in my briefcase and follows me like a shadow wherever I go. If you haven't started to build a file of story material, do it now. Publications like *Reader's Digest* contain an amazing amount of very interesting material. Buy a filing cabinet dedicated to stories. Get fair dinkum about writing up a journal.

My dad Big Max used to say, 'The faintest pencil is better than the best memory'—which brings me to the diary or planner. Without one of these your life will continue to be a journey without a rudder. My diary is my bible—a blueprint for making dreams come true and a tool for recording the memories in ink.

The weekly compass is a great help to getting a busy lifestyle in perspective. If your desk, office or life is in chaos, buy a good one and eliminate the suffocating effect of too many pieces of paper. None of which you can find when you need it.

There are occasions when even a diary can't predict exactly what will occur. Life's pathway is full of unexpected turns and happenings. In my wildest dreams I never expected to come face-to-face with that famous comic-book hero, The Phantom! I had just sat down after about an hour on my feet entertaining a wonderfully receptive audience at the Western District Aussie Rules Football Club in Brisbane.

Be a student of people and places . . .

It was a hot, sticky night and the sweat was pouring forth from my brow. Showing a lot of suave and decorum, I patted my leaking brow and glowing cheeks with the bright red paper napkin I hadn't yet used. They do stain.

Sitting on the main table at any function can be very much 'spotlight on sport' with 200 sets of beady eyes dwelling on your every movement. It's very difficult to pick your teeth in private if the steak has been too tough, or if the gap between your front teeth is clogged with a delightful piece of golden corn so elegantly gnashed off the cob earlier in the night.

The idea is to appear unruffled by all the attention and act naturally. Which is exactly what I was doing—casually chatting away with the club president and signing autographs.

Then I watched a strange character making his way to the official table. I couldn't believe my eyes! The humidity was stickier than a desert drover's armpits and here is a guy dressed in full-length trenchcoat, cravat, sunglasses and top-hat.

It was a capacity crowd. Yes, they were hanging from the rafters that night. As the masses made their way to the public conveniences in the foyer during the break, this joker forced his way against the traffic flow to the front of the entertainment room—where we were seated!

I said to the president, 'Have a look at this bloke—I bet he wants to get in my ear!' I couldn't help but add, 'He's a real live one, this fella!'

He arrived, as large as life, in front of the decorated trestle and introduced himself: 'Mr Walker—the ghost who walks.'

I thought to myself, 'Oh, oh, I wasn't wrong—he reckons he's The Phantom.' It was very difficult to prevent myself from laughing. A sly grin crept out from under my moustache! He thrust his hand towards me in a positive manner of greeting and said, 'From one Mr Walker, to another, it's an honour to meet you!' Needless to say his hand was very clammy, but a vice-like grip accompanied the dampness. Then he started peeling off his clothes, item by item. Off came the cravat, sunglasses and hat. Sure enough, he had the distinct black eye pieces to conceal his identity. As he took off his overcoat, he revealed the skin-tight grey body suit with the diagonal, black striped jocks. His belt supported some firearms and the famous skull sign covered his navel. Yes it certainly was him—the ghost who walks, the comic-book character created by Lee Falk, who died in 1999 at the age of ninety.

But why me? How was I going to explain this fellow at question time, soon to follow? He wasn't shy either. He quickly called for two glasses of milk so I could take the sacred oath—to serve the world, against evil.

Now milk is not one of my favourite drinks. But I thought, any minute now I'll be hearing the beat of jungle drums in the distance

The faintest pencil is better than the best memory.

saying, 'Drink the milk, Tangles, or you're dead!' Or maybe dozens of pygmies would come rushing at me through the club room doors.

What else could I do? I raised my right hand above my head and read the sacred oath:

I PROMISE TO FIGHT ON THE SIDE OF THE WEAK AGAINST THE OPPRESSOR WITH GOOD AGAINST EVIL, AND TO DO EVERYTHING IN MY POWER TO DESTROY GREED, CRUELTY AND INJUSTICE WHEREVER IT EXISTS, AND MAY MY CHILDREN FOLLOW AFTER ME.

Cricket commentator Bill Lawry was nicknamed The Phantom because he always had a Phantom comic in his back pocket during his playing days. I later discovered the man they used to refer to as a corpse in pads was a member of The Phantom Club of Australia.

Today there are more than 3500 members of the club. They share good times and a large range of recreational activities. I was proud to accept a life membership of the club, and it really is quite amazing just where and when you run into Phantom 'phriends'. Worldwide, there are 100 million devotees in sixty-three countries.

For the uninitiated: 400 years ago the lone survivor of a pirate raid was washed up on a remote Bengali beach. On the skull of his father's murderer he swore an oath to fight crime. Generations followed him. The pygmy Bandar people believed it was always the same man. 'The ghost who walks,' they said. So the legend grew. A name whispered, loved and feared—The Phantom.

He's pretty good, The Phantom. But I wonder how well he'd cope batting against the fearsome pace attack of the West Indies. Maybe they'd respect him too much to get him out? Good question.

It's amazing how a perfectly normal beginning to a fun night can be turned into a deadly serious commitment to fight evil at all times. All it took was a couple of milks.

I repeat, 'Long live the ghost who walks'—and that applies to Bill Lawry too!

4

The Birth and Growing Pains of a Good Speech

A good speech is when the price of the dinner, the carpark and the babysitter were worth it.

ALFRED HITCHCOCK

A good speech can be written on the back of a business card.

MAX WALKER

Speaking in public is the one thing that scares the living suitcase out of human beings most. Not sharks, crocodiles, spiders, the big one—DEATH—or maybe heights. No, it is being invited to stand up and speak . . . 'Ladies and Gentlemen . . .' Research suggests that the situation of being asked to stand up and speak in public is one of the most feared predicaments we can find ourselves confronted with.

I have often compared the situation to climbing onto the blocks prior to the start of a swimming final—standing naked! There you are in your birthday suit, good or bad body, goosebumps—a bundle of nervous energy before the race. There is no turning back or turning your back to the world. It is now—not yesterday, not tomorrow—judgement time.

Why not have that judgement be a positive one? Take control and be prepared like an Olympic swimmer. Athletes train 365 days a year for their chance at glory. For many it will be their only chance at Olympic gold. For the rest of their life they might have to wonder: If only I had done this . . . or that . . .

The reason for you standing on your feet is to create and deliver a memorable speech. Let's give you the benefit of our experience. Mike has written more than 20,000 opening lines and approximately 750,000 jokes. In cricket terms, my aggregate of 'talks' outside of television and radio is close to 3000—far more than the total number of runs I accumulated in the Test arena.

Having a speech written for you is in most cases a luxury that neither time nor money will afford. I have never enjoyed reading speeches written by somebody else, but many people in the corporate and entertainment worlds are having chunks of words and full-scale speeches written for them every day. Attempting to regurgitate another person's words with emotion, meaning and candid humour is not easy. The constant parade of politicians captured looking often less than convincing on television, confirms how difficult it is to spit out someone else's words.

Okay, down to making it happen! First, make sure you know your audience and your topic. Find out everything you can. The more research you do, the less bland, boring and predictable your speech is likely to be. This is why you may get more relevant information by watching what people do rather than listening to what people say. This is especially relevant in sales of products.

It will all come so much easier if you can develop an attitude of genuine love of people and a curiosity for what makes others tick. Be a student of people. Ask interesting questions. The more interesting the question the better the answer. Often a person will answer the question with the answer they think you would like to hear. Ever filled in a questionnaire on sex or dieting? How many times, how much? It makes you smile doesn't it?

> *Don't speak too fast. Calm down, take a deep breath and smile.*

Begin with an open mind and a blank sheet of paper. I like to list all relevant information on an A3 size pad—the pages are large enough so I don't run out of space. This way you can keep an eye on everything as you think. I like a 'scatter gun approach', where the number and variety of ideas at the start is more important than the purpose of the speech. Even though a thought or idea might seem irrelevant at first, it may become significant to the end result.

Use shorthand and symbols that feel comfortable—bullet points, globules, squares, arrows, lists, numbers and colours. Use whatever it takes to get the information organised on paper.

You may suffer from writer's block during brainstorming and run into a dead end . . . clean out of ideas! Persistence sometimes works, but I find that going for a quiet walk through the building or outside around the block, is great to release a few endorphins and shake up the grey matter. Mulling, I think it's called.

Invariably when I return to the worksheet, my thoughts have crystallised. Go back to your subject headings. These words will act as a trigger to stimulate thought.

From the initial jottings, sketch a broad skeleton (see page 109) for your talk. This will act as a framework to fill in around the major elements. Think of the big picture and don't get bogged down by detail and trivia. This is a most critical part of the creative process. Let's call it the pyramid—starting with a strong foundation and peaking at its apex. The pinnacle representing the key factor—the final message.

As in any building, the stronger the foundations the more secure the design solution. The more homework and research that is done in preparation for a speech, the more flexibility, credibility and fresh humour is possible.

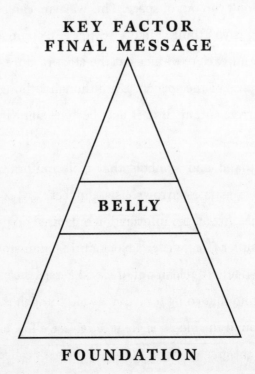

KEY FACTOR
FINAL MESSAGE

BELLY

FOUNDATION

THE GOLDEN RULES

- Know the person for whom you are writing. Know everything about them and how they think and react.

- Know the audience you're aiming at. There's no point in doing jokes for your friends. It's the audience that you need to get to laugh.

- Be concise. If a joke can be told in five words and not six, tell it in five.

- Like and respect your audience. Don't talk down to them.

When filling in the skeleton, let your mind wander a bit. You may have written or spoken on the same subject in the past, but need to gather some new ideas. Perhaps there are some people who might be able to give worthwhile insights into your theme. Write their names down and circle them so they stand out on the page.

Planning pays off when working out your speech priorities. It's like a cricket captain with his batting order. How can the team score the most runs from the given players? On the dressing room wall he pins up his list, from number one to the end. In simple

LIFE / SPORT / BUSINESS... EVERYONE HAS THE RIGHT TO MAKE A DECISION — WINNER OR A LOSER

WHAT WE ACHIEVE OR RECEIVE IN THIS LIFE IS VERY MUCH DEPT ON ATTITUDE.

■ **FLINDERS STREET STATION**
- COMING 2 BOTH ENDS KICKED IN → JUST WAITING FOR SOMETHING... ANYTHING TO HAPPEN!
- LIKE CATTLE ... NO DIRECTION → THEY WILL NEVER FEEL THE EXHILARATION OF WINNING AGAINST

AT NO STAGE IN THEIR LIFE WILL THEY FEEL THE EXHILARATION OF WINNING AGAINST

THAT'S OKAY FOR THEM ...

BUT I'D LIKE TO THINK EVERYONE HERE HAS THE POTENTIAL TO BE A HIGH ACHIEVER

■ **NIKI LAUDA ... ATTITUDE ... LEARN FROM MISTAKES ... PREOCCUPATION**
PICK UP THE RECEIPT.

→ IN SPORT THERE IS NO PERFECT PLAYER ... ALTHOUGH SOME WOULD HAVE US BELIEVE

VERY GOOD AT TIME MANAGEMENT ... THEY MAKE CHOICES ... SPUT SECOND OVER YEARS.

BE PRO-ACTIVE NOT REACTIVE — IF YOU DON'T MAKE THE DECISIONS SOMEONE ELSE WILL!!!

... IDEAS. DON'T BE
commit the   IF IT WILL M
energy behind ✱ BUSINESS &
the idea.

■ **CHANGE ... WSC .. against public opinion**
MAKE DECISIONS IT WILL FORCE THE PACE.
NIGHT CRICKET ... JOEL GARNER.
DO IT IN THE MIND DESPITE THE OPPOSITION ... MANY TIMES Z CORRECTION.
... SELF VISUALIS

■ **BIO COMPUTER ... BRAIN**

■ **SELF ESTEEM ... HORRIE SMITH.** — KEY TO MY SPORTING SUCCESS
WHEN A SCHOOLBOY I HAD 2 IMMEDIATE GOALS... BURNING PASSION **HONE**

■ **PLANNING** — BRINGING THE FUTURE INTO PRESENT
GOTTA HAVE DIRECTION "BLUEPRINT" — GOAL = PLANNED FOR ELLST.
ASK QUALITY QUESTIONS OF YOURSELF — GET QUALITY ANSWERS ..
1. HOW GOOD ARE WE?
2. ARE WE SUCCESSFUL % OF REPETITION
   DOING TODAY WHAT WAS SUCCESSFUL YESTERDAY
3. ARE WE TOP OF THE CLASS — WHY NOT.

■ **LIFE IS LIKE GOLF ...**
FOLLOW THRU!
WE AS INDIVIDUALS MUST COMMIT TO THAT
GENERALLY THAT COMMITMENT IS ENOUGH TO

■ **RESEARCH & PREPARATION — KAPE COFFEE ..**

■ **MINAX TIME-MANAGEMENT ...** Doing things right v d
comfort zone
160 hrs / week. BY.Y
KANI — ATTITUDE...

■ **TEAMWORK — NOT LETTING SIDE DOWN**
RICK McCOSKER   OVERCOMING PAIN / FEAR Z DESIRE / PLEASURE

■ **CROCODILES.**
high ethical standards the cornerstone of con
HONESTY / CREDIBILITY / TRUST ... MONEY CAN'T

FINISH ...
COMMUNICATION IS A CONTACT SPORT ... YOU'VE GOTTA
Bottom line is people.

terms, you have to have a great start, a good middle and a great ending. The challenge is to connect all three parts seamlessly.

You may want to transfer the ideas to a computer at this stage. Because I don't enjoy using a keyboard during the creative process, I stay with the pen or pencil on paper. I have better 'vision' with the ideas laid out on paper rather than a computer screen. No two people are the same, so do whatever opens those creative gates of spontaneity for you.

Having selected start, middle and finish, it is time to get serious. Let's write the speech. Nobody gets it right first up! Don't agonise over precise wording, sentence structure or length. If your elements, anecdotes or data fail to connect, leave a hole, a colour, a symbol or brackets to let you know where it needs more work.

> **Don't use a story unless it is relevant and fully illustrates a point.**

You may prefer to dictate into a tape recorder. This might get you thinking more like a speaker, and works well for some people.

In terms of method of communication, the written word and the spoken word are poles apart. Remember this when you are writing—it is a talk, not a read. No matter how clever your words may look on paper, a speech is only as good as it sounds to its audience. Readers have the luxury of being able to reread or check back if there is something they don't understand—listeners can't do this.

LADIES AND GENTLEMEN

Usually a printed text avoids repetition, but a spoken text often benefits from being able to repeat and reinforce meaning—like some sports commentators! Not the annoying ones!

As a general rule, clear, simple, unmistakable words and phrases are more effective than complicated sentences.

When pulling together your exploratory first draft notes, consider blending information from observing the world around you. It is freely available, and all you have to do is look for it.

You could check almanacs for birthdays and details of major events. Daily papers are wonderful for up-to-the-minute snippets on any subject. Headlines from newspapers can be a good source of interesting lines.

> *Word pictures of personal experiences can be the glue that holds your speech together. Bring feeling to your anecdotes.*

Word pictures of personal experiences can be the glue that holds your speech together. Bring feeling to your anecdotes and bring yourself into the story.

Listen to how you have been introduced and, if possible, 'back announce' your introduction. Choose a point from the introduction, and react to it in such a way that you can move from your comments straight into the presentation. Try writing your own introduction.

At a luncheon in Hong Kong for the Australian Chamber of Commerce, the MC had done his homework before introducing me. After listing several of my achievements, he went on to say, 'and Max was once described as being able to speak under water with a mouthful of marbles. Ladies and Gentlemen, that remarkable all-

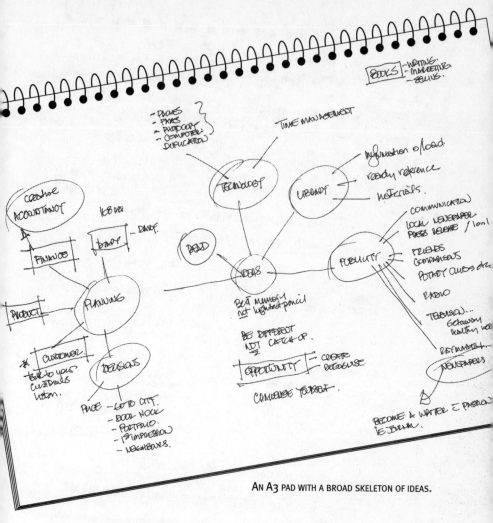

AN A3 PAD WITH A BROAD SKELETON OF IDEAS.

rounder, Mr Max Walker'. On arriving at the lectern, grinning like
Luna Park, I was presented with a stocking mesh bag containing
20 odd marbles—cat's eyes, blood suckers, milkies, the lot; as well
as a pair of blue speedos which I'm sure would have changed the
pitch of my voice had I been able to squeeze my important pieces
into them. His planning proved to be a great prop, and allowed me
the opportunity to explain how ABC commentator Drew Morphett
was moved to utter such an outlandish claim.

It occurred way back in 1981 at the conclusion of my inaugural

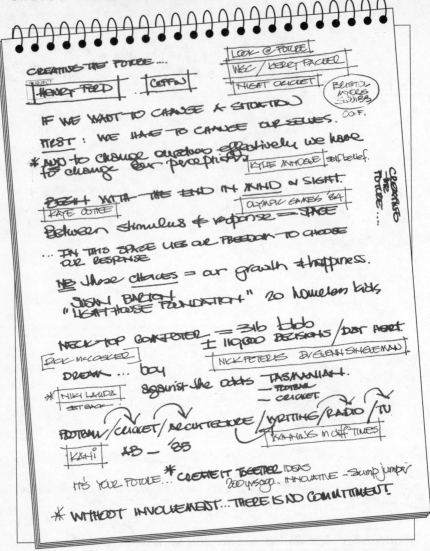

radio commentary assignment—Victoria versus South Australia at Kardinia Park, Geelong. In attendance were relatives, press, stray cats, dogs and seagulls.

My stint at the microphone ran in two-hour blocks, three times a day over four days, without commercials. I had no alternative but to keep talking. Fortunately it happened naturally and easily. Drew was asked by a person of authority, 'How did the big fella go?'

Yes, it was a memorable answer.

Writing 100 jokes a day By Mike McColl Jones

For most of my television working life I've written up to 100 jokes a day for comperes like Graham Kennedy, Don Lane and Steve Vizard, many of these during the show as it was going live to air.

When I started at Channel 9 writing for Graham, I met a man who was to become my mentor and close friend, Freddy Parsons, whose illustrious career spanned vaudeville, radio and TV. Fred created the 'McCackie Mansions' for Roy Rene 'Mo', wrote for Jack Davey and others through the golden era of radio and then shared his great talent with TV viewers, creating such masterpieces as 'The Wilsons' for Graham and Rosie Sturgess.

The first advice Freddy ever gave me was, 'Never think about tomorrow until you've conquered today'—never concern yourself with the next show until the credits have rolled on this one.

The other early advice Fred gave me was to always start with a blank piece of paper, and never to use joke books. At first I did buy a couple of joke books, but gradually I found that the stuff I was writing was more effective, so I haven't used a joke book since.

Once Don Lane first came to do a show in Melbourne and asked me to write for him. He brought three of his own writers down with him. They were using my office and I was fascinated to hear them say, 'Let's look for a Philip Brady joke in the book.' I interrupted, 'Don't bother, you won't find a Philip Brady joke in any joke book.' Philip is a very distinctive character and you have to know that before you can write about him.

Many times I've been asked to think of a joke either moments

APART FROM HER MAJESTY, I NOTICE SO MANY LADIES ARE WEARING THOSE JEWELLED HEAD PIECES TONIGHT. APPARENTLY THERE'S A "TIARA BOOM TODAY"

(BERT IS HANDED NOTE). ..... I'VE GOT A MESSAGE FROM THE AUDITORI... (AROUND) .... APPARENTLY THERE ARE TWO PEOPLE WHO GOT IN HERE TODAY WITHOUT PAYING (STARE AT ROYAL BOX)

NOTES TO BERT NEWTON, WHO WAS HOSTING THE ROYAL COMMAND PERFORMANCE.

eased from Long Day J to the studio, and wh the delay?

he was late getting to the studio, and oduction girl went up to her and said "why the delay?

at the cab driver had taken her to Channel 7 by mistake, a

he production looked at her with her huge round eyes and

illing him".

And one of my all-time favorite stories.

This didn't happen at Channel 9, but at another TV station

A noted legal man, a lawyer, had written a book about his

was called "The Lawyer who Laughed", and he was a gue

In those days, a particular production crew member use-

unfortunately, this man had only about five per cent of hi

Green Room and take him to the studio.

heavily, and he was pretty well primed when he had to

When he arrived, the man's wife gestured to him and s

early blind", to which the production

MIKE'S TYPED-UP JOKES, READY TO GO.

ON THIS IS A PRETTY LAUGH
UP, BUT NEVILLE WRAN...
IS YOUR LIFE."

THE DRESSING HOVE AT THE
OPNA HOUSE IS STUNNING
TONIGHT. I SAW ONE WITH
SEXY OFF THE SHOULDER BLUE
SATIN, BEAUTIFUL DIAMONDS ON
DROP EAR-RINGS — THE GOWN
HAD A SPLIT UP TO THE WAIST...
AND THAT WAS JOHN MICHAEL
HOWSON.

before a show or during the show. You don't have time to go to any joke book under those circumstances. It has to come straight off the top of your head.

It doesn't matter whether you're writing 100 jokes a day or preparing a speech for a 21st. The technique is the same:

Always carry a small notebook on you and have it by the bed. If you get a good idea, write it down.

I like using large art pads so that you can have several trains of thought running at the same time. Start in the centre and work out. This is great for preparing speeches too.

It's easy to say 'don't worry', but never think about how many jokes you have to do—just do them!

The skeleton for the Australian Chamber of Commerce talk was a truly spontaneous document, but a very necessary process and working tool.

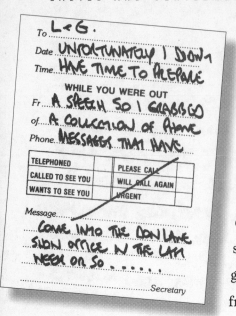

To L & G.

Date UNFORTUNATELY I DON'T

Time HAVE TIME TO PREPARE

WHILE YOU WERE OUT

Fr A SPEECH SO I GRABBED

of A COLLECTION OF PHONE

Phone MESSAGES THAT HAVE

TELEPHONED		PLEASE CALL	
CALLED TO SEE YOU		WILL CALL AGAIN	
WANTS TO SEE YOU		URGENT	

Message

COME INTO THE DON LANE

SHOW OFFICE IN THE LAW

NEED OR SO . . . . . .

———————Secretary

One example of a different approach is what Mike calls his message pad speech. He once wrote a speech on 20 or so phone message pad sheets. Carefully planned, it all made sense, but was different, the premise being, 'I didn't have time to prepare a speech'. It was written as if he had grabbed a handful of message pages from hotel reception. 'Let me read them to you'. Paul Hogan, who was in the audience that night, reckoned it was one of the cleverest speeches he'd ever heard.

Paul's offsider for many years, and now a successful businessman, John Cornell, was invited to speak 'briefly' at Kerry Packer's sixtieth birthday. The event also doubled as a twenty-year reunion of players and key personnel involved in World Series Cricket—a milestone in the many and varied entrepreneurial successes of Mr Packer, as we players referred to him. When World Series Cricket was starting off, in the midst of incredible publicity, Kerry Packer's brother, Clyde, visited Sydney from California and when he stepped off the aircraft, journalists asked him to comment on arguably the biggest cricket story this century. Clyde looked at them and said, 'I am not my brother's wicket-keeper'.

John Cornell is a very astute writer and has always had a keen eye for what makes people laugh. Wearing a scriptwriter's hat, he set about using one phrase and repeating it as the conclusion of each anecdote. The phrase was . . . 'Now that took balls'.

I don't need to fill in the anecdotes—they were memorable. But more memorable because of the manner in which the major elements were linked. His performance, beautifully crafted and executed, was all over in 10 minutes. Having written and rehearsed it until delivery was perfect would no doubt have given him enormous satisfaction. He left the lectern and spotlight to a standing ovation, and a smiling Kerry.

Another way to make a speech different is to convince your listeners that you have unearthed

> *Success or failure— we all have a choice.*

several old report cards of the major players or high-profile names in the room.

Merv Hughes, the retired fast bowler with the fertilised moustache, could be discussed like this: 'Merv Hughes—he'd better be good at cricket and footy because he's not going to make it as an academic'.

For Christopher Skase: 'Christopher seems quite talented, but a curious thing happens at exam time when he always complains his asthma is too bad for him to take the test.'

Another approach is to think of an ideal ending, then work backwards. This is a particularly good method when you're short of time.

What makes a memorable climax? Look for a way to encompass the spirit of your message. Appeal to the gathering's shared hopes, fears, selfish or humane interests, and try to twang a chord.

One that I have used successfully, and I can say this on the basis of many people asking me to send them a copy, is the following:

> To dream anything that you want to dream—that is the beauty of the human mind.

> To do anything that you want to do—that is the strength of the human will.

> To trust yourself to test your limits—that is the courage to succeed.

This is one of the many quotes I've collected over the years. I keep them all handwritten on beautiful paper in fountain pen ink. The book cover will last a lifetime—it is made of timber. Unfortunately I do not know the author of this inspirational cluster of words. If I did I would say thank you from the bottom of my heart for the impact they have had on audiences around the world.

To gain maximum effect and to make the ending even more special, have a photocopy of your quote folded away in your pocket. Use the power of silence, of thought, of expectation . . . a little theatre. What has he got in there? Slowly take the quote from your pocket while capturing the attention of as many of the audience members as is possible—a slow even sweep of your eye-line from left to right.

Then read with passion, but be familiar with the words. The audience needs to see your eyes, not the top of your head. Pause and wait for the applause. Acknowledge the reaction of the audience and walk away feeling a job well completed.

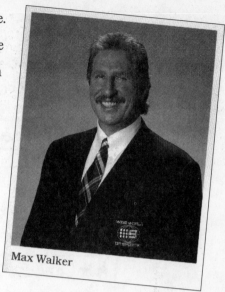

Max Walker

I love language. Recently my seven-year-old daughter provided me with a wonderfully creative sentence. Because we were going overseas to Kuala Lumpur for the Commonwealth Games she was going to miss two weeks of school. Her teacher, Miss Murray, was smart enough to give the trip her blessing only if Alexandra wrote in her journal every day.

Her first entry read: 'While travelling in our taxi to the airport, I watched my mum put on her kissing paint.' Kids are hard to beat.

This one is from an adult in a canteen we ate in often, describing the food he was eating: 'These meat pies are really rat coffins'. Needless to say, I looked closely after every bite. He went on to give credibility to his comment by suggesting he had been given one across the counter with the corner bitten off like a pocket on a billiards table—teeth marks visible in the firm, brown pastry.

Whether you start at the top of the page or the end of the page, if you have laid the bones of the speech down correctly and firmly,

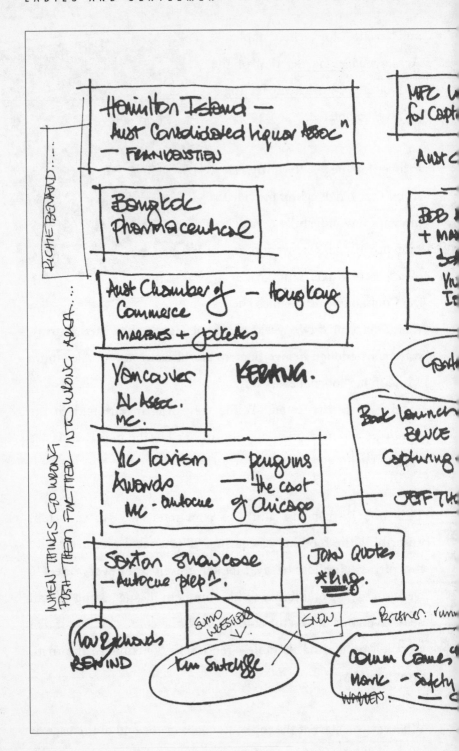

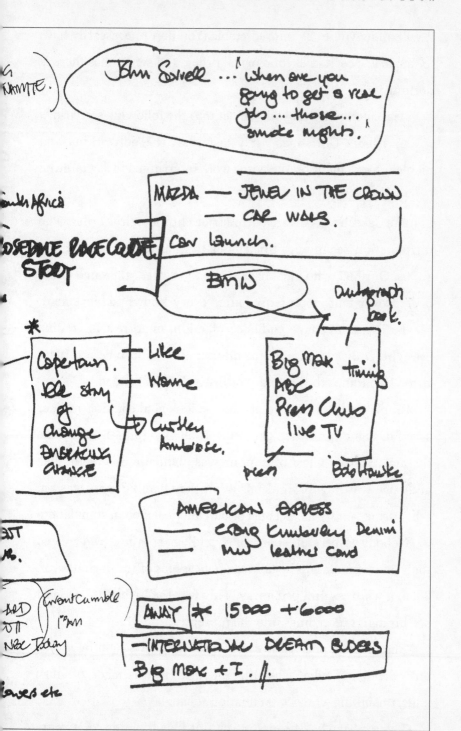

A BRAINSTORMING PAGE.

it will allow you to be unpredictable. You don't necessarily have to tackle a speech in chronological order, and sometimes there is nothing worse.

Please don't ever let yourself get into the following scenario:

At a bank Christmas party last year, the networking and nibbles, not to mention the wine, were interrupted to say farewell to a long-serving member of staff.

The speech was arranged in strict chronological order. The introduction began with this chap's first day at the bank in the 1930s. Our MC, who must have started his career the same week, peered over half-moon lenses after every known achievement. Maybe it was to gauge audience reaction, or to rest his failing eyesight. Only a handful of the attendees were born before 1940. After 10 minutes the Second World War had just ended.

People's glasses were empty and he looked like taking another seven or eight minutes to get to the 1956 Olympics. By this time the embarrassed guest of honour was clenching his teeth. The audience was now brain dead. What they wanted most was another drink, a tasty morsel on a biscuit and real mental stimulation.

Nobody gave a stuff about 1961, and most of the crowd created their own stimulation by talking about issues of the current year. Then a waitress dropped a tray. This was the highlight—at least she brought proceedings into the present.

The thickish pile of cue cards in the speaker's right hand was an indicator of what was still to come. He was made of stern stuff, unsmiling, with no inclination to laugh.

This rooster had been spitting out 'dead' words for twenty minutes—time to get off the perch. It was only supposed to be an introduction. His delivery was monotonous, sleep-inducing and totally forgettable.

Be daring, be unpredictable, be different. It is not a crime to be original. In fact you will be probably be applauded for it.

If you are writing the speech for someone else, it is important that you capture their spirit, style and unique turn of phrase.

If writing for yourself, the same applies. Don't read large amounts of material you have pinched from another source. It may sound okay read silently inside your head, but it is not you. The key is to find your own voice.

> **Read with passion, but be familiar with the words.**

Television is a disarming medium. Hesitation, change of eye-line and physical imperfection are magnified. Keep the eye level of your conversation and the pitch of your words horizontal.

'Never talk down to people who look up to you'—this little gem came from boxing legend Muhammad Ali. When he dominated the pugilistic landscape, his press conferences were refreshingly frank and unique. He would tell the world when he would turn out the lights and put his opponent to sleep (often he was correct). 'The Greatest' would also recite poetry he had written.

Today he walks and talks awkwardly but still with power, dignity and a unique delivery. One indelible image of Muhammad Ali for me is not so much from the boxing ring, where he did win Olympic gold, but in 1996 at Atlanta. Billions of people held their breath in awe and in expectation as his cameo with the Olympic torch ignited the world—it lasted only a matter of seconds.

> **Be daring, be unpredictable, be different.**

Bert Newton introduced 'The Greatest' to the packed Melbourne Hilton during the Logie presentation in 1979, and immediately their rapport was obvious. As they played with each other verbally, Bert threw in a phrase he'd been using on the Don Lane Show.

'I like the boy,' said Bert, after Ali had said nice things about him.

Suddenly the mood on stage changed. Ali was looking angry (and one thing no one ever wanted was for Ali to be angry. He could cause a severe injury even when he was feeling good!). Bert was nonplussed. The audience thought it was a set-up at first, but then they realised something 'serious' was going on. Ali's friends were yelling to him, 'He said Roy . . .' because unknown to most of us, especially Bert, addressing somebody as 'boy' is highly offensive in America.

The tension was electric. Ali sensed it was a fight and the audience could see the situation was for real. Bert was ad-libbing away. 'I'll even change religion,' he offered Ali.

Things finally sorted themselves out, but viewers will never forget the time Bert met 'The Boy'.

Ali summed it up beautifully, body positively confrontational, aggressive, eyes wide: 'I'm the man, you're the boy.'

Bert agreed and used his most disarming weapon—the smile!

Once you have written all of the words, this doesn't mean you have finished. Congratulations, you have only completed a first draft. A useful idea is to prepare drafts double spaced, to make redrafting easier. What you have created may be only the foundation. During the rewrite or polishing stage you can play with each subject, each paragraph and each word to improve your presentation.

Just because you've written it down once, it doesn't mean you can't scrap it altogether if you are not happy with it. Be prepared to lose some of your efforts—even the words you like most. The Australian author Bryce Courtenay suggests sometimes having to cut out all the things that you really like.

Absolute worst case scenario: you hate your first effort. It requires guts and conviction to start again and quite possibly from an entirely different direction. But sometimes this is the best way to go.

The great comedy writer, the late Fred Parsons once said, 'Always write down the second thing you think of'—meaning there was always a better way of saying anything.

It is not sufficient to silently read your script. Reading the speech out loud will give you a chance to pick up words that interrupt the natural rhythm of the sentence. Once the speech is finished, you should practise it several times in front of somebody else or a mirror. You can never read a speech too many times. It helps produce a more relaxed performance.

When you become comfortable with your strengths at story-telling and relating facts in an interesting manner you will probably want to bypass the stage of writing out the whole speech word perfect.

You will focus on structuring the skeleton in the best possible order.

You may like to write only the first linking line into an anecdote or example and then the closing or relevant link to the next element in your speech.

This is the way I like to operate if my engagement is a specific theme at a corporate level.

The key is to find your own voice.

Once your point, story, agenda, quote has been accomplished, you can plan to use the power of silence, or a comment like, 'Where was I?' or even apologise for digressing, before getting back on track. Doing this several times can help create a tapestry for thoughts and messages.

Refer back to your master plan (the A3 page) to check with your original thoughts. Sometimes, halfway through writing the speech you may realise that you could improve it by going back to another idea.

If a computer is not your preferred medium, the good old reliable 'cut and paste' may help at this stage. It's probably better than using a computer, being able to see much more than the limitations of a screen.

Even though you might check your 'work in progress' with a couple of close friends, don't blab the contents of your speech to the world. Otherwise you will dilute the impact.

We all like a laugh. But some advice to people who think they are funny, but in fact are not: Don't even think about trying to be funny. We have all watched and cringed as some poor unknowing soul has launched into a presentation story that they thought was funny.

Except perhaps at funerals, a humorous approach or a few humorous points will always lift your presentation. But the humour should be appropriate for your theme. Humour should not distract—it must support. Not all humour is jokes—and not all jokes are funny. Never forget the great rule of comedy: When in doubt, don't.

Not everyone needs to tell a joke. Too many speakers use a randomly chosen joke with a view to getting an easy laugh or in tennis terms, a free point. Genuine wit is preferable to gags. A story told from true life experience, embellished to capture humour, will usually win the sympathy of the audience. A public speaker is not a stand-up comic. A speech is meant to be relevant to the occasion. People listen to learn about a subject, enjoy the debate or celebrate the occasion.

In the mid-1980s, the Australian Test cricket team was beaten by New Zealand in series both at home and in New Zealand. At one after-game

125

dinner following a heavy defeat the chairman said, 'Ladies and Gentlemen. In conclusion, I would like you to raise your glasses and drink to absent friends, and in that I include the names of the complete Australian batting line-up.'

Okay, the speech is nearly ready—we're over the hump, past the halfway mark and can see the finishing line. The task now is to figure out what is going to be the best and most effective way to 'break the tape' finish.

It is very important to know exactly how you want to leave the audience. With a laugh? With a question? With a quote? With a challenge or dramatic moment. And preferably wanting more.

A major decision to be made by you, the speaker (unless relying on memory), is the choice of format with which to represent the words—hand-held cards, hard copy in a binder, autocue, etc. One helpful technique for newcomers is to work up the hard copy and underline or highlight the key words, in the same way a television newsreader does. Leave a little room for ad lib and always have a pen and highlighter handy on the day or night.

I will never forget the first time I had to read autocue 'live' on television. It was truly terrifying. I still feel for newcomers to screen, non-blinking, eyes popping, taut grim face, tense muscles, lunging forward, talking breathlessly at the camera. You are allowed to smile. You can sit back a little more relaxed and eyes do need blinking to keep the eyeballs moist.

The first day Nicole Stevenson co-hosted the *Wide World of Sports* with me after an early 'read', she leant across and placed my finger on the side of her neck. She said, 'My heart-beat—at least 160!' Yes, there is real pressure in front of the camera and an audience of a million plus. It is important to work out how long the speech will last. As a general rule, most people speak at about five words a second. Tasmanians like myself speak a little slower say, three words. For example, if you're given five minutes, we're talking 300 seconds, which is approximately 1400 to 1500 words. This in turn is about six pages at 250 words a page. Interesting way to look at it, eh?

> **You can never read a speech too many times. It helps produce a more relaxed performance.**

Sometimes unpredicted events offer a chance to make the most of a situation . . . and turn it to your own advantage.

During a 'warm up' for Steve Vizard's *Tonight Live* on Channel 7 Mike discovered a honeymoon couple in the audience. Steve introduced them early in the show, welcomed them to Melbourne and invited them to watch the show in a more appropriate way. He called the staging crew to bring on a double bed and placed it near the desk so they could watch the show, as they should be on their honeymoon—in bed!

It was a fun show. After most acts, Steve asked them how things were going . . . 'anything you'd like to tell us', etc.

When Mike worked with John Howard before the 1996 election, he suggested a few things to him such as the use of small dictaphones . . . a more relaxed wardrobe for weekend press conferences and to book a separate room near to the function room, a place where he could disappear and go through his speech quietly without interruption.

During the second TV debate with Paul Keating in February 1996, Mike told the opposition leader that if he did a line about the Worm, he could 'win' the debate . . . he suggested John wait for the PM to say something that was a bit over the top, even by Paul's standards, and then say 'Hang on Paul, not even the worm would swallow that!'

He did, and it proved even to the PM there is nothing like a

COURTESY MARK KNIGHT/HERALD SUN

cking wit who penned Howard's winning one-liners

❝I always felt John Howard had more right to the word 'bloke' than Paul Keating ever did❞

ster of mirth: Mike McColl-Jones had the write stuff for a joke-hungry John Howard

...Jones was jokes for people you know," he said. "If they can't say them confidently, they won't believe them.

...found him a really ...made it

the prime minister and tried to bring this out."

One of the jokes he sent to Mr Howard originated from an image he saw while he was driv... k and Christoph...

like — a 4-wheel drive vehicle that never gets mud on it'." Another of his jokes which Mr Howard used was: "That's as likely ...

turning point for Mr Howard. He'd had a dire week which included forgetting details of his family tax package, stumbling down stairs and being caught unawares by the release of plans to cut tax on savings.

In a bid to turn the tide, Mr McColl-Jones sent Mr Howard a joke on the day he fell: "That's the last time I listen to any of my staff who say 'break a leg'."

When he saw Mr Howard on the Saturday immediately before the first debate he was already determined to pick himself up from the setbacks ... previous week.

Y HERALD SUN

prepared ad-lib. The media gave that 'hook' and John Howard maximum exposure.

Mike's been writing prepared ad-libs for nearly forty years. The exercise has become a way of life and a business. A professional shadow.

For the average mere mortal who cannot afford the spare room, the spin doctors, fashion consultants or someone who's writing your words, there's still one thing you both have in common—an audience! And at the end of the day, they and only they will judge how your efforts have been received.

129

BEFORE YOU MAKE A SPEECH

- Who is the event organiser? Are they reputable, and is it appropriate for me to participate?

- Why am I doing this?

- What kind of audience will I be speaking to? Male, female, older or younger? How many will be attending?

- What is the 'theme' of the event?

- What should I call my speech?

- What messages am I trying to give the audience? What would I like them to take home and talk about?

- How much can I take for granted that the audience will know about the subject? And myself?

- How can I build upon this perception or knowledge?

- Are there one or two areas I disagree with or need to change?

- Should I anticipate a hostile audience?

- Are there prejudices or issues I need to be aware of, especially at question time?

- What shape and size room will I be performing in?

- Will I be speaking from a podium, stage or lectern? Will the lectern have lighting? Will it have a sill?

- What type of microphone—lapel or lectern, on a stand or hand-held?

- Will I have a space for notes?

- What time should I arrive at the venue, and what time am I scheduled to speak?

- How long should the speech be?

- Who else will be speaking before or after me? Ask questions about their format and how their subject relates to or differs from yours.

- Should I supply an introduction, or will it be written by another person?

- Is it worth setting up a face-to-face meeting or briefing? Can it be done by phone?

- Anything else I should find out?

Introductions too are very important! Saxton Speakers' Bureau has set introductions for all of their speakers. It is often appreciated more than we could imagine—not having to research and construct a set of prose suitable to introduce a statesman like the ex-Prime Minister of New Zealand David Lange. Tough assignment.

After I completed the scripted introduction, the Hon. David Lange strode confidently to his lectern approximately 20 metres to the right of mine. Massive applause—finally silence. He was the first speaker of the morning session for AMP's national conference in Melbourne.

> *To people who think they are funny, but in fact are not: Don't even think about trying to be funny.*

Unfortunately the unthinkable happened—serious interference with the microphone. Static, static, then more static. Like a batsman at the non-striker's end I stood alert and ready for a sharp signal. An MC can never relax or take things for granted.

David Lange was the complete professional. In sensational ad-lib, he took one glance at me and stated appropriately: 'Never have I been paid so much to say so little in such a short time!' He feigned to walk off-stage then accepted my call for the quick signal. A 20-pace stroll across the black carpet separating our two lecterns solved the immediate problem. The technical hiccup was rectified while the gathering enjoyed morning tea.

David Lange was able to turn a huge negative into a memorable plus. Let me say, too, his speech was magnificent for its depth of material, and was presented with true political gusto. What an orator!

During a briefing before speaking at a function to be held at Royal Melbourne Golf Club I admitted to often using two or three adjectives where one would surely do. The adjective is defined in the *Shorter Oxford English Dictionary* as 'forming an adjunct to a noun substantive; or dependent on a noun substantive, as an attribute. Those who appreciate and widely use the adjective may be described as being adjectival, are prone to adjectivity and will make every effort to deliver their prose written or spoken, liberally adjectived, or presented adjectively (that is made more adjectival)'.

In other words we think adjectives are good, the multiple use of up to five adjectives even better, but alliterative, multiple adjectivity is best.

A morning coffee with John Gourlay, chairman of the National Stroke Foundation Charity, provided one of the most incredible introductions of my life:

'It is now my predilection to introduce our speaker, a speaker with a predilection for augmenting his nouns substantive who will tonight present an eloquent, erudite, esoteric, embellished enunciation on the inevitable evolution [e]ccuring on this earth.'

I had to think, is that really me he's talking about? (I was the keynote speaker.) John went on to say: 'Change! In other words, what is changing our lives and how we should adapt to these changes. Ladies and gentlemen, Mr Max Walker.'

Let's get serious. Now that you have constructed your speech step by step with the help of the skeleton, go through the work one more time. Make sure you are absolutely satisfied with the result. Honesty with oneself is a wonderful trait to have at this point.

If you are relatively new at piecing together a speech, write it out in full with the benefit of your skeleton headings and notes. Once this is complete, don't read it again to yourself but ask someone else to read it out loud to you. In other words place yourself in the audience.

> *We think adjectives are good, the multiple use of up to five adjectives even better, but alliterative, multiple adjectivity is best.*

Question yourself on its ability to arouse interest. Very good speakers have their points of interest well spaced throughout their speech. This way they know if interest falls even for a few seconds. Then they can revive the interest and energy at will. There should be no definite lines between these steps or building blocks. They must blend seamlessly into one another. Try to mention something so interesting that even the most casual customer in the crowd will want to sit forward to hear more.

Check that the finished work has a nice blend of high levels of interest. The first one should be placed very early after the opening. This is when you create and confirm interest in what you will be talking about. The hook.

One evening at a sportsmen's night, I was the last of four speakers. The previous gentleman had got out of control, and so had the noisy audience. I stood up at around 11.00 p.m. This is the time of night at these fundraising functions when a well-watered crowd takes no prisoners.

The last speaker had been a shocker—talking under the influence and went on for too long. How do I resurrect this night? Most of the audience are ready to go home!

Only a dramatically controversial approach would have any chance. I suggest I would talk about sex the night before a match, drugs in sport and apartheid in South Africa. They went from noisy to quiet in one longish sentence. The challenge from here was to creatively hang on to their level of interest. This is exactly what happens every time we are invited to the microphone.

A word of warning: never say anything so controversial that the majority of the audience will want to argue against you. Their attitude towards you will be negative all night—and mostly they will be listening more to their thoughts than yours!

> *Try to mention something so interesting that even the most casual customer in the crowd will want to sit forward to hear more.*

Let Mike and I ask you a simple question right now. What are your main interests? You might say reading this book and that is very kind of you, but let's be honest, you are interested in this book because you have an expectation that it might be of help to you as a speaker and it may well make you occasionally chuckle. I am certain we would be correct in reckoning your main interests are the same as ours: family, ourselves, business, sport and leisure-time activities or hobbies.

The same will apply to your audiences. So when you begin to speak to them, think along these lines and you will be interesting to them. If you are going to talk about their business or general wellbeing don't waste time. Tell them straight away how you can help them.

This is the 'you, we, I' principle. Think in terms of the other person's interests and you will be well on the way to success. It is part of the equation to find out what the audience want from you. Answer the want and a good result will occur. Don't answer the wants and there can be no guarantees.

> *Never dawdle at the outset. The first two minutes are dynamite. Dive straight into your subject as quickly as possible.*

Mostly people will come to listen in the hope of being entertained, to learn something, to feel proud, to feel sentimental, to feel pleased, to find out how to make money, self-preservation and to benefit health, even faith. Give them what they want and you will gain their confidence and support—at the same time boosting your own confidence.

Apart from agreeing to give your speech, the crucial decision to make is exactly how you will execute or perform your task. There are basically three ways to do it.

TIPS FOR A GOOD SPEECH

- Know your audience or do not speak.

- Know your subject matter.

- Ask 'Why will the audience want to listen to me?'

- Before actually constructing a speech:

  — think about it for several days

  — research, research and research

  — ask questions—material you will not find in textbooks.

- What kind of speech am I going to deliver?

  — educational/informative

  — to persuade (a point of view)

  — inspirational/uplifting/ motivational

  — special occasion—toast

  — after-dinner speech.

- Brainstorm the main facts that apply to each step.

- Cull irrelevant facts.

- Spend time creating a good opening and closing sentence for

MASTER BLUEPRINT

1 Opening

2 Major point of interest

3 Creation of credibility and confidence

4 Body of the speech (the wants)

5 Close

1   Read your speech

Generally you should only read your speech if you have been invited to lecture, or if it is to be reproduced or reported. Thus it must be accurate. Remember, though, that few speeches that are read out are enjoyable for the listeners. True, it can be more polished than one without notes, but unless you are an extremely good reader then a monotonous torrent of words will sound dull and boring.

One way to practise becoming a better reader is to read stories to your children or grandchildren or even someone else's children. I have always read stories and told made-up spontaneous stories to my children. They will remember those stories and the telling of them long into their adult lives. When I began my career in television, this became an invaluable ritual which had a marked impact on my on-air persona. I would even read aloud to my wife. Roald Dahl's short stories were perfect: about ten to twenty pages long and very unpredictable endings. My wife went to sleep, and I became a better reader of print.

Seriously, how many people can read well aloud? Believe me, if they are unable to convince their kids that what they are reading is for real and entertaining, then how can they expect to enthusiastically set about reading ten or twenty pages of A4-sized paper?

So if you must read your words, practise. Practice will enable you to get light and shade into the text—a change of pace and inflection in your voice. This is a fairly difficult task, but if you underline names, numbers, dates and nouns for emphasis, this alone will make your task easier. Place 'hooks' around your descriptive words as well and you will be more in control of the

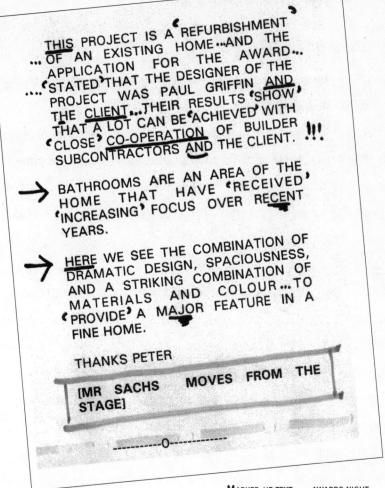

MARKED-UP TEXT . . . AWARDS NIGHT.

changes in the level of your voice . . . equal breathing spaces.

Ideally half an hour a day would be great before the big day arrives. This way you will be more familiar and you will feel much more competent. You will also be able to spend more time experiencing eye contact with your audience. A must.

With practice you will be able to actually read one or two lines ahead, giving you more time to scan the audience. Colour-code segments.

2   Impromptu or off the cuff

You will discover the effective off-the-cuff speech is not totally off the cuff. Usually it means that before attending the luncheon, dinner or meeting, much consideration has been given to the possibility of speaking.

So if you reckon you have even the remotest possibility of being asked to speak, toast or respond in public please take some time to roughly outline a possible skeleton. Deal only with one or two aspects. If you are not asked to speak then you will not have wasted much time. Be prepared.

3   Fully prepared speech using notes or cards

This is the most common scenario—much time has been spent piecing together the finished product before it has to be delivered, either partly or fully written out. You will have memorised some of, if not the whole speech. You now have personal freedom to develop your talk along any line you'd like. Flexibility.

The end product here is a polished, effective speech that sounds like you—natural and spontaneous, yet structured. This is the ideal set-up for most speakers. You might ask: how do I remember a speech like this?

I would not recommend writing out the speech in full and attempting to memorise it. We are not actors, and remember, they too, forget their lines. I would not recommend referring to a pile of papers during the speech—a recipe for disaster. Odds are, you will lose your place (even with a large typeface), you'll get spooked and you will put in a shocker. Entirely forgettable—you might not recover!

Expand each element by:

- giving statistics
- presenting evidence to prove the statement
- telling an anecdote
- retelling a humorous story or describe events
- presenting a historical fact or two
- giving an analogy
- using a quotation or an appropriate piece of poetry

You only need to use two or three of these, in whatever order suits.

You can't afford to lose eye contact with your listeners while trying to find your place. I have tried this, thinking an ad-lib would enhance my speech. It did initially, but threw me into a tailspin with worry when I could not quickly find my 'pick-up' place.

Many speakers prefer to simply use notes to which they can refer. If you choose this method, make sure your notes are in large lettering. It will help to use arrows, boxes and colour. The brain thinks better in graphic form. Be aware that once you stand up and the pressure of the occasion embraces you, it is possible your 'fantastic' memory may let you down.

Try to get all your information on two A4-sized sheets. Any more will confuse. The alternative is to try numbered cards. But keep the cards to a minimum. The card should have maybe the first sentence into a new element then maybe three or four bullet points or facts, and of course the card number. Write only on one side of the card. Cards are very effective and very popular. They should be rigid.

Having said all of this, my preferred method is to merely memorise my list of headings (a good speech can be written on the back of a

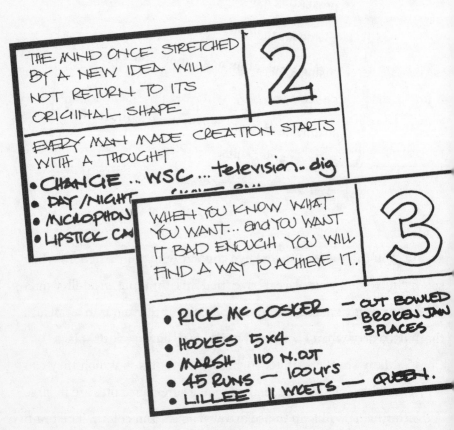

CREATE A LEAD-IN SENTENCE AND NUMBER YOUR CARDS CLEARLY.

business card). You will only be able to do this when considerable research and structure have been put into the planning stage. Understand what you have to say and memorise it till you are comfortable to talk to the subject matter. Maybe there is one lead-in sentence you will need to write in full—do it and don't forget it is acceptable to produce a quote from your pocket, or you may prefer to tape it to the lectern before the function begins. This will prevent the two or three speakers before you walking away with your material.

Remember notes are natural—never be afraid of your notes if you are going to use them. Don't hold them in your hands—no one likes to see a speaker waving sheets of paper around. They are a distraction.

Ask for a lectern to be made available. (Make sure the lectern has a lip so that your sheets of paper will not slip off—a common problem.) If you are speaking from a dinner table or board-room table, make sure you will be able to read your notes. Also check your seating so you won't have your back to the room full of people. Your every move will be an unnecessary distraction.

If there is no lighting on the lectern make sure the house lights are up. I find it is better to be able to see the audience's eyes. A spotlight on the speaker and room in darkness is to be avoided. You are not a singer. You need to be able to see body language and hear the feedback in front of you. This we will talk about more in Chapter 6.

Allow me to indulge with the following: good old-fashioned blood, guts and determination are three basic ingredients that the average

Australian sports fan can immediately relate to during a day at the 'big match' or an evening spent in front of the silver screen.

I guess there is a certain safety in the comfort of our loungeroom, feet up and overflowing esky at your side, or even in the company of half a dozen bare-chested mates under a blazing sun at the Sydney or Melbourne Cricket Ground.

But for those who are given the responsibility of representing our country, state or club at a chosen sport, there is no such safety. From the moment you walk through the gate onto the playing arena you are on your own. Like speaking. Easy game for overheated spectators, biased pressmen or anyone else who cares to take a 'shot' at you.

ACTUAL CONDENSED SPEECH NOTES.

Generally there is a feeling of apprehension, fear of failure and the heavy burden of a rapidly pounding heart as blood surges through the tightening arteries to the extremities of your body. Adrenalin is released in great quantities as the contest begins—there can be no turning back now.

> *From the moment you walk through the gate onto the playing arena you are on your own.*

One of the gutsiest performances I've ever seen on a sporting arena occurred during the Centenary Test Match between England and Australia at the MCG in March 1977. The game itself produced one of the greatest encounters in the history of Test matches played between the two historic arch-rivals. The atmosphere of the

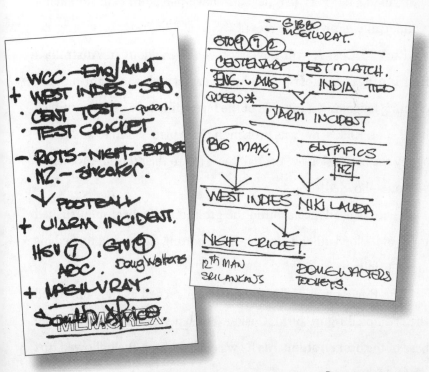

POCKET-SIZED KEY POINTS.

Never forget these rules:.

- statistics—make them live
- quotations—must be appropriate
- anecdotes—bring yourself into the story. Someone you spoke to. An incident that happened to you or maybe something you witnessed first hand.

sportsman I felt very privileged to have played in front of such a wonderfully appreciative crowd.

Rick McCosker will never forget the incident in Australia's first innings. A short-pitched delivery struck the right-handed opening batsman on the side of the face while he was attempting a hook shot. Rick's jaw was broken in three places, and to add to the agony the ball dislodged the bails as it fell to the ground. McCosker was out—bowled!

There was silence around the ground as medical men rushed to his aid. Blood quickly drenched the batting gloves and turned his face a bright crimson.

The Englishmen were obviously concerned as they encircled the crumpled figure of McCosker. His bat was still resting at the base of the broken stumps as he was helped from the hallowed turf of the MCG.

I first saw the injured batsman as doctors stretched him out on a table in the dim Australian dressing room. There was too much blood for me to handle. One glimpse was enough. Half his face was swollen like a football. It was really quite a sickening and gut-wrenching sight to see one of my team-mates badly injured like that.

Anxiety would be a fair way to describe the feeling in the Australian camp as McCosker was taken to hospital for exhaustive tests and X-rays. The X-rays revealed three fractures on the left side, and his damaged jaw had to be wired. That wiring was to stay in place for more than three weeks.

On the lighter side, Rick is a very quiet guy at the best of times but this was ridiculous. Now all we would get out of him would be a nod or a shake of the head with maybe a deep grunt in approval.

Doctors warned him not to take any further part in the game. This was like a red rag to a bull. McCosker was a player no matter what, and he couldn't get back to his team-mates soon enough. Such was the vast pride the man felt in representing his country at cricket.

It is history now that Rick McCosker did bat for Australia in the second innings, but down the batting order instead of his normal opening position. As Rick walked through the green dressing-room door with incredible determination and purpose typical of the guy, and 65,000 people stood up and applauded as he walked down the path towards the white picket fence. Our players in the dressing room area pulled back the sliding glass windows to hear the roar. I have never heard that sort of noise from 65,000 Australians.

He was bandaged heavily under his chin, over his jaw and around his forehead. He looked like a character from a slapstick

movie. On his head Rick had the coat of arms on the baggy green Australian cap. I'm sure that was the only thing holding McCosker together that day. He was going to represent his country no matter what.

The hairs on the back of my neck stood up and I think most people at the ground would have experienced the same sort of sensation. It was indeed a very moving moment.

The crowd cheered and began singing, 'Waltzing McCosker, Waltzing McCosker . . .', as he strode positively to the wicket, tapping the face of his cricket bat into the palm of his left hand, a nervous habit used to relieve the tension.

Can you imagine how he must have felt during that emotional walk to the wicket to do battle with the Englishmen once again! How difficult it must have been to suppress all the negative thoughts of being hit in the face by a speeding cricket ball.

He took guard on 'middle and leg' as usual and cast an eye around the ground at the opposition field placings. The big crowd cheered as he crouched down over his bat. Anti-hero and England captain, Tony Greig, urged his fast bowler, John Lever, not to relax. McCosker's grim determination to be part of another Australian victory was evident as he hooked the fifth delivery he received

behind square leg for four. The 'outer' was ecstatic—the chanting continued.

Rick didn't score a great deal of runs, but together with Rodney Marsh (110 not out) the pair added some 30-odd runs. When the final result is considered, I think Rick McCosker's contribution to our win was enormous.

The courageous batsman from NSW received a tumultuous ovation as he left the scene. I just happened to be the next man in and, as I passed Rick at the white gates, I knew it was going to be a difficult act to follow. I'd been dropped down the batting order an extra place, which also put more pressure on me.

When Lillee took the final wicket late on the fifth day of the Test match, Australia had managed to score a memorable victory against England by just 45 runs. Exactly the very same margin of runs as in the first encounter between the two countries 100 years before.

Sitting in the dressing room after play had been completed, with a beer in one hand and a cigarette in the other, Doug Walters made one of the most profound statements of contemporary cricket. With a puff of smoke and a cheeky twinkle in his eye he said, 'Well, fellas, in 100 years of Test cricket the Poms haven't improved one bloody run, have they?' How true!

Doug was trying to make Rick laugh. He was sucking champagne through a straw from a beer glass . . . his jaw wired in three places.

Just minutes earlier, Dennis Lillee had been chaired shoulder high from the oval after taking six wickets in the first innings and five in the second. It was not the case, but this match could so easily have been Dennis Lillee's last official Test match for Australia. Remember, he didn't tour England in 1977 because of a recurring back injury. Three stress fractures of the lower vertebrae were the original problem way back in 1973. Also he had signed to play cricket in Kerry Packer's World Series Cricket during 1977–78.

It must have been tough for McCosker to do anything but grit his teeth during his stay, because his jaw was wired in three places.

Rick was to be my room-mate on the 1977 tour of England that followed, but because of his jaw being wired, he wasn't able to travel until three weeks after the team arrived in England. Consequently, I had a room to myself which was nice and quiet for a while.

When Rick arrived in one piece, I thought, 'This'll be great— someone to talk to.' No such luck. I thought my 'roomie' had forgotten how to talk! After a couple of nights I had to say to him, 'Mate, all this noise is killing me. I can't concentrate on my game, I can't go to sleep. You're gonna have to stop asking me all these silly questions!' It didn't take him long before he was chewing the cud and back to normal, telling tall stories and making runs.

When you consider Australia only won the Centenary Test

match by 45 runs, Rick McCosker's performance was a match-winning innings.

For the record, I did get a hit. I scored 8 of an unbroken 10-run partnership with Rodney 'Bacchus' Marsh before my captain Greg Chappell declared at 9/419. I still don't know whether Marshie was embarrassed because I was outscoring him 4–1 or he was just plain tired after his century. But I do know that it was another 50 nipped in the bud, as so often happened during my career with the bat. It was either a case of running out of partners or running out of time.

I can still vividly see Rick McCosker in the dressing room. He was sitting on a bench among the sweaty ol' shirts and smiling through those clenched teeth at the rest of us singing our victory song:

"GREIGY" – YOU ONLY MISSED IT BY THIS MUCH !!!
CENTENARY TEST MATCH, M.C.G., MARCH 1977.

'Under the Southern Cross I stand

A sprig of wattle in my hand

A native of this native land

Australia you . . . beauty!'

Rick always played the game the way it ought to be played—competitive to the back teeth, but more importantly, like a gentleman.

As you can see, the anecdote comes to life by being in the story. The numbers mentioned have credibility, take on more strength, and they come alive. Also the quotation of Doug Walters is appropriate to the telling of events.

The audience shares the privilege of being inside the dressing room enjoying the victory.

Insider information may also provide a catalyst for a topical opening: 'Yesterday at precisely 3.15 p.m., Charlie Fitzgerald did something he'd never done before in his life—he consumed an alcoholic drink—but wow, what an excuse!'

So basically from here, all that is left to do is to get on our feet. We stand and deliver our efforts. Until then, please go to the opposite page and begin the create your own masterpiece. Fill in the blank space!

Ladies and Gentlemen...

Good luck,
Max and Mike

Rising to the Occasion —
Tips for Speakers and Hosts

Speeches at weddings should be like a mini skirt.
Long enough to cover the subject, but short enough to
be interesting.

FATHER BERNIE MACKIN, PARISH PRIEST AT ST MARY'S, ALEXANDRA

In a lifetime your brain only stops twice ... once when
you die and the other when you stand up to speak
in public.

BOB MILLER

Here we take a look at some special occasions where the approach
needed depends on the circumstances. However, the basic rules
about speaking always apply.

Speeches are an important part of all the special 'biggies', from
a child's christening to the most difficult speech you will ever have
to make—the funeral of a relative or a close friend. And the ones

that consistently cause the most anguish are the wedding speeches.

Being a host, Master of Ceremonies (MC) or presenter at a special occasion or event takes a lot of planning and effort. Attention to detail, humour and an understanding of the audience might make the difference between a successful event and a flop.

Weddings

The wedding speech is usually very straightforward, but preferences and traditions vary, and personalities certainly play an important part here.

A relative or old acquaintance usually proposes a toast to the bride and groom, and a smiling groom gets the opportunity to reply on behalf of himself and his bride, pausing predictably to capture the applause from guests, as he says for the first time: 'On behalf of my wife and I . . .' The groom then usually proposes a toast to the sometimes envious bridesmaids—usually his wife's very best friends. These days it is usual for the bride to say a few words too.

The best man responds and sets about the taxing task of 'getting right' his toast to both sets of parents. Anyway, that is how it is supposed to work out—but we all know differently, don't we?

On the day or night, there will always be someone else who wants 'just a few words, please'. Be prepared for the celebrations to 'throw up' a totally unexpected offering, either formally, or without direction or notice.

Marriages are very sentimental occasions. From wedding vows

to toasts—parents symbolically saying goodbye to their children in order to create another 'family', which will extend the family tree.

The degree of sentiment and the pace at which alcohol is being consumed usually means that shorter speeches will go down better than long-winded erudite orations.

Everyone involved wants their efforts to be right. With the best intentions in the world, the reality and results are generally different to expectations, but hopefully memorable.

How about this for a scenario? It's a group of five—been through the good times, the bad times and the downright unsavoury times—through school, puberty and adolescence. Manhood beckons. Inseparable lifelong friends, until the female of the species initiates the crack. Hairline at first, it was soon to open up like the San Andreas fault. How could our mate love her more than us? After all we've been through!

At first the telltale signs weren't obvious: 'I've got to get away straight after practice. Only got time for one beer.' In hindsight, the creativity of excuses was extraordinary. True love knows no boundaries!

Dulling the senses with copious quantities of all kinds of alcohol was a teenage hazard, and it was during one of these thirst-quenching brain-numbing 'truth' sessions that Ossie let the unexpected news slipped out.

'I'm in love. She's beautiful. We're going to get married!'

'What! When? Let's have another drink?'

'Geez, she must be bloody good. When did all this happen?'

'I—I've been meaning to tell you all. Really!'

And on the other side . . .

'But he's a really nice guy.'

'Emma, how could you? Didn't you take precautions at all?'

'Were you drunk?'

'Tell us you didn't know what you were doing?'

A few months later . . .

'You guys coming? Your invitations will be there tomorrow. I thought one of my best mates might propose the toast to the bridesmaids.'

'You're joking. Us, stand up and talk at a wedding!'

'Well, it's gotta to be one of you guys. I ain't got anyone else. And by the way, guys, there's no way round this. Emma's brother's gotta be my best man. Okay?'

'Well . . . only if we don't have to talk.'

'Forgot to tell you guys too—it's black-tie for the top table.'

One of the most important ingredients to the success of any wedding is the toast to the bride and groom, and the toast to the bridesmaids. And let's not forget the 'telegrams'. In the past they used to be much awaited. Somehow technology—email, mobile phone and faxes—has diminished the expectation.

Regardless of all the fun, mateship, bitchiness and family politics, someone has to stand up in public and string more than a handful of words together that encapsulate the commitment of marriage and the sensitivity of the occasion, with a touch of mischief and humour.

Phone call from hell (TO UNCLE BOB)

'Now, I know it's short notice—we're talking four weeks away. It's a long story, and I'll fill you in later, but I'll be forever in your debt if you can do the honour of proposing the toast to the bride and groom on the night.'

Bob is stunned on two fronts. The marriage itself, which is totally unexpected. And him, of all people, being asked to make a speech. This is Bob's worst nightmare. His conscience tells him to say 'yes', but he wants to say 'no'. Unlike his own 'patch of dirt', this is unfamiliar ground—with the very real potential for public humiliation.

Where does he start?

Uncle Bob has to start somewhere. All he's got is a blank piece of paper—and a lot of doubts! He needs to talk to his brother (Emma's dad) about the baby days, the little girl, the teenager and the woman now to be married—in other words, a young woman's life.

It's a time-consuming process. Bob also needs to talk to Emma's mum and her two sisters. He also needs to research the groom.

A toast to the bride and groom BY UNCLE BOB

I'll never forget my wedding—that, too, happened in a huge hurry. In fact, I met my wife on a rabbit-shooting trip out the back blocks of Casterton. Didn't catch any rabbits, but Vera and I have been together for thirty-nine years.

Ladies and gentlemen, and Reverend Parker, it is indeed an honour to toast the bride and groom.

We're here this evening to celebrate the coming together of this wonderful young couple in wedded bliss.

It's amazing with a little bit of research, how much dirt can be scraped from a selective fingernail.

Let's start with Emma. She entered the world with little more than a whimper, and hit the scales stark naked at eight pounds four ounces, with a cheeky grin that still endures. I notice that the big shock of black hair from day one is now blonde. Must be the Torquay sun.

As a five-year-old, she gave the little boy next door a blood nose, not because he peeked under her dress, but because he dismembered her coathanger and stocking-mesh fairy wings. I think it was a fair penalty. She has always been able to look after herself, particularly when things get a bit rough. If I were you, Ossie, I'd be a bit careful in close, and definitely don't try to dismantle her fairy wings.

At twelve she was captain of the hockey and softball teams, but more importantly, she was a better footballer than her brother Nigel. When Emma was sixteen, she had her first serious 'crush', and we all thought that this might be it.

She quickly moved on to become the most beautiful beach butterfly, and I dare say, a perfect match for the 'Grub'— Ossie. No offence son, but you do wear that nickname well. And in fairness you have scrubbed up an absolute treat tonight. Congratulations!

Mrs Beecher, Headmistress of MLC, probably best

summed up Emma's potential when she said, 'I hope she marries a millionaire, 'cos she's not going to be a cost accountant.'

Which brings me to Ossie, who's about to become a member of the family. It would be fair to say that Ossie's had a good upbringing, and at least he has read Dale Carnegie's bestseller How to Become a Millionaire. Maybe he also read Mrs Beecher's report card.

At eight years of age, he had the best paper round in Anglesea. Trouble is, at eighteen, he still had the best paper round in Anglesea. His excuse is that it gives him more beach and book time.

His four mates with us here tonight are responsible for him looking so shabby. His buck's night was last night, and without getting into the sordid details, he's shut the door on a pretty memorable first twenty years of his life. From now on, he'll answer to only one person—his wife!

> *Weddings can be wonderful events for everyone—not just the bride and groom.*

I'd like you all now to stand and drink a toast to their happiness—the bride and groom—Mr and Mrs Chambers.

Ladies and Gentlemen—the bride and groom!

Weddings can be wonderful events for everyone—not just the bride and groom. All the homework and attention to detail will pay off on the night, and hard work and planning will make sure there is no reason to have to say sorry or be disappointed.

If you happen to be the anointed one to speak:

- *Be yourself, do your research and have fun. If you do, so will all the guests.*

- *If you happen to be the groom—responding to the 'toast to the bride and groom', remember you must be sincere.*

- *Don't forget to mention your in-laws, even if you usually only communicate with them through a solicitor.*

- *Checklist of phonecalls on groom's side. Mum and dad, footy coach, even a quote from an old girlfriend will bring a good laugh but be sensitive.*

You might find a quotation that fits the occasion. Here are some old favourites:

> *Girls have an unfair advantage over men. If they can't get what they want by being smart they can get it by being dumb.*
>
> YUL BRYNNER

> *A man would prefer to come home to an unmade bed and a happy woman than to a neatly made bed and an angry woman.*
>
> MARLENE DIETRICH

WEDDING RECEPTION

THE ORDER OF EVENTS

1. The MC welcomes guests and invites them to either sit down or stand to greet the bride and groom as they arrive. The preferable one seems to be that all the guests sit . . . and the MC announces the couple's arrival. All the guests then stand and applaud the wedding party as they make their way to the official table.

2. The MC then speaks briefly about the order of events.

3. Priest or minister may say grace.

ENTREE

4. Today, many weddings have the speeches slotted between the entree and the main course, with the best man reading the telegrams/faxes between the main course and dessert.

5. The first speech is made by the person who proposes the toast to the bride and groom, usually a relative or close friend.

6. The groom and/or the bride or both respond. After responding, the groom proposes a toast to both sets of parents.

7. The father and/or the mother of the bride and groom responds.

MAIN COURSE

8. The best man toasts the bridesmaids and reads the telegrams or faxes. (Sometimes the bridesmaids respond.)

DESSERT

9. The bride and groom may want to perform a bridal waltz. They may be joined by the wedding party guests.

10. Goodbyes . . .

A man in love is incomplete until he has married.
Then he's finished.

ZSA ZSA GABOR

Mike's daughter Catherine was married recently to Mr Craig McGrory, and included here is part of Mike's speech. He arrived at the lectern, smiling. Fumbled in his inside jacket pocket, reached into another and finally found the sheet of paper. He inspected it and looked very puzzled. Here's his story:

'I can't believe it—one daughter, all these years to prepare a speech . . . words fail me. I've left the speech on the dining room table. And you'll never guess what I've got—a bloody shopping list!

'Two pieces of rump steak . . .

'Until Catherine met Craig, she was a vegetarian. She hated meat—she wouldn't even drive down Bridge Road, Richmond because there was a steakhouse there. I remember years ago, we were all out to dinner at Mornington, looking at the menu, when Cathy suddenly burst out crying.

'We said, "What's wrong?"'

'She said, "Turtle soup . . ."'

'She was so upset. Anyway, we quietened her down, but in the next minute, she was bawling again. What's wrong this time?

' "Roast Lion." She'd been looking at Roast Loin of Pork.

'A packet of clothes pegs.

'Clothes pegs remind me of the day when Val came home from shopping to find Tim laughing hysterically, rolling about on the lawn while Cathy was pegged out on the line. She was so light, it only took a couple of pegs.

'I still can't believe it . . . I hope they're all enjoying my speech down at Safeway.'

Mike then went on to give a speech, with the items on the shopping list reminding him of things about Catherine.

Speeches at silver or golden wedding anniversaries are usually presented by faithful old friends who know the married couple well. On these occasions, your audience will understand the need to run a little over time—so too will the husband and wife. Indulge the occasion. I've even witnessed a fifty-year-old diary entry being read by the husband. Perfect.

WEDDING ANNIVERSARIES

1st	Paper
2nd	Cotton
3rd	Leather
4th	Silk
5th	Wood
6th	Iron
7th	Wool
8th	Bronze
9th	Pottery
10th	Tin
12th	Linen
15th	Crystal
20th	China
25th	Silver
30th	Pearl or ivory
35th	Coral
40th	Ruby
45th	Sapphire
50th	Gold
55th	Emerald
60th, 75th	Diamond

Funerals

One of the most difficult speeches you will ever have to make will be at the funeral of a dear friend, husband or wife, relative or business colleague.

The opportunity to speak usually arrives without warning, charged like lightning, releasing an outpouring of individual emotions which are difficult to harness.

You have a non-negotiable timeframe in which to both create your eulogy and deliver it.

> *The opportunity to speak usually arrives without warning, charged like lightning, releasing an outpouring of individual emotions.*

Such occasions need great care and diligence, as it is so easy to hurt and upset with poorly chosen words.

The fact that you have been called upon to deliver a funeral eulogy will certainly concentrate your mind.

Many people find the mere thought of death extremely unsettling. Others are 'spooked' by it, and in extreme cases refuse to accept the reality and finality of death.

When speaking at his mother's funeral, Mike wanted to embrace the entire congregation in tribute to his mother, but also realised that people had expectations, because of his talent for humour. The exercise of creating the words on paper in such a situation was challenging, but he succeeded. One of his ideas was the 'Fax from Heaven'.

Many of you may not realise it but St Joseph's here in Hawthorn has a unique claim to fame—it has a direct fax line to St Peter up in Heaven, and although Mena has only been there for less than a week, I'd like to read you some of the things she's achieved in heaven already.

On her first morning, she visited the local supermarket to check the service and prices. She recognised the manager who had been in charge of her local store in Hawthorn before his sudden death a few years ago.

During the afternoon, Mena met with Helena Rubinstein and showed her how to get her hair bouffant early in the day. St Peter introduced her to Cecil B. De Mille, who was asked if he'd like to see some home movies . . .

Less than a week, and already Mena has been picked up by the police three times. Once for going too fast, once for going too slow, and once for poking her tongue out at the officer because he asked her age.

She's reunited with Hec and they've got a lovely apartment together. The only thing is that she hasn't worked out how to tell Hec that these days she enjoys a bottle of wine and a few brandies before bed.

According to St Peter, Mena is the only person ever to make three trips to Heaven. It took her that many to get her jewellery up there.

And St Peter adds a note: 'Tonight I'm taking Mena to meet "the boss" at "the cloud club". I can't wait to see his face when she looks him in the eye and says, "Call me Ninnie". '

From the immediate members of the family, thank you dear Ninnie for being such a wonderful mum.

Nothing in the world will prepare you completely for death or the prospect of eulogising a deceased relative or friend.

Once you have started to come to terms with your sorrow because of losing someone you cherish, you have the opportunity to become a great source of comfort for many other people. These people are your audience. Don't get preoccupied with only the deceased. You have an enormous challenge and responsibility.

'Finding' in your heart the right words in this situation is one of the most sensitive assignments a person can be given to perform.

I have been privileged to speak at several funerals now—each time very intense in the presentation, albeit for only a few minutes, but ultimately very satisfying.

A good eulogy will be remembered and treasured for years. It is a gathering to send off a friend and the mourners will appreciate the following:

- *Words of comfort to family and friends.*
- *Memories. Recall the special moments which will bring both tears and smiles.*
- *Best qualities and happy images.*
- *Inspiration—celebrate a life well lived, and its impact on others.*

We watch television and see images of national and international grief, but some of the best eulogies are those that the general public will never hear. There is no reason you can't do the appropriate thing when you are called on. So when the call comes your way . . . answer it! Just do it . . . celebrate a life in spoken words and word pictures. Have strength.

It starts when you first hear the bad news. That is the first encounter. The grieving continues on every mention and thought of the dearly departed. A never-ending number of questions. Why? Why? Why? It attacks your senses on every level as arrangements for the ceremony are made.

The really difficult funeral is accepting to talk about your immediate family, mate, lover, friend or relative. And having agreed to speak, the composition of words will never be more difficult. The words should come naturally from the heart —snapshots of a life lived well—happy, poignant, perhaps even humorous. Smile through the tears with words.

Look at both the strengths and frailties that made the person's life special. Everyone's journey from birth to death is fascinating, and your words will help all concerned cope with the loss and celebrate the life.

The famous Footscray Football Club No. 3, 'Mr Football', Teddy or E. J. to his mates, was one of the truly great sporting characters this country has produced. Ted Whitten's deeds are folklore among the football community. In the western suburbs they named a bridge after him. In the Northern Territory they recognise the best player on grand final day by presenting him with the E. J. Whitten medal. His deeds on and off the playing

'Finding' in your heart the right words in this situation is one of the most sensitive assignments a person can be given to perform.

PLANNING A FUNERAL SPEECH

1 How did the death occur? Old age or lengthy illness will be less traumatic than death by accident, or at an early age.

2 Who needs to be mentioned? Family, friends, interstate or overseas mourners, business colleagues, dignitaries.

3 Any no-go areas? Find out if there are estrangements, dislikes and personal things that should not be mentioned.

4 Best qualities? Seek out the person's best traits—be positive and emphasise them. Bring them to life with words.

5 Major achievements? Life's highlights will be appreciated by friends, relatives and work colleagues. Use an anecdote or two here if appropriate.

6 Things that meant a lot? Maybe use a common saying or quote from the deceased. Use associates in life's journey to supply other material, and don't forget to include your own point of view. Humour can be a tonic if used carefully.

arena are legendary, but unfortunately cancer cut short a life lived wonderfully well.

I'll never forget his last season on the Sunday morning *Footy Show*. Ted's body was buckled with pain and the finger-cracking handshake had disappeared. He asked not to be slapped on the back in the typical male-bonding greeting. In a few short summer months he had withered to a fragile shadow. He understood our united concern for his comfort and well-being. His character and sheer zest for living life his way overshadowed any thought of him not fronting, not being part of the Sunday morning gang.

'Don't treat me any different to what you ever have—for God's sake, don't go soft on me!' We didn't and he loved us for it.

On his last appearance, he made a point of individually saying 'hello' to each of us. They were moments of immense significance. The handshake and that depth of feeling deep in his failing eyes I will never erase.

You see what is happening here on these pages—once you begin to recapture the moments, it's difficult to stop.

St Patrick's Cathedral in Melbourne overflowed with men, women and children at Ted's State funeral. What an event!

Mourners crammed into each row of seating. It took me less than half an hour of sitting precariously on the end of the pew to cramp in the hamstring. Ted would have smiled. My pain—facial!

Everyone, I'm sure, walked away with a different memory.

It was the first funeral to be hosted 'live' like the *Footy Show*. Eddie McGuire in the chair. Ted would have enjoyed the fuss. The only things missing were the giveaways, competition and prizes. The chosen speakers did Teddy proud.

Ted Whitten Jr, or 'Young Teddy', allowed us a window into Ted the parent: 'It was at times difficult living alongside a legend and to remember that he was simply Dad, and we did the sort of things kids do with their dad . . .' Heart-rending.

But E.J.'s real 'final send-off' occurred a couple of weeks earlier, tracking the white boundary line of the ground that Ted had played on a hundred times. The legend and his son were driven around the MCG boundary. He was able to say his final goodbye to the public he loved beyond the white picket fence. The huge concrete coliseum became a sea of tears.

> *Look at both strengths and frailties that made the person's life special.*

It is so important to acknowledge those family members present, and it is here that much research is vital.

Recently I was honoured to speak at the funeral of a remarkable man and friend, John Tripodi. John was a mentor and inspiration to all those involved with Breaking the Cycle, a scheme for finding work for long-term unemployed young people. I'd only known John for five years but his impact on me will remain indelible as it will with the hundreds of people who attended the church, and the many thousands whose lives were touched by him.

It was an honour to be one of five people who were asked to provide a snapshot of his life. As it turned out, I was the first of the group to provide my picture of the man.

Regardless of all the experience you can have, nothing can quite prepare you to speak at a gathering like this.

With the permission of John's wife Bernadette and sons Oliver and Edward, on pages 174–175 is a portion of what I had prepared.

I've stood behind the microphone many times in my life, but on this occasion, my eyes scanned the church to the overflowing rear pews—it was packed. I glanced down at my notes, which, by the way, is a very good idea—a safety net at a time when many different thoughts are traversing the landscape of your mind.

I thought I'd know how I'd begin, so I looked down again. Silence . . . but somehow my script didn't seem to fit. I took another deep calming breath, cast my eyes to the heavens and then I followed my instinct. I began with something along the lines of, 'If John were to walk in here now, he'd be unstoppable—bulletproof. A huge smile—that fantastic attitude that we all knew so well. To him, nothing was impossible, so now, let me start where I thought I might . . .'

Death has no sense of timing. There's so much to organise, and so little time to do it. Where do I start? Who do I talk to? In

Everyone who had the priviledge to know my sister Lexie will have admired her amazing vitality and zest for life! Many times she remarked, "There's no way known they're going to miss me." And no matter what the crowd or what the occasion, you could not help but be impressed.

Even as a child, she attracted the fair share of attention. Those mischievous brown eyes would light up at the prospect of joining in with me to sneak a chocolate from behind the counter of the family store in Hobart.

In her early school years, her academic and sporting achievements were exceptional. Her hand/eye co-ordination, and the right parents, made her a natural at any sport she tackled. Yes, the kid from the corner shop already seemed somehow special.

Her grades continued to be high when she entered the Friends' School, a Quaker college, in 1961, but it was as an athlete that this young woman began to bloom. As a member of the Sandy Bay Harrier Club, she was selected to represent Tasmania at the Australian Athletics' Championships in Perth.

the case of my younger sister, Lexie, who died suddenly after suffering a burst aorta at the young age of thirty-eight, I sought the help of former Pentridge prison chaplain, the much respected man of the cloth and friend, Father John Brosnan. He suggested I write the eulogy. He would read it. It proved to be the toughest blank sheet of paper I've ever had to fill. Many hours and many tears later I was through, but I guess—never finished. (Remember, you have to stop and let go at some stage, otherwise you'll torment yourself too much.)

Lexie received a great sendoff, in the presence of so many friends and acquaintances. Again, I reprint a few paragraphs as an example.

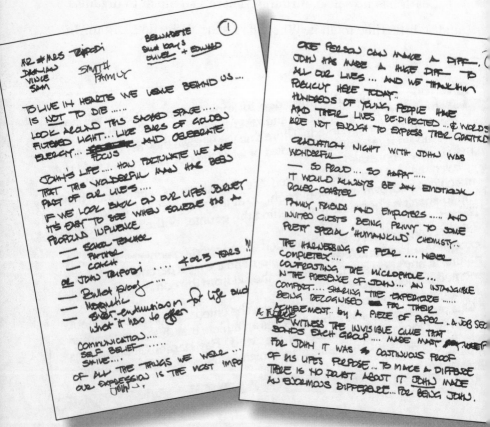

Death is a shadow we all have to confront throughout our time on this planet. Every so often, creativity and preplanning can be an unforgettable addition to the proceedings inside the church.

In Chapter 2, I described many of the characters who gave Channel 7's *World of Sport* on Sunday an almost religious following. The Gospel according to Louie, Jack, Woofer and Uncle Doug.

Even in death, Uncle Doug Elliott was larger than life. For years a Labor politician, he was TV's original heavy-duty spruiker.

Many of Unca's friends, television and radio celebrities, and a whole bunch of local people gathered on the mighty Murray River in Kerang for the big fella's last hurrah.

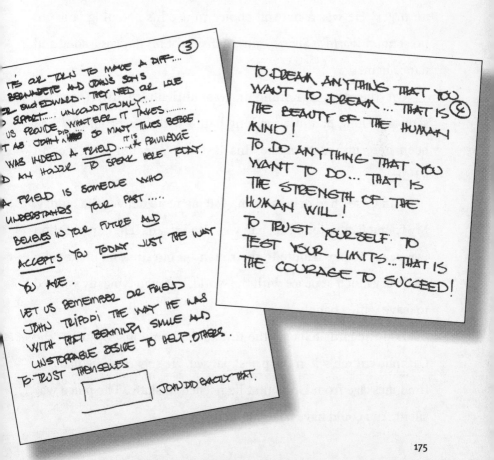

The then Premier of Victoria, John Cain, and several other high-profile dignitaries were present. Doug would have been proud of his legacy as final funeral preparations began. It didn't take long for the anecdotes to begin circulating among the congregation . . . many of them old, but relevant.

Some people had driven the 250 km from Doug's home territory of Windy Hill, base of his beloved Bombers—the Essendon Football Club.

During the 1980s Doug was Mayor of Essendon. The image of Doug complete with full regalia—black cloak and gold chains—is indelible. He loved the pomp and ceremony of the office and was a kind of contemporary town crier. Despite the robes, he was always an urger! He was a natural choice to use his booming voice to present on *World of Sports*—an extension of his days as a song and dance man!

On the day at Kerang it was difficult to dwell on the sadness. Doug had lost his long battle with cancer and he had been determined to make this last day one not to forget in a hurry.

Ron Casey had driven from Melbourne to deliver the eulogy. My friend Father John Brosnan was also present. The congregation was ready to pay tribute to their man—a fair dinkum bloke who died very much at peace with the world, but who typically wanted to leave with a bang!

Lou Richards tells me the funeral had only just begun at the Catholic church when the priest paused. He suggested he had one final message from Doug that he needed to share. The place was silent. You could have heard a pin drop.

'Up here . . .' Doug's voice boomed, ricocheting off the walls and high ceiling—taking everyone by complete surprise.

Lou thought, 'Strewth, he's through the Pearly Gates already!'

The voice kept going, focusing attention on the words.

'Up here—in Kerang . . .'

Yes, Doug had taped his final farewell using a lifetime of experience in the trade of communication to make it memorable. He spoke of his love for his family and friends, then went on to mention individually a lot of his friends he knew would be present in the congregation.

Predictably, he even gave the sponsors one final free 'airing'. That was still not the end, although it may have been a logical conclusion! 'After the show,' Doug announced, 'there's sandwiches and cakes, a few pies and plenty of booze over here to your right . . .'

Imagine what hearing that voice . . . those words . . . must have been like for Doug's long-time mate and the genial host of *World of Sport*, Ron Casey. He had to gear himself to follow that. Together they had created a television institution, been through so much together, but now Ron was alone. He would have to 'tough' this important occasion out by himself.

At the best of times the President of the North Melbourne Football Club is an emotional man. Wiping tears from his eyes unashamedly, Ron began: 'How do you follow an act like that?'

The man with the heavy-rimmed glasses and distinctive voice had landed his message one last time in his own inimitable style.

More recently, images of Senator Jim McClelland, using state-of-the-art technology were beamed onto large screens in a Sydney church as the great orator said goodbye to that gathering.

Don't miss the opportunity to speak in celebration of a life close to you. As the twilight of your own life becomes apparent it would be good not to reflect on an invitation rejected. So say 'Yes'. No doubt someone will step in when your own journey ends . . . it won't be any easier for them.

Birthdays

Birthdays are also special, and so they should be. It is nice to celebrate the birth date of a close friend, colleague or family member. The mere fact you have bothered to remember will have a very positive effect. Card or call will be equally effective. Isn't it nice to be the one remembered?

Birthdays are part of our investment in each other—a reason to celebrate the passing of time. On special occasions a good way to recognise that passing of time is by the use of words—a heart-felt speech!

The earlier birthdays are wonderful to look back on, even if the video camera operator is no Steven Spielberg—lots of floor, ceiling, people walking in front of the camera, and missed moments because of no film or flat battery. Mum and Dad might utter a few words on behalf of babe, but only if pushed. More important is the ritual of tiny fingers messing up the cake and candles and singing Happy Birthday.

We also have to take responsibility for what happens in the future. In years gone by it was the twenty-first birthday that was recognised as the first 'big' one, but now it seems that eighteen years of age is also celebrated as the moment for being able to tear along the perforation line from family ties. At eighteen you can get a driver's licence, you get to vote, you can drink in a pub, you go to university or get a job—become responsible.

Whether eighteen or twenty-one is the chosen symbolic number to hold a special party doesn't matter. But it might require a speech or two. Usually a toast and a response from the birthday boy or girl. As a rule these moments of mischievous honesty tend to become much remembered and even cherished later in life.

Insights and perceptions for the speech can be constructed in the same way as for a wedding speech. Research needs to be done, with targets such as mum and dad, relatives, school friends, teachers, employers, and sports coaches.

A decision needs to be made about the use of photographs, graphics, videos, and slides. How true the old cliché: 'A picture is worth a thousand words.'

Twenty-first birthdays offer fantastic potential for the use of slides or videos to tease and have fun about the early and formative years before becoming the now mature specimen worthy of a celebration.

> *Birthdays are also special . . . The mere fact you have bothered to remember will have a very positive effect.*

Slides are an easy way to do this. Simply organise a screen that can be seen by all, and an automatic slide projector. Match up to each image an appropriate and preferably humorous anecdote. Work hard on searching for unfamiliar and unforgettable pictures. The element of surprise will be rewarded by universal acclaim.

A picture is worth a thousand words.'

After the twenty-first birthday, it is popular to recognise the milestones reached at ten-year intervals—30, 40, 50, 60, 70, etc.

My wife's friend Kristie celebrated her 30th at a popular watering hole in the inner Melbourne suburb of Richmond. They came from interstate and just around the corner to toast the ol' girl on her thirtieth. The gathering consisted of granny, mum, dad, brothers and sisters—as well as the necessary thirsty mates. What are friends for—to make you smile, squirm a little, and be merry?

Two pages of rhyming couplets were penned to put Kristie's life into perspective. Kristie's reaction was very playful as she picked up on many of the subtle suggestions and the poetry became a catalyst for Kristie to bring more laughs to the celebration of her passing the thirty-year mark when she spoke.

Dining out is one of Kristi's passions
Places like Marchetti's Latin were always in fashion
There, she'd order tiramisu and a drink from the bar
But, Kristi, did you ever get caught with your hand in the lolly jar?

Kristi went back to Sydney for a squizz
And there she became a marketing whizz
She loved long walks around Cremorne Point
While, back home, the burglars were casing the joint.

As a cricketer, when I turned thirty, the major change in my life was the way in which journalists described me. Instead of words like 'brilliant', 'unplayable', and 'match winner' being used, they were replaced by 'veteran', 'ageing', 'war horse', 'consistent', 'experienced' and 'evergreen'.

They didn't affect the way I felt or performed—merely the descriptive space in newspapers. My family seemed just as happy to have an old medium-pacer who reckoned he could bat.

On my wife's fortieth I asked the florist to get me forty magnificent roses—not cheap, but her reaction was priceless. Kerry chose to have a few close friends and family instead of a large party. After the toast, her reply centred purely on saying thank you to the special people who had shared and shaped her life.

Fiftieth birthdays can be huge, and generally a matter of how much we can justify spending. The speeches at such occasions are often significant.

The man responsible for getting me to the Nine Network way back in 1985, John Sorell, the head of GTV9 News Department, had a memorable fiftieth celebration.

John has won several Walkley awards for his ability with words. His father, a judge, and a Tasmanian, proposed the toast. At almost eighty years of age he was articulate, clever, humorous and unhurried. John had limited the old man to five minutes—a legacy of producing television news.

His dad pointed out, 'I rarely get the opportunity to discuss my son—his achievements, and his shortcomings in front of such an illustrious collection of people. And I don't care what John thinks, it will be impossible to cram his life into five minutes. I am his father and at my age I will indulge in a few extra minutes . . .' (no one argued). The judge summed up his case in an unforgettable manner sourcing archival newspaper columns, life in television and the boy growing up in Tasmania.

John Sorell also received a video, put together by his newsroom editors in their quiet time. The link between different elements was John staring at camera, then quaffing a drink—better than commercial breaks—and funny.

At fifty you can do whatever you would like—that is, unless your husband or wife decides a surprise party is a better idea.

The late Peter Bakos, very small jockey and a good friend, returned home from a day at the races at about 7 p.m. The place was in darkness. He reached for the light switch to the lounge room—and a hundred people burst into song. When he stood on the dining-room table to address the 'race-day crowd' with a mischievous face and bushy moustache he used his 'height' and size to maximum effect.

'This is the most uncomfortable table I've ever stood on. I'm standing up here not so you can see me, but so I can see you . . .'

Peter was a winner on the sportsnight circuit for thirty years. His Rosedale racecourse story is legendary. He was one of the few speakers who would actually time himself to the nearest second—

a word-perfect hilarious performer. But he was also a worrier. If he ran three minutes over for a half-hour talk, he would worry about what he said to make it run longer.

When family friend Ann Ledger partied on her sixtieth she chose NOT to speak, but her children more than compensated for this, each in their own special way. It was done backyard-style—Hills hoist, fruit trees and a trestle-top bar—wonderful ambience. The dog next door barked as the sun set.

A call for 'quiet!'

Speech time!

Steven spoke first and began: 'As mum's favourite child it is only natural that I should initiate the ceremony . . .' (He thanked the guests and those who had helped with the catering.)

'Now I am going to ask Cameron to come forward,' he finished.

Cameron started: 'Being mum's biggest favourite I have been called upon to talk about Ann's achievements . . .' (He went on to summarise Ann's sporting achievements, career, interests, skills and role in the family.)

'And being mum's favourite I take it upon myself to declare the toast . . .'

After a sip from the champagne flute (plastic) Joanne continued the running sheet: 'Well, being Mum's favourite I've been asked to say a few words about our mother and our memories of her when we were growing up . . .' (She then reminisced about childhood events and compared her own experiences of motherhood.)

Last and by no short measure least, Kristie had her say . . .

'Hi, being the youngest and Mum's truly ruly favourite, I get to talk about her 'relationships' . . . A friend of my mother's . . . is a friend for life, and usually ends up being a friend of mine . . .' (She covered her mother's character, generosity, and romantic streak as well as other relationships.)

The great Don Bradman had people hold parties in different parts of the country to recognise his 90th birthday. The format is up to you. Whether it's your birthday or someone else's, a few thoughtful well-chosen words will always be a wonderful contribution.

The host with the most

A good umpire at a cricket match always goes unnoticed. But without them being firm, fair and honest the contest would turn into an almighty shambles. Being an MC or host is similar. You need to take control of proceedings, and let everyone in attendance know what is going on in a personable yet unobtrusive way. It is your duty to tie up every possible loophole and be ready to overcome any problem that might crop up. And I mean any! You are the insurance policy to make sure the event flows according to plan. Take control.

> *Whether it's your birthday or someone else's, a thoughtful well-chosen few words can be a wonderful contribution.*

In 1997, as a member of the Saxton Speakers' Bureau, I was invited to be Master of Ceremonies at their Ultimate Showcase. The running sheet offered to a creative market a snapshot

(10 minutes each) of the synergy that exists between practitioners of a number of creative disciplines in the fields of lighting, sound, staging, theatre, video production, venue operators and the producers and designers of special events like this. The showcase was complimentary and ran from 8.00 a.m. till 2.00 p.m.

I arrived in Sydney at 6 p.m. on Sunday night expecting several reads of the script and dinner with my wife at 8 p.m. Sometimes, even the best plans go awry.

My brief as MC was to welcome guests and introduce approximately thirty different windows of talent. On this occasion we were using a device called an 'autocue'. It uses a mirror to reflect a scrolling collection of words (the script) onto a piece of glass. Many politicians use the autocue in order to be precise. With natural movement of the head from left to right, glancing around the room, it gives the impression the speaker is not reading from a prepared script.

Thus my performance depended on the autocue operator, and not 100 sheets of typed A4. Having a Virgo star sign, I'm accused of being too preoccupied with perfection and detail (a nice trait to have as an MC). By 10 p.m. and after five apologetic phonecalls to my wife, the autocue operator, Annie, and I had to settle for delivered pizzas.

In hindsight, it was a worthwhile investment in my performance and the showcase. Had I not been prepared to commit that much time to getting the script, breathing points and pauses correct, the next day might have been a disaster. There was no value in 'dying' in front of all of those prospective clients. It could have been a humiliating experience, and one that I might never have gotten over.

I'd like to think that anyone contemplating being an MC (or bus driver) is prepared to invest as much time as it takes to ensure their performance is seamless.

I have acted as compere or host on many occasions, and Mike has worked on mega productions like the Logies. One piece of advice that you must heed is: after reading the equivalent of thousands of words several times, don't trust your own eyes for the final read. Get a fresh set of eyes to check it. You may have been reading the same mistake so often that it now seems correct. Make sure someone else checks it for you.

> *I'd like to think that anyone contemplating being an MC (or bus driver) is prepared to invest as much time as it takes to make their performance seamless.*

A host's best friend is a highlighter and a handful of coloured felt pens—thick if your eyesight is at all in doubt.

Even if your total presentation for the night has been scripted (and that's a bit like being locked in a jail cell with nowhere to go for three hours), you must read and understand every word before you get on your feet. It's preferable to read the script at least ten times (more if you need to), to have a good chance of success.

Now, we come to the speaker's safety net—the little bag of tricks that will consistently save you time and time again. It can also enhance your performances.

Like a cricket umpire's purse in which he carries all that necessary equipment—things like sun cream, mosquito repellent, bandages, painkillers, etc.—the speaker has a 'magic bag' too.

It's a fair bet that at some stage during the night, at very short notice and sometimes at no notice at all, the preconceived order of the night will change. For example, a name might change because that person didn't turn up, or perhaps the boss wants to accept an award, because he's the boss. Or perhaps bits of the original text is wrong.

MC is another term for 'paper magnet'. The instant you assume the role of an MC, you're likely to be assailed from all sides with names, numberplates, anniversaries, birthdays, ideas and public announcements from everyone—most of them outside the official channels.

I was once asked to tell Mr —— to 'Please leave the seminar immediately and return home because your house at Emerald is about to catch fire!' The message was from his wife.

Sadly, sickness and death have no sense of timing. These are rare occasions that tax an MC's sensitivity in the handling. How much do you share with the rest of the audience, while making contact with the necessary person?

Quick thinking is required when official and unofficial pieces of paper arrive at the lectern mid-sentence. One evening, just before closing the events of the night, a piece of paper was handed to me. I was to tell the audience to use the back doors because there was a problem with the two side doors. I quickly suggested I couldn't tell that story about the two old ladies in this company (everyone was curious as to which joke I was referring). I got a laugh and at the appropriate time was able to mention the back-door exit.

Officially, there will always be some 'housekeeping'. Information like times, venues, buses, raffles and the most popular one of all, 'Ladies and gentlemen—last drinks!'

Be selective and attempt to do the job with originality, flair and style while allowing the individual specialists to perform to the best of their abilities.

One idea that I've seen used with a lot of success is this: 'Ladies and Gentlemen, may I have your attention. Would the owner of the car with the registration number NSJTRWQKLYD 1947624 017286 please remove it from where it is parked. Your numberplate is stopping the traffic on the Hume Highway'. It gets their attention!

> *Quick thinking is required at other instances when official and unofficial pieces of paper arrive at the lectern mid-sentence.*

I would urge all potential MCs to go beyond the sometimes pathetic three or four lines of lifeless information you receive in order to introduce person A on the running sheet. Try to meet them if you can, to see what they look like, and to try and establish some kind of rapport. Ask them a couple of background questions: footy teams, hobbies, family, famous relatives, etc. Share a fact or two with the audience.

As a rule, introductions should be no more than one minute long and should address three points:

1 *who is speaking*

2 *what are their credentials*

3 *the topic on which they are speaking.*

The most effective way to get this right is to write your own and give it to the MC on the night. If you are the appointed MC don't be afraid to write up your own version based on the information you've received, plus the extra research.

This removes one of the most onerous tasks from the organiser of the function. An important point to take into account is not to fall into the popular mistake of saying 'Ladies and Gentlemen, please welcome . . .' and at this stage turn to the speaker and say, 'Mark Taylor.' The former Australian cricket captain may be well known enough to the audience, but a visiting New Zealand speaker on politics will be disadvantaged, because everybody applauds, but no one actually knows who he or she is.

It is a good idea to ask for the sort of equipment and technology you will require, for instance, a lapel microphone and a lectern with lighting. Talk to the audio-visual people if you get an opportunity so that there are no surprises.

The two most important parts of the performance, for either a speaker or an MC or host are the START and the FINISH.

I like to pull out four or five highlights of the night, or day. Actual quotes are even better, but a preselected quote in the right position will also normally work.

I recently back-announced Dr Rosie King at the 'Best of Health from Bedroom to Boardroom' Seminar in Sydney. She presented a very entertaining lecture on 'Good Loving and Good Sex'. It had been a fantastic hour of entertainment, with her tongue planted firmly in her cheek. In describing the difference between erotic and kinky, Dr Rosie used the example of 'To be erotic, you only use the feather—to be kinky, you use the entire chicken'. In closing, I used the title of one of my books *How to Hypnotise a Chook* as an obscure link between her quote and my literature. Presented with a huge grin, and a suggestion of being outrageously kinky, it worked!

The lesson here is to listen to everyone who leans on the lectern. You're bound to get an opportunity to exploit a line or a situation later in the proceedings.

> **The two most important parts of the performance, for either a speaker or an MC or host, are a bit like reading a book—the start and the finish.**

As far as dressing is concerned, never 'under-dress'. It is advisable to take the 'middle ground'—wear a suit and sober tie! Find out beforehand what the general dress is. Don't wear formal gear if it's going to scream out like a boil on your bum.

I once orchestrated a night under the lead-light ceiling of the Great Hall in Melbourne's Arts Centre. It was the BHP Awards for Excellence. We had a rehearsal. The hosting was split between television presenter Carmel Travers and myself.

On the night I opened the proceedings together with Carmel. There were three minutes of ad-lib banter between us—the usual way to get people relaxed, feeling comfortable, happy and ready for what was to happen over the next four hours.

During the rehearsal I had left my folder on the lectern,

assuming that my notes, running sheet and everything else I required would be absolutely safe there.

When I stood at the lectern ready to start and opened the cover of my folder, I discovered to my horror when I looked at the top right-hand corner of the script, the number 16. Yes, we were 16 pages into proceedings and to my under-standing, I was to present award No.

> *Don't wear formal gear if it's going to scream out like a boil on your bum.*

1, and Carmel was pretty sure she was to present award No. 2.

The senior BHP executive, whose duty it was to welcome and say a few words on behalf of the company had grabbed a few extra pages to jot down some notes plus his speech, not thinking they were the vital pages 1–15 for the first part of the night. Out of the corner of my eye I could see the culprit shuffling my precious pages at his table. Not a worry in the world, oblivious to his crime.

Thank goodness I was working with a true professional, who nevertheless took more than a little cajoling on the basis of 'ladies first, gentlemen second'. I suggested she present the first two awards. Saved by a videotape clip and the room going to black . . . I raced across the stage to Carmel's folder, grabbed pages 7, 8, 9 and 10 in order to present awards 3 and 4. The 'quick-fingered' executive was asked to come forward on cue at precisely page 10.

By the time he left, everyone was smiling—especially me, and the proceedings were back 'on track'.

I was playing MC at the Victorian Tourism awards in the early 1990s when, late in the night, my professionalism was tested.

Even though I was a Channel 9 personality, in my capacity as the major awards night presenter, GTV 9 boss, Ian Johnson, allowed me to be part of a live cross into Channel 7's *Tonight Live* with Steve Vizard. The timeslot was between 10.30 and 11.30 p.m.

Our cross was to be at precisely 11.06 p.m. Our plan was to cross to the final award—the best five-star accommodation in Victoria. The Grand Hyatt won the award—again! And alongside me on stage was the most amiable executive of the hotel, a Frenchman called Philippe.

In order to keep the 11.06 p.m. commitment, we had scrambled through more than 30 awards in better than even time. The timing was perfect—the award was ready to be announced on television. Philippe had the trophy in his hand, and we were expecting a perfect cross, when the TV director's voice in my earpiece stated abruptly: 'We'll get back to you in about three minutes—we've got to go to a commercial break'. Silence in my ear. Unrest in the audience. Stretch!

After the commercial break, comedian Richard Stubbs (who was hosting that night), decided it was appropriate to get his audience back on track with a 3–4 minute routine of stand-up comedy. Talk about 'dancing on your feet'—I'd only just met Philippe. Everyone else on the night was allowed two questions only to stay on time.

Well, I reckon we covered the decor of every room in the hotel, including the kitchens. We seemed to get a second wind at about the four-minute mark when I established he didn't much like Aussie rules, but loved soccer. This was stretch . . . plus tax!

As I started to ask about the recipient's school days, on this gala five-star accommodation night, the full bravado and cutting wit of

Richard Stubbs punctured the ambience of the room via loud speakers.

Within seconds, both Philippe and myself were on the defensive, covering ground we'd already traversed so painfully in the preceding minutes.

A quick 'goodbye' and 'thank you' from Richard before their show resumed with a nude woman in a shower segment.

People hype the marketing power of TV, but on the night I had to wonder—was it really worth the effort? Especially at the expense of all the other winners!

Every so often you may be asked if you are willing to dress up as part of a theme night. For three hours my five-year-old daughter, Alexandra sat with her eyes fixed on her dad's head. I had accepted an invitation to compere a gala dinner for the Australian Consolidated Liquor Industry on Hamilton Island in the Great Barrier Reef. The only snag was, I needed to be made up to look like Frankenstein: green shoe-box-shaped head, jet black triangles of hair as in the Munsters and a dirty great bolt protruding from either side of my neck. The ugly scars across my cheeks would have frightened a dog off a chain on a dark night. The theme of the night appropriately was 'the after-life'. Wearing an uncomfortable abrasive hessian-bag dress-up suit, I was as far away from formal attire as possible.

The company faithful joined in the spirit of the theme as they paraded through the doorway and into the ballroom. Nurses with dagger handles protruding from white blood-stained uniforms,

Count Dracula lookalikes, guys with machetes parting their blood-drenched hairdos, zombies, walking wounded and dead people—fantastic scenario.

The decor of the room was stunning. The ceiling was dressed to mimic a gigantic spider's web and in the sagging middle suspended precariously on nylon was a huge black hairy spider. The evil environment pervaded every corner of the room. Three skeletons dangled from the hangman's noose below exposed timber frames. Arms and legs pushed out from coffin lids, flesh a dead grey-green colour. Eerie and cold to the touch.

The night was almost purely ad-lib. Scary but rewarding as I let go of the steering wheel and went with the energy off the party.

It was a hot, steamy, sweaty night. The gravel rash between my legs caused by the rough-textured hessian trousers lasted a week—the legacy of a night of chewing the microphone and light-heartedly bagging the amateur pantomime cameos that each sales department were forced to perform.

The brief was not to take 'after life' too seriously and make sure everyone had fun . . . and a drink. Brilliant—and late! Next morning the chemist sold out of Berocca vitamin B tablets.

'GOOD EVENING, AND WELCOME TO . . . THE AFTER-LIFE.'

Even when the MC or host endeavours to make sure that every aspect of a function goes to plan, it almost certainly will not. It is a difficult enough exercise to get your own act together let alone the other 'talent' on the night.

Each speaker or act should be responsible for establishing their own rapport with the audience. After they have been introduced skilfully, then they are on their own. If they pull up short, the audience should not really hold the MC responsible for their shortcomings.

> *The brief was not to take life too seriously and make sure everyone had fun... and a drink.*

However, it is your role to get speakers on and off on time. A keen ear and curious, perceptive mind will help you achieve this. The host is there to present and thank, not to outshine the rest. And don't for a moment take your mind off your own performance.

Back-announcing a speaker with a pertinent comment is part of your task, but do it with good grace and make sure you are complimentary. This is the perfect opportunity to feed into the program a little of your humour and professional ability. Always keep an eye on the clock.

One of the most satisfying functions in 1998 for me was the Melbourne Football Club Captain's Lunch at the Palladium Room at the plush Crown Casino. This was a day to celebrate legend, success, leadership and the heart and soul of the red and blue club. There were no videos, no dancing girls and no gimmicks—pure football, charisma and words.

Only two captains didn't make it: the oldest, Alan la Fontaine, who was seriously ill in Sydney and the now schoolteacher Carl Ditterich.

From multi-talented gentleman Percy Beames, who was three days short of celebrating his 87th birthday, to current captain Todd Viney, they were marched onto the stage and seated behind a long, elevated top table. In the middle were greats like Beckwith Cordner, McMahon, Barassi, Alves Flower and Lyon. My task was to interview all 17 of them in approximately 45 minutes—mission impossible.

I decided we would chunk each cluster—one before main course, after main course and after cheese and biscuits. Each chunk involved five or six captains. I began with the oldest, Percy Beames: 'Times have changed since you first arrived in Melbourne, Percy?' I asked, knowing both his ability as a newspaper journalist and that there was a memorable anecdote, which would be told in response.

Wonderful as his first answer was—about spending his first night in the big smoke from the country in a house of ill-repute—it lasted seven minutes. At this point he hadn't mentioned getting a kick or winning a premiership. He wanted a second question—which I grudgingly gave while checking my watch.

I'm dividing five into eight minutes and not getting a satisfactory answer. Nevertheless, having researched my facts, I was able to paraphrase the personal achievement and club performance of each of the captains.

The guys would have loved 45 minutes each and would have been fascinating. But I was able to tell them all before coming on stage they would possibly only get one or two questions each, and to concentrate on a memorable and if possible humorous reply.

We compared notes individually, and I was able to get the job done on time. They were fascinating and funny. Everybody left lunch wanting more. Planning had made it work—it always pays dividends. Great captains make great team players.

Let me tell you about a time when attempted planning was foiled by an over-protective publicist.

Patrick Swayze, star of the Hollywood blockbuster, *Dirty Dancing*, visited Melbourne for the premiere of the film based on the

Dare to be a little different.

best-selling book *City of Joy*. World Vision used the occasion as a fundraising event. The two stars of the movie were special guests at a black-tie after-movie gala dinner.

The publicist was adamant her man would only talk for two minutes. (Well, what's the point of research!) I would say hello, he would say hello, and we would all get down to eating and drinking.

Worse still, not only he, but also his Indian-born co-star would be on stage together. At least the Indian had played cricket and knew of me—we liked each other immediately.

My first question to Patrick after introducing him to the adoring crowd was, 'I bet I'm the first real live Tasmanian you have ever met.' His answer proved to be very playful. And you bet it went on much longer than his allocated two minutes. This guy and his mate were about to have some serious fun. All plans were thrown out the window. The publicist was nowhere to be seen and

World Vision supporters were in raptures. Be prepared for the unexpected.

For the next half an hour we talked about Tasmanians, wrong-uns, rickshaws, rock bands and dwarf-throwing! I could not get them to 'walk'. This was before main course. An hour and a half later, Patrick again walked from his seat to the front of the fabulous room dressed in a tuxedo and bow-tie. He politely asked if he could say a few more words. Earlier he had forgotten to mention World Vision and its wonderful work worldwide. He enthralled and appealed to the well-heeled gathering for financial support—it was very successful. He talked non-stop for another 25 minutes.

Thank everyone involved.

The Power of the Publicist. Could be the title of a new book!

Here we had need for spontaneity. At no point was I trying to upstage, merely giving the audience value for money. If Patrick had left after two minutes, the room would have been dead. Instead we created the mood, and made sure the program moved along in the right direction.

Presidents have the Secret Service, Popes have Cardinals, Governors have Aide de Camps, Royalty has Men and Ladies-in-Waiting, and MCs, hosts and comperes have people like Mike.

For the best part of forty years, Mike has been the 'shadow' to some of the biggest names in show business. Not only does he write for these people, but also helps 'get them up' for their performance, and carries spares of everything in his pockets: spare scripts, running sheets, pens, blank cards, rubber bands, paper

MIKE AND THE KING OF TELEVISION GRAHAM KENNEDY.

clips, and scraps of paper which might contain a joke or a suggestion to pass on to the writers.

His chores include making sure all scripts and props are placed properly on the desk or out in the host set. It's wise to have a good working relationship with the crew and floor manager. Check the compere's dress and make sure everything that is supposed to be done up is done up. Bert Newton once did a KFC commercial with his fly open for the entire five minutes. Those were the days when they were allowed to make commercials 'live' and entertaining—and I might add, successful! Part of his job is also to make sure the compere is happy and relaxed, ready to go. They each have vastly different nervous traits prior to 'going out there'.

The wrap-up or finish is very important. This is where you get to say thank you. Knowing how to thank people and which ones to thank will set you apart from the part-timers! In principle, it is no different to being a keynote speaker.

Dare to be a little different. Be caring. And above all be professional. Take notes during the night—insights, snapshots and perceptions of how the evening has run and why. You need to pull this all together in shortish sentences. It's late and we don't need another speech.

But we do need to thank everyone involved. I like to make a list of possibles before I walk on stage to open the night. This way you only have to add one or two and it will not spoil your well-prepared finish.

6

A Speaker's Kit Bag—
Tricks of the Trade

*For the things we have to learn, before we can do them,
we learn by doing them.*

ARISTOTLE

It's a fact that you project who you are.

NORMAN VINCENT PEALE

When you make a speech it may be the only time your audience will have the opportunity to be impressed by you. You owe it to them, as well as to yourself, to take your performance to the max. This is a great self-starter or thought to ponder . . . especially when feeling tired and lethargic—maybe you have had to travel a long distance to make your presentation. Self-esteem will usually do the rest.

This chapter will provide a travel kit of experiences, ideas, tips and possibilities. Not all of the advice will work for everyone. But these observations drawn from true life experiences will come in handy in all kinds of situations. Upmarket, downmarket, good and bad. From assembly halls crammed full of school children to corporate boardrooms. From the basic sportsnight to mega conventions, the journey has provided much insight into what can work and what will not. Accept what can work for you and use it to your advantage.

Everybody at the main table heard it—a single muffled click. All eyes were on Tom. Yet nobody could have guessed what had happened? Expecting the worst, Tom's tongue quickly confirmed his initial thought.

'My God—my teeth's broke! Whatever am I going to do?' the mainlander pleaded, half choking. A quick reconnaissance of his upper denture revealed the extent of the fracture. Like the faultline of an earthquake, it was unstoppable. In football parlance the tremor had travelled the whole way—from full-back to full-forward—separating his two buck-teeth.

I guess you can't beat bad luck. But who do you reckon was seated next to the hapless import from Melbourne? You guessed it—my old man, Big Max. The interstate 'keynote' speaker was scheduled to make a speech in 15 minutes' time. The occasion was the annual Building and Architecture Forum in historic Hobart town. Gathered inside the magnificent old sandstone structure were builders, engineers, subbies, architects, local council and Public Works Department personnel, and guests. 'Structural Design of Prefabricated Off-site Components and the Future of Plastics in the Construction Industry' was the title of his presentation.

Despite Tom's internal structural failure he was impeccably dressed. Purple, wide-lapelled and double-breasted suit, cantilevered shoulder cushions, Brylcreemed, slicked-back hair, white loose-studded collar and paisley tie. But no amount of dress sense could disguise his look of despair. The next hour had the potential to spin totally out of control.

The bespectacled 34-year-old academic from across Bass Strait was decidedly crestfallen as he extracted from his mouth a handful of unfortunate teeth. A gaping split—right down the hey diddle diddle. Also extracted from his mouth was the culprit—an apricot stone!

Above the clatter and chatter created by the audience of crusty old builder types trained in traditional techniques by master craftsmen, a certain prickle, tension and expectancy that had nothing to do with the fractured fangs, was already developing.

> *These canny codgers were not about to be lectured on 'what to do' and 'what not to do' by a sharpie with a Mafia-style hairdo wearing shiny dancing pumps.*

These canny codgers were not about to be lectured on 'what to do' and 'what not to do' by a sharpie with a Mafia-style hairdo wearing shiny dancing pumps, even if he did have more Australian letters after his name than a French sailor has French letters attached inside the back of his cap.

No speaker's bible could prepare a speaker for this scenario. His earlier hypertension and sense of fun were replaced by the gloom of the unknown and self-doubt. He had been advised that Tasmanians

 were suspicious and sceptical of people who came from the mainland. The theory being: if you cut the connecting rope then they'll float away. Most maps do leave Tasmania off, don't they?

For Tom it was akin to being in another country. The visitor had to trust someone, somebody he had known for less than three hours. It was fortunate he didn't know my old man very well. As a publican, Big Max had developed his already mischievous character to XXXL size, just like his building overalls. His humour was warped, but regulars in the main bar at the Empire Hotel loved him for this and encouraged him at every chance to entertain with well-practised jokes and stories.

The question Big Max had to answer was 'Is this going to be yet another practical joke in the making, or will I "burn" my new-found friend in front of an audience of strangers?' Both options had appeal.

At this stage, only the top table were aware of the predicament. To speak or not to speak was the question. The situation was not getting any better, and a long series of grotty one-liners began to be offered in consolation. He didn't have to be Albert Einstein to deduce he was not entirely among friends.

Then, like a bolt from the blue, his only chance—Big Max— uttered those very Australian words, 'She'll be right mate. Trust me.' He added, 'Don't panic yet cobber, we've got almost 15 minutes to get you a gob full of teeth.' Then he was gone. No one missed the loveable local builder, least of all those who had paid good money to be present.

The hero suddenly returned. As he parked his bum on the leather-padded chair, he dug his hand deep into his coat pocket. He could well have been a bar-room trader of watches. As Big Max opened his fist below tablecloth level, Tom caught his first glimpse of the possible solution—a set of unfamiliar and ugly shaped upper dentures—similar to what grandfather used to keep in a jar of vinegar in the bathroom.

'Try these for size,' said Big Max, gesturing. The exchange of dry dentures must have resembled a clandestine drug deal going down.

'You sure?' Tom didn't know what to think. Were they Max's spare set? It was certainly not the quick-fix job he'd hoped for. Preparing to pop them in, he found it difficult not to think this was a set-up—after all, he was trusting a Tasmanian. But there was also a positive train of thought tracking through the cuttings of his mind, suggesting that it may just work out okay.

For the past ten minutes, Tom had contributed very little to the small talk on Table No. 1. He reckoned more than 50 per cent of them wanted him to fall flat on his face. He dared not eat . . . and couldn't smile. But he could drink, and drink he did!

'Well, are you going to whack 'em in or not?' challenged Max. 'But be quick! You'd better give 'em a rinse in your beer . . . otherwise it might be a bit painful sliding them in on unfamiliar tracks!'

As Tom sheepishly dunked the answer to his problem into the beer glass he lost his tenuous grip between nervous thumb and forefinger. The tide rose quite substantially as they floated on the surface like a dirty, craggy, iceberg. Big Max broke into a grin, busting to share the laugh. In they went. Then out they came, quicker than on the way in, like a kid swallowing a nasty medicine.

'No bloody way. Way too narrow!' was the dejected verdict.

Big Max pocketed the first set of porcelain uppers and reached into his pocket. 'Try these for size then!'

No guts—no glory. Same procedure among several deep breaths, head bent low and away from the table. Hand over mouth but no toothpick. A combination of beer and saliva trickled from the corners of a half smile. Did they fit? Would they work?

'Max, this is bloody unbelievable—they actually fit like new. Thanks! Let's have a beer.' Colour was again present on the face of the keynote speaker.

Big Max couldn't help himself: 'Never worry, never fear when you know Big Max is near.'

By now the buttons of perspiration were beginning to evaporate. The chairman called for silence. Tom's moment of truth had arrived. He gripped the lectern with both hands, a little shaky, a little squeaky. He quickly realised the value of thinking rapidly on his feet—a lot of his original 'opening' had gone out the window with his false teeth.

So, with his audience summed up, he finally began. The body of his talk (which could have realistically been his corpse) received major attention. He didn't miss a beat—articulate, informative, to the point—the odd injection of humour making it a memorable address for everyone. Even the non-believers were standing, loudly clapping their rousing seal of approval. There was a future to be excited about. Change never occurs easily.

A transformed, reinvigorated man returned to his seat. As he sat down he could feel his own teeth biting through his trouser pocket. What a night!

First to shake his hand in congratulation was his newfound friend, Big Max. 'Bloody beauty. Absolutely sensational. They loved it—ten out of ten!'

Back in his comfort zone, he offered one more acknowledgement to the crowd, with a hand-signal more appropriate to royalty, similar to the old-fashioned stop signal. Before cars had indicators—open palm forward! Policeman.

Quickly his attention turned towards his neighbour, now his trusted mate, who had saved his life, or at least his reputation and credibility within the building industry. 'Max, don't let me leave tonight without taking note of your dentist's address. I really would like to send him a thank you note. The teeth feel great, and if there is a cost please tell me how much.'

Now for the finale—worth waiting all night for, thinks the builder with the crewcut hairdo on his right. 'My dentist's name is Gordon Lyons. But look, there really is no need . . .'

Tom interrupted, 'But I insist, I must . . .'

'Look, there were really only ever two options. No dentist in Australia is still open this late on a Saturday night,' Max stated. 'So you see, I just slipped around the corner to a friend of mine who runs a 24-hour, seven-days-a-week business. Well, that's the way it has to be—he's an undertaker'.

Tom's guts began to recoil into serious anxiety mode. He couldn't believe what he was hearing.

'My mate suggested I grab the four sets of teeth from the shelf in his preparation room, and said you might get lucky.' Big Max showed him the two 'untried' sets of clackers from his other pocket and, with the contagious grin of a comedian, began to chuckle at his own joke.

The next bombshell was that the undertaker required them all back by Sunday night, because he needed them for funerals on Monday and Tuesday. A tennis-ball-sized lump of peanuts and whatever else Tom had put away earlier that evening began to surface behind the borrowed teeth.

> *A smile is the lighting system of the face and the heating system of the heart.*

'You've gotta be *%$#@!$# joking,' he barked with the scowl of a Doberman watchdog.

'Tell me these teeth don't—or should I say didn't—belong to a dead man!' he pleaded.

'Well, you may be right. They might have belonged to a dead woman! To find out for sure you're gonna have to ask the undertaker,' jibed Big Max. 'Well, don't feel too bad. If I had more time I was going to slip back to the Empire hotel.'

'Why would you want to go back to a hotel?' he naively asked.

'We've always got a stray set or two on the counter after a big weekend,' he chuckled, enjoying every word of explanation. 'We sometimes accumulate up to four homeless and unemployed clusters of teeth waiting to be collected on a Sunday morning. That's two hundred a year!'

The point of this yarn is never to take things for granted—when you least expect the unexpected, it happens.

Smile! Very hard to smile without teeth though.

Remember, a smile is the lighting system of the face and the heating system of the heart. A smile will enhance your words . . . round off your presentation.

My dad, Big Max is like a magnet for a laugh. I guess it gets down to attitude. He will always seek out the funny side—a reason to smile.

As a teenager I was privy to him telling the most outrageous anecdotes and fibs across the front bar at the Empire hotel in North Hobart.

He would often refer to our time in the pub as the 'Institute of Experience'. For a young adolescent, how true. That period of my life unconsciously coloured my understanding of the good, bad and ugly sides of society.

As a hotel proprietor, Big Max understood the business of selling beer. A warm, happy, comfortable environment—throw in the ability to tell an engaging yarn and the clientele would always buy another drink. Depending on the quality of the stories, 'one for the road' had the tendency to multiply.

> Always look for the funny side—a reason to smile.

I am certain my passion for the telling of an engrossing story blossomed in the shadow of my father and mate. So much so that Big Max and I are one of the very few father–son speaking combinations in this country. I'm proud to say how wonderful it is to be invited as a 'double' act to various functions. Then there is always the constant minor conflict of who will speak first.

Neither of us will ever forget our invitation to the National Press Club in Canberra. The one-hour speaking engagement would be televised live nationally.

On arrival, we were ushered towards a magnificent leather-bound visitor's book—I signed first with the fountain pen provided. My father was told, 'Mr Walker—your own single page.' My old man was completely blown away, as he scribbled his combination upper-case lettering merged into linked script autograph. Names like Paul Keating, Bob Hawke, Gough Whitlam, Sir Robert Menzies signed with black ink, John Gorton, Malcolm Fraser and Billy Snedden demanded attention in earlier pages. Yes, it certainly was illustrious company.

Other signatures included visiting dignitaries and celebrities. Now there was young Max and his dad from Hobart, Tasmania. Part of the press club history.

Big Max was seated across the table from former prime minister, Bob Hawke, whom he got to know in ACTU days. To suggest there was added pressure to perform was an under-statement. We were both nervous for each other. One hour of live television with no commercials could be an ordeal.

A red light shone brightly on the 'on air' camera. It is now or never. The chairman, Ken Randall, introduced what he believed to be the only father–son combination of speakers in Australia.

Symbolically, the chairman tossed the 20-cent coin high into the air—end over end, head over head. We waited like two Test captains on the outcome. Big Max won the toss and promptly asked yours truly to speak first. It could have been a Test match. The vast crowd of politicians, public servants, press and businesspeople applauded. I could sense this was going to be a memorable luncheon. Expectation everywhere. What would the first hour throw up?

Big Max obviously thought, 'Well son, you're on your own and I've got half an hour to suss out this crowd.' He understood the benefit of being able to interpret the early crowd reaction while I was speaking.

The content may well have been a roast, but it was merely two men—father and son—indulging in a bit of verbal jousting—nothing sacred. My father the builder, me an architect—more conflict in the making. But more appropriately, a lifetime together. Memories.

Exposing your own sense of humour is one of the best ways to win audience support. So I decided to share a small window into how a father and son, builder and architect, Big Max and Little Max might co-habitate—the odd couple.

He worked hard all day as a builder while I studied most of the day at the Royal Melbourne Institute of Technology. Then after three energy-sapping hours of football practice at the MCG, I would return home to our flat in Camberwell. Dinner? We ate a lot of take-away Chinese meals and fish and chips—health food of a nation!

Homework one night was an assignment to design a dozen condominiums using the contents of a dozen Redhead matchboxes. After dropping randomly the contents of the matchboxes like 'pick up sticks' onto a metre-square piece of Masonite (the base), I presented my Master Builder father with the completed design. I was proud of the aesthetic quality of the glued and coloured structure. My site plan, floor plan, side elevations and typical sections showed a student's flair for colour and design. It was midnight. 'Well Dad, what do you think?' I asked, looking for support.

Architects—all pretty drawings and no responsibility!

Never one to miss an opportunity to score a point for the builders he replied. 'Not bad—but I've got one serious question. You see that cantilevered roof, balcony or floor?'

'Yes—I admit you need to use your imagination!'

'It's not my imagination that is the problem. How are you actually going to support that overhanging structure?'

Without thinking I shot back with: 'That's not my problem, I'm only the architect—you're the builder!' I grinned and Big Max beamed. He had nailed me again.

'Nothing's changed since I went to building college. Architects —all pretty drawings and no responsibility!' The concept struck a chord with the crowd—connection made. Subject relevant.

It's not always the belly laugh that is important, but sometimes the wry smile or appreciative chuckle that are better indicators that all is going fine. Watching Bob Hawke's face light up, I was sure in his days as ACTU chief he would have heard similar comments. I always attempt to have myself 'involved' in each story, incident, fact or anecdote—a reason to be talking about the stuff. This way you will not become captive to reciting what someone else wrote or said. Sure, gain stimulation from around you, but use your own words. It will give your performance and yourself more credibility. A sort of verbal heartbeat.

I contemplated telling a wonderful anecdote about my early days as a kid when both Big Max and Little Max played cricket in the same team. Time was against me so I decided not to start and then have to cut it short.

My innings of half an hour at the lectern complete, I rotated the strike. I wished my father good luck like a partner at the fall of a wicket, but deep down I worried. I was not sure if Big Max would stick to his part of the deal—the important part. That is finishing at exactly 2 p.m.—not 1.56, or worse, 2.07 p.m.

Fingers crossed—he was working beautifully. Later he was to confide in me that the ordeal was like following Sir Donald Bradman to the crease after he'd peeled off a century at a run a minute.

Normally politics dominated this room, but not today. He challenged my schoolboy experiences, criticised architects and revealed a fascinating life behind the bar and on building sites.

And, most interestingly, my old man decided to tell my (our) story about the fence picket. Gee it was odd listening to him tell the yarn. But he had a valid reason to tell his (our) story, because he was in it. This is how I've told it many times before.

At the age of about eleven or twelve I was lucky enough to play cricket in the same team as my old man. I should tell you that curators in Tasmania are not too flash. They turn up about every three months to cut the grass. And even though this particular game was a grand final—Mathinna versus Oatlands—I don't think anyone would have seen the match. It certainly wasn't televised. And just because it was a Grand Final made no difference to the fact that there had been two and a half months between haircuts—the grass stood a metre high.

The situation didn't worry me because I had the ability to hit the ball in the air, but several of our other players were a little bit inhibited by this sea of green.

So, imagine the scene at the ground. Thirty-five of our relations and their dogs have turned up. The buzz; the barking; the horns tooting all the way around the ground—you can feel the tension. Electric.

> *Every speaker loves that high-energy response.*

We required 17 runs to win. Normally we would romp in. But this time, it's just a little bit tight. There's only ONE ball remaining. And to make matters worse, there's only ONE batsman left: my old man. Now how good a player is Big Max, to be batting number 11 behind me in a Sunday afternoon competition?

The state of play doesn't improve. The previous batsman to be dismissed has chopped down so hard on a yorker, he's broken the handle of the only bat in the club. We used to drop the bat and run up and down between the wickets in those days. Sponsorship was unheard of back then. Bats were hard to come by.

No way was the opposition going to lend us their only bat. The old man walked out the gate, grabbed a picket from the fence, confidently strolled to the wicket and took block. My old man is a dead-set impostor. He possesses one shot and one shot only—that is, a slog straight down the ground! Fair dinkum, my old man would not be good enough to snick a ball to third man. Still, the opposition were not going to let him off lightly—no matter what the odds!

The fast bowler has the ball in his hand and is giving it heaps. He's polishing it up and down; really giving it plenty! But all the polishing in the world won't make this cork composition ball shine!

Now I should mention there's a lot of science involved in polishing a cricket ball: Total maximum utilisation of one half of a cricket ball up and down your trousers, right? I've been involved with my body for a fair while now and I can't come up with a better groove than the groin for polishing a cricket ball. Every fast bowler worth his salt has been known to rub a cricket ball up and down his trousers. Apart from one, Jeffrey Thomson. Tommo holds the ball in front, belt buckle high and gives it the gyrating pelvic girdle.

In the fast bowler charges, through the long grass. Up high on the toenails in the delivery stride. (Tasmanians have got real long toenails). With a huge grunt he lets the ball go and the old man gives him the big Colgate smile back down the track.

I'm NOT OUT nought at the other end playing for the 'red inks' (NOT OUT). Now anyone who knows anything at all about the game of cricket will realise this—you must not bowl a ball pitched middle or leg stump to a tail-end batsman, otherwise you'll end up being hit straight down the ground on the first bounce for 4 or, depending on how much right hand is on the bat, a whack through mid-wicket for 6!

So what does this bloke do? He bowls the big, rank half volley—it doesn't swing a lot because there's not much red paint left on the ball. And like most number 11 batsmen, the old man plays straight down the track. Plonk. Almost trod on the ball, which has got to be a bonus. Where do you think the ball's landed? Pitched middle and leg stump! Half-volley! head down.

So the old man hits through the most magnificent on-drive you've ever seen. We take off, run 1, 2, 3, 4, 5—and there are five guys scampering around at deep long-on. Can't find the ball anywhere in the long grass.

As we crossed for 6, I shouted to my partner: 'Dad, that's it. You can only run 6.' He said: 'Bullshit son, keep running, keep running'; 7, 8, 9, 10 and there are now eight fieldsmen way out at long-on . . . can't find the ball anywhere. 11, 12, 13. The old man has now got heartburn, dyspepsia, the whole catastrophe! You just don't come in first ball in a Grand Final and chip 13 off your toes, do you? I mean, that is really not on—no matter what grade of cricket you play. 14, 15, 16—There are now ten of 'em out there at long-on—and still they can't find the ball anywhere.

The wicketkeeper is the only bloke left—standing over the stumps ready for the run out. The rest of them are stamping down the long grass with their boots. A quarter of the ground is trodden absolutely flat. The rest of the grass is a metre high.

Seventeen runs. What a fantastic performance! To get up and win the Grand Final, another flag for the dressing-sheds back home—against the odds. You little beauty!

Great sportsman that he was, the old man looked across to the opposition captain, who was a bloody long way away at long-on, and walked in his direction.

'Do you really want to know where the ball is?' he asked with a grin. Then he turned over the picket—and wedged deep into a nail at the end of the piece of timber was the cork composition cricket ball. Unbelievable!

Could only happen in Tasmania!

Leave your audience believing everything you've said ... and believing in you!

The story lost nothing in the way he told it. Because he was the one holding the picket he described it differently and in more detail—red gum, giant square headed nail, splinters. He also squeezed a few laughs at my expense, but it was a wonderful yarn shared with a captivating smile and matching the enthusiastic feedback from his audience.

Provided you have a credible reason to talk about a subject, your own point of view in the structure of the telling will make it so much more believable.

So, my dad, the raconteur of the long run, was rewarded with much laughter and a standing ovation at 1.58 p.m. Thank you very much. Mission accomplished.

It was worth the travel, the nerves, the preparation. His applause was well deserved. Every speaker loves that high-energy response. Such was the feedback to Channel 2, they have since replayed the program several times. While travelling to Asia on a cruise ship, my dad bumped into several Australians who said they watched the telecast in Bangkok. It's a small world, and you never know who is watching or listening. This is why every time you stand up in front of an audience you must aim to perform to your absolute best. No excuses.

After this appearance in Canberra, we both received more invitations to speak. Leave your audience believing everything you've said . . . and believing in you! It is a perfect way to market your talent.

> **Back then, speakers were expected to travel hundreds of kilometres for no petrol money— maybe a free meal (if you were lucky).**

After becoming a regular speaker you will understand which functions to attend free of charge and with a smile . . . and when to ask a fee. A speakers' agency can be an enormous help when and if you become good enough to be speaking professionally.

In Australia, public speaking for a fee didn't just happen—and wouldn't have happened if it had not been for the persistence, foresight and strength of character of an intelligent woman named Joan Saxton. After five years of voluntary speaking in Australia, she decided to set up Australia's first speakers' agency.

The year was 1965. 'Beatlemania' was sweeping the world, we were shortly to embrace decimal currency, our imaginations were fired by the space race, and because of television, the spoken word was even more in demand.

But the concept of actually paying a fee to a speaker was almost impossible to grasp. So strong was her belief that speakers should be given a fee for their talent to entertain a gathering, that Joan approached the Yellow Pages to take out a listing. At first they wanted to list her under 'entertainers'. She wouldn't have a bar of that. A lesser person would have wilted! Reluctantly they agreed to create a new heading for 'Speakers' Agency and Speakers'. Today that heading lists many agencies and names—no longer the solitary name of Joan Saxton Speakers' Agency.

JOAN SAXTON

In the formative years, it was not unusual for Joan to have to handle an inquiry from Yellow Pages about the possibility of supplying loud-speakers—such was the ground-breaking nature of her business. Most callers had never heard of speakers expecting to be paid.

At one function in the early days, when the possibility of having to pay a fee came up, the president couldn't hide his discomfort. Joan asked him a simple question: 'Would every person here buy the person on their right a drink?'

'Of course,' he replied.

'Well,' said Joan, 'that's about all a speaker's fee will amount to.'

It was a most unpopular idea for a business. Not even top-flight academics were paid to speak then. On one occasion, after asking for a fee for the speaking services of the brilliant professor

W. H. Frederick, she was told bluntly: 'I thought professors were supposed to profess quite freely.'

She admits it was a hard, hard slog and the helpers she had in other states had a hard time too. Joan reckons that if you pioneer anything, then don't expect to make any money for some time. Today, the foundation stones laid by Joan are supporting the sixth largest speakers' agency in the world.

England's first lecture agency in London began way back in 1879, so the British soon became used to paying for fine speakers. The concept exploded in the US where today it's not unusual for an ex-president, astronaut, army general or business guru to be paid tens of thousands of dollars for one performance.

Listen and learn from other fine speakers, then practise, practise, practise!

Joan believes that people still do not respect the spoken word, or the amount of work and experience needed to succeed in the public speaking profession. Nevertheless, people who are good at the craft today can earn a considerable income in good conditions, and in Australia they have one person to thank— the matriarch of the microphone—Joan Saxton.

It is wonderful to attend a school play or pantomime where children are performing—eager little people walking up to a microphone to say their given lines. The experience will enhance their opportunities later when they seek employment. Employees love people who have an ability to express themselves, and this is especially important during the job interview.

How can we develop this skill? Are you born as a story-teller or can a person acquire the elements to get better? Joan's advice in a nutshell is listen and learn from other fine speakers, then practise, practise, practise!

A call to Toastmaster International is a good place to improve your skills. Join their sessions.

When I look back on my own development—keen to listen to the very best teachers while at school, fired up by various sporting coaches, spellbound as my father cast his words like a web across the bar, then as I got older seeking out the better speakers on the circuit and learning from each—it seemed a natural thing to do.

An insatiable appetite to learn and a genuine curiosity for our environment is a helpful attitude to acquire. Develop a keen eye for detail and language. The rewards will be a more credible speech, whoever you talk to, especially in the linkage of story and subject matter—a smooth change of gear into a new subject. Be relevant. Cultivate a good general knowledge.

Practise using microphones. People are so often terrified at the mere sight of one. Seek out a lecture on microphone technique. This will definitely help you understand the intimidating beast.

The three most common types of microphones are: fixed lectern, hand-held and clip-on.

The fixed lectern or lectern-mounted microphone is the most restrictive. You can't move away from the lectern, but it is ideal for a speaker who has many notes to refer to. If you need to demonstrate visual aids use a wireless hand-held model . . . it will allow the freedom to move around but can restrict the use of your hands.

For some speakers they are a blessing because they no longer have the problem of what they do with their hands; hang on with one and express with the other. I like this approach. You can walk closer to your audience yet still make the big hand gesture.

A clip-on microphone is attached to your clothing at a fixed distance from the mouth and allows you to use both hands while presenting your speech. Very popular today.

But always position them correctly, otherwise they can exaggerate noises such as breathing or turning over pages.

Always check the sound system beforehand. Know where the on/off switch is. If it fails, simply ask for the sound to be turned off and carry on without it. Don't fall for the on-again, off-again scenario. In the end your efforts are likely to be sabotaged by poor quality sound. If the sound system plays up once, it will almost certainly do it again. Be direct . . . don't gamble!

The subject of microphones brings to mind Kuala Lumpur in 1997, where Super 8s cricket was being launched. The dinner was lavish—the King of Malaysia's son, several high-ranking politicians, dignitaries, celebrities and famous cricketers, past and present, were in attendance at the Hilton hotel.

Former Australian Test captain and selector, Greg Chappell, masterminded the festival. Before I spoke, I asked Greg if there were any minefields—things I should not talk about, including local customs.

'Naah!' he said. 'No problems . . . not at all. You'll be right!'

I was the after-dinner speaker—humorous anecdotes from fine leg to third man to be digested between main course and sweets.

The before-main course entertainment involved two comedians seated at a desk, TV-presenter style. (A send-up of cricket guru Richie Benaud and Sunil Gavaskar, the legendary Indian opening bat.) They called themselves Richly Boring and Sunny Skar. Richly predictably had a cream jacket with nine powder-blue dots on the pocket.

Richly Boring and Sunny Skar began with enormous wit, playing on cricket terminology events and names. But soon they crossed the unchartered boundary line. The pair verbally hooked and cut their way into local politics. Richly sported a silver hairpiece; Sunny was a black-haired local of Indian extraction, with a rapid-fire accent.

I wasn't aware of the significance of names named . . . or the incidents talked up, but they were obviously scoring boundaries at will. Then the sound system suddenly failed. I was naive to think it was coincidence . . . a minor technical problem!

The comedians didn't miss a beat. They continued going for the jugular. Obviously blood was being spilled on the lush carpet beneath the chandeliers. Laughter was suppressed in fear of self and the entertainers. The King's son and his minders were apparently not amused. A phantom pulled all the plugs.

I can only speculate about the train of events that led to that total power blackout. No sound, no lights, and no windows—the room was pitch black except for the nervous glow of cigarettes like silkworms in the dark.

When order, sound and lights were restored, Richly and Sunny were nowhere to be seen. They had vanished into the night along with their set, like magic. I never did find out what exactly happened to them. I wasn't game to ask. Freedom of speech is not so free in that part of the world.

As for my performance—line and length—never strayed from Australian humour—the perfect diplomat. Never mentioned playing against Gavaskar or commentating with Benaud.

Be careful when speaking overseas. Research and beware of the meaning of words. There is a lot of difference between speaking in Asia, the United Kingdom, Europe, South Africa, New Zealand or the USA. Find out a little about local culture.

The venue—Marriott hotel, Times Square, New York, Australia Day 1992. The black-tie event of 600 plus had an audience consisting of 60 per cent Australian expatriates. My brief was to bring nostalgia, rumour and news from Down Under.

On the night, who would I pitch at—the Australian component or the rest? I followed my gut instinct as well as a very loud Aussie-born singer in an extremely large room—like an echo chamber! Her words reverberated off the polished surfaces like ballbearings rolling around a pinball machine. I wondered whose decision it was to allow her to sing before I spoke. Poor planning.

Timing for my talk rekindled memories of the time I had to speak after a rock band and singer, on a moving ferry one balmy night on Sydney Harbour. It was only marginally easier to keep my champagne glass on the slippery Laminex tabletop than to recapture audience attention for an intimate and quirky chat. The speaker system was hopeless. As we navigated our bumpy way across the wake generated by other craft criss-crossing the picturesque harbour . . . the sound from the tweeters and woofers disappeared into the moist night air. Tough night at the office.

Outside the Marriott hotel, the New York sidewalks were clad in snow. The temperature was minus 3 degrees Celsius. I decided to satisfy the Australians. The rest had no idea what a chook was, and wondered whether I was fair dinkum in talking about hypnotising and kissing crocodiles.

When I suggested we were catching mosquitoes in rabbit traps, my countrymen laughed at the image conjured. But the others found the humour too difficult to grasp.

I am pleased not to have missed the opportunity to speak in that part of the world. A learning experience and a memorable trip. Hey, I'm talking about it now, aren't I?

Enthusiasm is contagious. I hope our enthusiasm for the prospect of taking centre-stage is catching. Never say no, provided you know your subject matter and your audience's expectations.

When preparing for your diary entry it is a help to open a file. Include everything necessary to be successful. Try using my checklist as a front sheet. There are two columns—things change!

The following checklist helps me keep track of all the details needed when planning a speaking engagement.

Speaker Checklist

	Now Prior	2 Weeks
ARRANGEMENTS		
1 Organiser: Name:		
Title:		
Business number:		
Emergency number:		
2 Briefing contact: Name:		
Title:		
Business number:		
Emergency number:		
Organisation/division:		
3 Function:		
4 Date:		
5 Time: Arrival		
Speak:		
Duration:		
6 Venue: Address:		
Phone number:		
Fax number:		
7 Dress:		
8 Audience: Age range:		
Company level:		
Ethnic mix:		
Gender mix:		
Spouses included?:		
9 Travel: Flights:		
Taxis/cars:		
Parking:		
Admittance to building:		
10 Accommodation: Address:		
Phone number:		
Fax number:		
11 Other speakers		
DOCUMENTATION		
1 CV (sent?)		
2 Photo (sent?)		
3 Introduction (sent?)		
4 Program (viewed?)		
SPEECH CONTENT		
1 Briefed:		
2 Speech must include:		
3 Speech must not include:		
4 Introduction to my speech:		

The invitation was to speak at the 1999 Shell New Zealand Cricket Awards dinner just before their team left for a tilt at the World Cup in England. It was much easier than my New York assignment!

Christchurch was my destination, dress black tie and my topic, cricket and laughter.

Apart from coach Steve Rixon and a handful of guests from across the Tasman, my audience would be totally New Zealand. It would be in everybody's interest if I selected several New Zealand anecdotes to include in my talk.

During that week, rioting by spectators and player safety were front-page headlines from the West Indies. To be topical, I began with a blending of the week's events in the Caribbean . . . and recalling the mass hysteria and rioting the 1979 World Series Cricket Australians had to endure in Georgetown, Guyana. Players barricaded under siege in their dressing rooms for two hours. Sixty thousand dollars worth of damage occurred in 45 minutes. Militia police with perspex shields and submachine guns finally dispersed the crowd. A relevant start with emotive impact.

I followed this with the infamous 'under arm' incident at the MCG in 1981. This was the last one-day international I played for Australia. Trevor Chappell gained an indelible notoriety for delivering the final ball underarm. The NZ Prime Minister at the time suggested it was almost an act of war . . . sheer outrage.

I had to suggest that story was being told due to special request. Fortunately, the locals laughed with me and at me, and I thank them for their sense of humour.

They didn't stop when I referred to the streaker who invaded the centre wicket area during the Third Test between NZ and Australia at Eden Park, Auckland. Greg Chappell hit him on the bum with his double-scoop bat several times before police apprehended the culprit. The temperature was only 8 or 9 degrees Celsius.

I mentioned Alan McGilvray's last stand at the microphone as a test commentator . . . then wished Steve Rixon and Steven Flemming, the NZ captain, good luck for the World Cup.

I finished with an inspirational quote. In hindsight it was worth the extra effort to tailor my presentation to NZ ears. The NZ women's team present were happy to have defeated Australia in the Rose Bowl series. I was able to congratulate them with a beautiful cricket quote from a young Englishwoman who loved cricket.

You can never do too much homework for a presentation.

'Do you reckon you could present another similar talk on the same night?' the voice on the other end of the phone inquired. I had already committed to one.

'How far apart are the venues?'

'Not far.'

'Will I have to drive myself?—I don't need the hassle of being confronted with a FULL carpark sign if we're running skinny for time.'

The bloke surprised me. 'I tell you what we'll do. You agree, and we'll drive you and your wife from one venue to the next in a limo. That's if she can stand listening to you twice in one night. It might be a bit much, even for your wife!'

'What about the fee structure?'

'Exactly the same for each talk. Can't be fairer than that.'

'Okay,' I confirmed. 'But how much time in between talks?'

'One hour exactly.'

I still only had a fee and a date. No detail of who the client was or how large the audience was going to be. But the night was black tie. As it turned out, I had agreed to talk to 15,000 International Dream Builders at the Melbourne Park tennis centre. Duration: 45 minutes, then hop into a limo to cross the tramlines and Swan Street to the Glasshouse, to repeat the performance.

They could have at least warned me I'd be speaking to 21,000 highly charged people on one night—up the degree of difficulty. I felt those blowflies start to bounce erratically off the inside lining of my stomach—nerves big time! As mentioned in Chapter 1, nerves and fear cause more alarm bells to go off among people invited to speak than any other factor. It also causes people to say NO!

The Green Room was full of VIPs who were dressed to kill— dickie-bird suits, best frocks, diamonds aplenty, dazzling. These characters were very successful, they were in a convivial mood and didn't have to speak to the masses. Relaxed.

I had been given a sneak preview of the stadium full of people on the way in. The stage was massive, brackets of speakers hung from the roof structure, a kaleidoscope of lights strobed the space, and high revving music was playing. I thought to myself, 'This is a larger crowd than Elton John played to.' It sure is set up differently to men's singles final day at the Australian Open tennis tournament. Very different to the basketball too. Darker! My heartbeat immediately climbed up to 160 beats per minute, similar to a triathlete, footballer, swimmer or bank robber!

Nothing could have quite prepared me for my introduction as I stood apprehensively in the wings out of sight, blood coursing vigorously through my veins. Even the varicose ones in my well-travelled legs were under the pump.

Huge strobes were deflecting coloured laser lights to all corners of the massive moveable ceiling. The banks of speakers were thumping an out-of-control digital music heartbeat. My heartbeat was in harmony—a freaky feeling . . . and energy-sapping!

To the back of the elevated stage was a gigantic polystyrene foam alarm clock. Special-effects smoke was being pumped into the stadium. The final sixty-second tick, tock, tick, tock sounded like a hammer banging inside my cranium. Was my memory box going to be able to handle this. 'What will I say—the beginning is so important!'

The booming voiceover said, 'It's your life, it's your time—take control.' The two-storey high rotating second-hand crossed the number 12 at the top of the fantastic clock. And at precisely the same moment, an anonymous looking man clad in a penguin suit and black tie smashed the face of the polystyrene 'prop' to smithereens with a huge sledgehammer. Pieces of the floating plastic foam were flying through the smoke—the overall effect surreal.

The image of a splendid wedge-tailed eagle appeared on a massive video wall four or five storeys high, beyond the shattered remnants of the clock. Soft focus gave way to sharp edge and the eagle soared on thermals zooming above the earth scanning for potential prey. The title of my keynote talk appeared in letters taller than me, emblazoned across the moving pictures: 'The sky is the limit'. I raised my arms like a prize fighter as I marched to centre stage. I hadn't yet uttered those wonderful comforting first words, Ladies and gentlemen. The applause was thunderous, intoxicating and memorable.

With a television monitor tilted to 45 degrees at my feet showing a digital countdown in large white letters, I let myself go with the energy. My imagination unlocked the door to their vision, their dreams. With every uplifting anecdote, incident or quote they stood and applauded, shouted, screamed.

> **Listen to your reaction. Harness all that energy if you can.**

I'm certain that the huge railway track which supports the roof was on the verge of exposing the magnificent Milky Way. We were believers. The sky was the limit. Confidence is a beautiful quality. Personally, I pushed it to the max, despite being alone in the presence of thousands. The experience was unbelievable. I spoke from the heart with uplifting passion.

My metabolism was raging as I walked off-stage. My wife Kerry was beaming and the crowd roaring. I thought, that's about as extraordinary as a talk might ever get. Savour the response—I did. Locked into the memory bank for easy recall.

Unfortunately there was no time to dwell in the present, share a champagne or even ask, 'How'd I go?' Before I had time to digest a handful of sandwiches and a soda water, the white limo beckoned. I felt like a wrung-out rag, mentally spent with barely another sentence in my system.

Another 45 minutes like that! You've got to be joking. Functions such as that one occur once in a lifetime, I pondered. But I was wrong. Start thinking positively. You need to do it again and 6000 people expect you to be good. Self-talk. Sports people do it all the time.

> **A certain amount of nervousness can add sparkle to a speech.**

So, like a tiring fast bowler I figuratively moved myself to fine leg for a rest and a recharge. I left my wife to mingle with the guests in a 'new' Green Room. I opted for solitude.

I evaluated what I said to the best of my memory, made a few jottings, tossed in several new stories for my own sanity and closed down my thoughts. Not easy when your nerve endings are jangling with excitement.

Before I knew what was happening I was again under the hypnotic spell of the mega-clock ticking away inside my head, the beauty of the eagle soaring high, in control, then bang, smash, crash, the clock was on the floor in pieces and I was on my feet clutching the microphone for support.

Yes, I had done it again, with a similar result. It was memorable—a real charge, and another image to replay on my mental screen if ever self-doubt threatens my confidence.

A certain amount of nervousness can add sparkle to a speech. Nervous tension is a perfectly normal reaction to any strong emotion. Emotion starts the adrenaline chasing around your body. Your heart rate increases, your blood pressure rises, and sweat glands in the skin work overtime to carry away the excess heat produced.

That's exactly how I felt as I walked into the Green Room at the tennis centre before Talk No. 1. Threatened. Wow! Listen to your reaction. Harness all that energy if you can.

Before you back out, remember that hyperaction, or reaction, is a natural byproduct of getting mind and body ready for

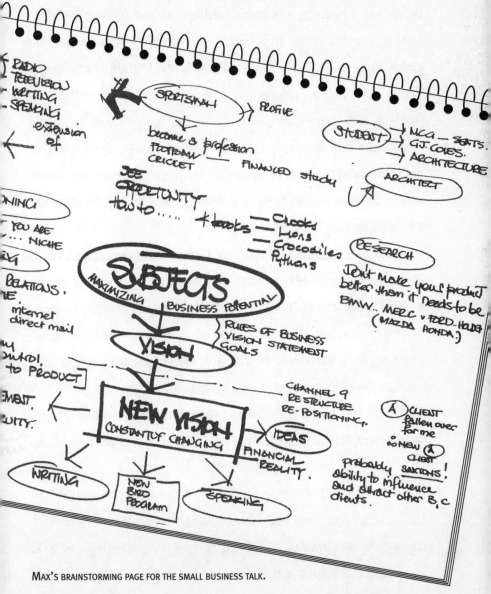

MAX'S BRAINSTORMING PAGE FOR THE SMALL BUSINESS TALK.

maximum performance. Like sportsmen, speakers need to listen to their bodies before going to the lectern. This will help explain why we are sometimes nauseous, tired or hyperactive.

I've seen it all, and it is not out of the question to see a batsman dry retch into the sink. The English opening batsmen of the 1975 Test series did exactly that before confronting the terrible pace twins Jeff Thomson and Dennis Lillee, plus of course, Tangles! Actors, especially on 'first night' are similarly affected. So too grand final competitors. Singer Patrick MacMahon is amazingly hyper-active before performing, so don't feel bad. Feel nervous, but not bad. Recognise that we live in an information society, full of computers and databases, driven by technology. But, it is our ability to communicate verbally that is directly proportional to the sort of success we can hope to achieve in almost anything we do. From classroom to career.

Depending on the function, it's advisable to take a book to read if you are to arrive early. Don't get caught up in small talk before you have to perform. You will be much better off in a quiet corner or room, reading your notes and clearing your head of noisy chatter. Your head will be filled up with enough chatter and unanswered questions of your own making.

Think about your performance, then start. Everyone has to begin somewhere. It is silly not to be heard simply because you are scared.

Sometimes it boils down to not having a clue about the subject. In this case it's okay and advisable to refuse. How often do you wish some poor soul lumbered with the task of presenting a paper, talk or speech had stayed home.

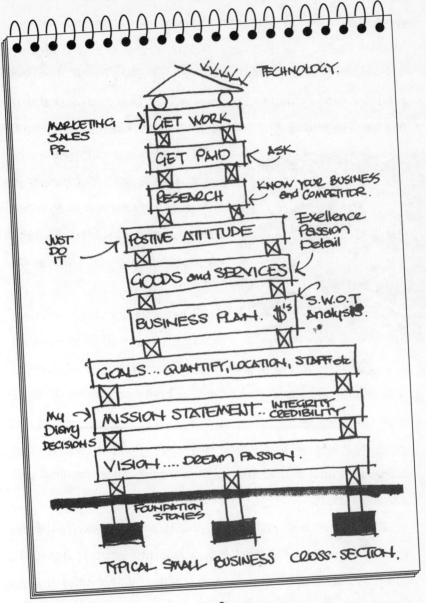

SMALL BUSINESS EXPO—DETAILED MASTER PLAN.

So, if you don't know, say NO. Otherwise start doing your research—books, people, photographs, phone calls, Internet, videos—whatever it takes (WEIT).

After weighing up the question and the subject, I agreed to

speak at the 1999 Small Business Expo at the Exhibition Centre in Melbourne.

I knew speaking about 'Maximising Your Small Business Potential' would require a lot of research . . . I devoted the best part of a week to getting my head around the vast subject.

> *It is a good idea not to drink alcohol before you speak— well, maybe one glass.*

My audience would want to take notes, take away information to help their business or how to set up a new business. Plus there would be an expectation of entertainment. Nice challenge.

What a target: men, women, old and young, all interested in progressing their unique businesses.

Where do I start? Think-tank . . . brainstorm on an A3-sized sheet (see page 233).

After much reading, personal experience and jottings, I decided a diagram would be my best approach to collating my material into a usable format.

My training as an architect helped. To be able to look at the big, broad subject and bring it all together into separate headings. Master plan, detail! (See the working notes on page 235.)

The diagram gave me the flexibility to ebb and flow with the interest shown by attendees of the presentation.

It was comforting to watch so many people nodding in agreement, then writing a note. To emphasise the issues and advice like a lecturer, there was a need to reinforce a comment a second time but couched in different words.

I had my start well planned. 'Just because you are in business and are your own boss will NOT guarantee your financial rewards and satisfaction.' The belly of my talk was structured around the diagram.

My finish was written on a piece of paper which I produced from my coat pocket: 'Remember one can never be too positive. Business will continue to be attracted to where it is invited . . . and it will always remain where it is appreciated.'

This was a perfect forum to take questions. I was able to talk specifically about what the questioner wanted. One question stimulated another.

Question time is a great barometer for whether your message is landing.

Maybe you've just been asked to propose a toast or vote of thanks. Don't believe you're not important enough to do the job. Merely keep your ear on the speaker and remember you're speaking on behalf of the rest of the audience. By all means, take notes and if the speaker is good, say so, and say why. The crowd will back you up. Then you can sit down.

> *A great majority of the audience will be nervous with you, for you.*

If you do know something about a subject, you'll be interesting, passionate and credible, and you won't make a stuff-up.

Persevere and initially only speak about things you are familiar with. Don't tell me you won't enjoy the sound of all that clapping.

Let me give you an understanding of how I gather my thoughts and prepare to battle through to the end. It works for 50 people and it worked for 15,000.

Having planned either precisely, or roughly what you will be saying (see Chapter 4), try to condense the lot down to no more than six or seven headings, or bullet points. Write these down in that little notebook that we always carry just in case we need to capture a thought, a funny line or language. If not, try using a business card. The theory here is to bring to the forefront of your mind the key areas or subjects of your presentation.

> **Gents, I shouldn't have to reinforce this, but check your fly.**

Now you only have a handful of words to remember. If you forget one, no one but you will know. You may even run out of time to fit in all you want to say in the allocated time.

Double-check your timeframe—in my case it is generally 45 minutes with no question time. But I'm more than happy to answer questions. Five minutes or so before you are to speak, allow yourself to stand up. Go for a nervous one. Whatever, but get physical. I like to touch my toes, roll my arms over like a butterfly swimmer and bang my chest in much the same way as a gorilla—many of you may think I'm a baby gorilla anyway. This will focus your senses and up your heartbeat.

It is a good idea not to drink alcohol before you speak—well, maybe one glass if you must. Remember, the microphone will take on the role of a magnifying glass and any slight mispronunciation of a word—the slur—will be amplified. Show some discipline until after the performance.

Okay, it is time to stop preparing your address. You've run out of time. Let go. You have prepared as best you can. Walk confidently to the lectern, be proud you are the chosen one, and that it's not someone else. The audience will relate to you.

A lot of people reckon they could successfully write a book. Ask them! But my goodness, most people are terrified at the thought of making a speech. A great majority of the audience will be nervous with you, for you. Feel better?

You've checked your clothes: shoes first. There is nothing worse than a well-dressed man or woman in shabby shoes. Old-timers reckon shoes are a dead giveaway to a person's character.

Gents, I shouldn't have to reinforce this, but check your fly—there will be nowhere to hide once you've opened your arms (and legs) to embrace the crowd.

Ties as a rule should be understated. Make sure you are not wearing lipstick as a result of the good luck kiss—save that for 'well done' later in the night!

Even under normal lighting a guy can take on the appearance of a lamington. Brush boys, brush!

Dark jackets with dandruff, particularly under fluorescent lights, look bad. Even under normal lighting a guy can take on the appearance of a lamington. Brush boys, brush! And don't be a badly dressed scarecrow. Women are always examined more closely than men. This may or may not be a disadvantage. Jewellery should be kept to a minimum for both sexes—it can be very distracting.

> **Between 30 and 90 centimetres, I am effectively blind to typeface ... by putting them across my five-times busted nose, I probably aged ten years.**

Where are your notes if needed? In your pocket with your business card perhaps.

For those of you who choose to read, make sure the script is lower case with capitals and not all capitals. It is much easier to mispronounce words and make mistakes when reading in capitals. If you need glasses to read, check that the lighting is sufficient, especially on the lectern ... and make sure the lettering is large enough to see. It is too late once you are on your feet and talking. A colleague of mine who has poor eyesight, thick glasses and very large typeface on his notes had the suggestion made to him that if ever he could not read his notes, he only had to hold them up ... for the audience to read.

Now where are those glasses? Once at a Melbourne Football Club match day lunch, I had scrambled quickly from the studios of Channel 9 where I hosted the Sunday *Footy Show*, to the Legends Room at the MCG in the Great Southern Stand.

I was more than 30 minutes late, and in my haste, I left my glasses in my *Wide World of Sports* blazer. Now, between 30 and 90 centimetres, I am effectively blind to typeface. Before I had a chance to read the menu I was called to take over from our stand-in MC, Bill Guest, the Melbourne Football Club's co-president. The first thing he reckoned I should do was to thank the sponsors—a list of more than 30 names in small type. Absolutely no chance— a large grey cloud passed over the ground, making the light inside the room even lower.

Thinking quickly, I publicly admitted my forgetfulness and asked if anyone had a pair of magnifying glasses I could have a lend of.

Quick as a school kid in a classroom wanting to leave the room for a nature call, Richmond Football Club president, Leon Daphne shot up his hand. I accepted his offer and put on some very delicate gold rimmed rectangles supporting pieces of finely ground glass. Very nice, although by placing them across my five-times busted nose, I probably aged ten years. My vision was now perfect. Thank you Leon for saving me from a huge embarrassment in front of my team's supporters.

Unfortunately the good deed wasn't rewarded. The mighty Tigers whimpered through the day and the Demons fired to gain a berth in the final eight. In fact, they defeated Adelaide, the 1998 Premiership team two weeks later in the finals. That was before Adelaide regrouped and went on to win the AFL flag.

I have said it before, but one of the biggest plusses you can have is a smile. It certainly requires less muscles to smile than it does to frown or be deadpan. (No one wants their speaker to be a soporific social butterfly with the look of an Easter Island statue.) If you can manage a genuine or sincere smile you will be well on the way to getting your audience on side.

A smile or a chuckle in the first few minutes will help your audience relax and believe me, they are going to enjoy, as well as learn from, listening to what you have to say.

The conclusion of a talk is just as important as the beginning. It should be a quick gathering together of the whole, and leave your audience with a big smile, a big finish.

At the end of 'Antarctic wife . . .' which is Joan Saxton's speech about existing for fifteen and a half months without a husband and coping with boys aged twelve and ten years, Joan says, 'At last he walked into our house, and I suddenly realised there were three wonderful words.'

The sentimental in the audience immediately anticipates the three words: I LOVE YOU, but not correct.

They are, 'ASK YOUR FATHER,' in a raised voice!

I accepted the opportunity to speak to Rotary, Lions and the Apex Clubs on more than 150 occasions before I deemed myself consistently good enough to ask a fee. I'm pleased I became familiar with the process of preparing a speech and doing it for no other reason than it was fun. The feedback was a nice massage for the ego. Don't be scared to grow your ego in the nicest possible way. Your audiences will make sure you keep it in check. The art of after-dinner speaking could be summed up by that wonderful old Henry Ford quote: 'If you think you can—or if you think you can't—you are bound to be right.' There is no shame in believing in your own ability, improving and perfecting that ability.

> **It gets down to timing, tone and nuance.**

To excel in the art of after-dinner speaking is a great social accomplishment. And believe me, it is an artform. As in the world of words, easy reading means hard writing. Only the most expert after-dinner speakers can afford to speak without considerable preparation. Don't risk it. Crash and burn!

Did you know that verbal impressions only account for 7 per cent of a speech's audience impact? Tonal impressions

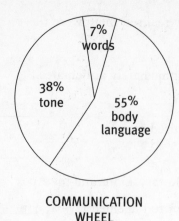

**COMMUNICATION
WHEEL**

account for 38 per cent and visual impressions account for a whopping 55 per cent. Body language is very important, but so often overlooked.

Man or woman, be attractive to look at on stage. You are the star attraction, so look like one, and speak like one. Play to your plusses.

It is an incredible stat: '93 per cent of your talk comes after you get the words right'.

Creating atmosphere is important. If you are a minister of religion, wear your dog collar. It will worry them to death at first, but if you turn out to be like the Anglican vicar, the Reverend Harlin Butterley, it will delight and intrigue them. I believe once a group of businessmen sitting at a table at one function took bets as to whether or not he was a real vicar.

Creating an inspirational, emotive atmosphere is a must for sporting coaches. To be effective they have to be heard, and they have to connect

RON BARASSI.

244

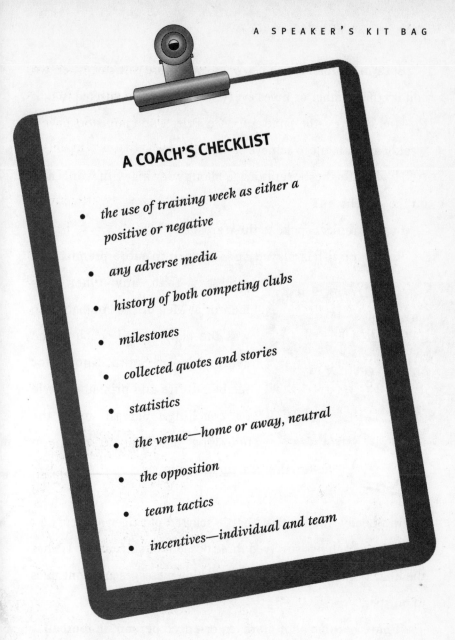

A COACH'S CHECKLIST

- the use of training week as either a positive or negative
- any adverse media
- history of both competing clubs
- milestones
- collected quotes and stories
- statistics
- the venue—home or away, neutral
- the opposition
- team tactics
- incentives—individual and team

with their players. They need to instil a sense of 'anything is possible, together we will conquer'—a self-belief.

Put simply, it gets down to timing, tone and nuance. There we see the coach extract every percentage point from the communication wheel. It is not just a matter of what these leaders say, but how they say it . . . and when!

Being a football coach becomes even more difficult when we add up the number of times every week they are expected to talk to—and inspire—the same audience. Priests and ministers have a weekly assignment to achieve similar results.

How do the best operators go about winning with words and on the scoreboard?

In AFL ranks I spoke to three greats.

Ron Barassi has played and coached in more premiership successes than any other. His mentor at Melbourne Football Club was the man named coach of the century, Norm Smith. Known for his blood, fire and brimstone style of coaching, Barassi used the following checklist to draw on material to fire up his team.

> **Visuals should never be used to prop up a weak presentation.**

Kevin Sheedy, the amazing battle-scarred old tiger and current Essendon coach has survived three decades of skirmishes. He has the knack of reinventing himself and his messages and continues to prosper.

'I have become a lot more experienced person, in football and in life.'

'You learn from your experiences and challenges if you are half smart.'

'You keep relooking at the years past. You appreciate that you did not do things right in some areas, and that you have been doing well in other areas.'

'Find out what the players need and do whatever it takes to give it to them.' (Kevin Sheedy)

This is exactly the attitude a good speaker must have—the parallels are there.

A lot of coaches have come and gone without success since Sheedy took over the Bombers in 1981. Almost 450 coaching games later, he reckons the way to get the message to the players is simple.

At the blue-chip Carlton Football Club, David Parkin prefers to 'theme' his battle plans and delivery. On his day, eyes popping, and veins bulging from his neck, David is irresistible as a motivator. That's why he's enjoyed multiple success on that last Saturday in September.

One of my first memorable encounters with the hot gospelling mode of delivery was at the hands and acid tongue of the late Mr Harold 'Nunky' Ayers who played football and coached alongside my father.

Nunky Ayers was known as Mr Football in Tasmania. At the invitation of our team coach Noel Ruddock, he coached the Friends' School first XVIII to a grand final victory against St Virgil's in 1966—only the third time in eighty-eight years that our school had won a football premiership, and a result to cherish.

Nunk delivered the half-time speech—a beauty.

'I can see 'em in there now with their rosary beads, crossing themselves and praying to the big fella upstairs to help them. But believe me, when they run out on the ground, hit 'em with everything you've got, and I promise you they'll bleed and hurt just like the rest of us!' he yelled as he chopped the air with a flat hand, laying down the law. 'Now follow me!'

Truly one of the great orators.

Nunk hunched his shoulders and ran like a wounded bull at the closed dressing-room door—boom, crash, clunk! The door was flattened. The human battering ram charged through. As captain I was first to follow. He turned and thumped me in the chest.

'You make your ol' man proud of you, son!' he quietly requested in an intimate moment shared. I think I did.

What had happened was that Nunky had gee'd up Val Evans, the curator, to remove the pins from the door hinges ten minutes earlier. Nunk hit the door from about seven metres in a wonderful show of strength—hip and shoulder. We never looked like losing. This was a Nunky Ayers special, perfected over many years, but it didn't always go the way of the coach.

> Audiences everywhere love something that moves, provided they can see what it is clearly.

The occasion was a combined Huon Football Association team against the Kingborough Country Football Association at Sandfly. This was the beginning of the running-through-the-hinged-door at half-time theatre—many football identities have claimed it for their own, but Nunk was the first. My dad, Big

Max, had wagered ten pounds (twenty dollars) on the Huon side. They were six goals behind at half-time, and his money was not appearing secure.

Nunky alerted the caretaker to undo the door hinges to the adjoining door. It would require a screwdriver to remove the hinges from the door jamb.

'I want to see the blood rolling out of your eyes and ears, and attack those bastards with hip and shoulder as if running through a doorway!' The coach stormed the door, intending to show the way it was done. But unfortunately the caretaker either forgot to, or couldn't find the screwdriver.

Nunk hit the door as though he was auditioning for a Hollywood movie. The door failed to budge, and Nunk ended up on his rump with an injured shoulder, embarrassed and the focus of everyone's laughter.

Climbing to his feet, he was ropeable—like a gorilla gone mad. Big Max reckoned what followed would make Ron Barassi, Kevin Sheedy, David Parkin and Alan Killigrew appear bland by comparison.

Well, it turned the game around. Big Max notched 8 goals in the third term and turned a 32-point deficit into a 5-point lead going into the last. Huon won by 14 points. Big Max never got paid his ten pounds, and assures me he never ever bet on sport again.

The players' dressing-room door is quite a prop by today's standards. But, if used properly, the effect will live on into the future in the minds of all present. Nunky proved that if at first it doesn't work, then don't give up. He made the best of every percentage point inside the communication ring—well-chosen words with passion and timing. His body language and tone of voice were exaggerated to extract an emotional response then the 'how to'. 'Just follow me . . .' crash through the flattened door—and ultimately victory.

When considering the use of props or visual aids, first ask yourself whether they are necessary. Will they actually enhance your performance? They are totally inappropriate for the after-dinner speech, for example. But they can have an effective role to play at lectures and business or motivational presentations.

Visuals should never be used to prop up a weak presentation. Take another look at how to polish up your words—then make the decision. Yes or no to visual aids.

Props aren't limited to slides, video or computer-generated graphics. And they can, if used correctly, add drama and impact to a talk.

The mere exercise of lowering the lights can create an expectation, an excitement and intimacy. But remember, when a speaker dims the lights he or she will lose eye contact with the audience. This can sometimes be similar to letting go of the steering wheel.

Let's assume you have decided to use visual aids. Consider these factors:

- **Use your energy to concentrate on your words first.**
  Videos, computer programs, slides and flip charts will cost not only money but also time. Your own freehand lettering

and sketching, if consistent and legible, can work as well as clinical typefaces and sterile graphics.

- A poor prop is worse than none at all—believe me they will stop listening to what you're talking about if they become preoccupied with sub-standard visuals.

- When using visual aids don't leave them on show too long. They become a distraction.

Professional lecturers at universities and schools prefer to use visual aids all the time. They believe it is impossible for students to continue to listen and concentrate continuously even to great lecturers without a break.

Lecturers also love student participation—it holds the rest of the class in a state of readiness and enhances their general level of interest. Demonstrations at front of class on stage are desirable. We all learn more quickly when we are allowed to actually do the things that we are being taught. I'll never forget my first couple of attempts at arc-welding in front of my architecture colleagues. The girls in our class only wore nylons to that subject once—sparks everywhere. Ruined.

Audiences the world over love an object that moves, provided they can clearly see what it is. Of course there is also the obvious video or film presentation.

Demonstrations with a working model are always a winner. These are used as often as possible when they marry up with the lecturer's subject. Congruant.

Magnetic boards are effective if available, but make sure you use lots of colour. Even with all our technology, the old-fashioned blackboard is still around and kicking . . . but it has some disadvantages. Writing becomes difficult to read after the board has been wiped or sponged down several times.

A better way is to use large sheets of white paper or butcher's paper clamped together by a spine of parallel pieces of timber. These are easily fixed to a fold-away artist's easel or stand. Black or any colour chunky felt pen can be used and the paper sheets either torn off or folded over the back. If these sheets or charts are going to be used several times, consider using linen sheets. They last longer and are easier to handle and transport than large cards. The size should be just under the one metre square, or whatever is available from your art supplier. This size, with large lettering, can be seen from any part of a normal classroom.

If you are working in a larger room or auditorium you will need to consider if this kind of visual aid is going to be visible.

The fewer points on each chart the better. They should be self-explanatory. If you have to explain what it is all about because it is complex and over-crowded with numbers, words and drawings, then it is not worth using. Keep it simple.

Illustrations are always better than numbers and words in terms of arousing interest.

VISUAL BACK-UP: A USER'S GUIDE

- *Don't overcrowd illustrations with too much information. Spread the message over two or three slides or flip-charts.*

- *Design the scale and look of your visual aids to suit your audience and the sort of impression you want to make. The way you put your message across will say a lot about you personally and perhaps your organisation.*

- *Upside-down or reverse-order slides or projector failure will reflect adversely on you. Double-check.*

- *Write all words horizontally, even on pie charts.*

- *Where there are several figures on display, highlight or circle the one central to your message. Bring it alive.*

- *Make sure colour combinations are legible. Don't get too fancy with colours—you'll confuse. (Pink, white and black—NO.)*

- *If you must show columns of numbers (please avoid this if you can), be consistent in their presentation. e.g. if years are displayed horizontally across the top of illustration, do not display them vertically on the next visual. Also don't use percentage on one slide and a mark out of 10 for the next.*

- *Check that your visual aid—size of letters and numbers—is legible from the back of the room.*

- *Graphs and graphics must always be honest. Never distort the facts with artistic licence. If you are caught out trying to cheat a little, your credibility will blow out of the back-stage door.*

- *If it is necessary to refer back to a particular slide or print, duplicate the slide or flip chart. Struggling back will be a distraction and it's not fair on the slide operator to have to 'discover' the correct image again. It mostly won't work.*

- *If you use a laptop for graphic presentation, make sure you have a back-up copy of your presentation.*

- *Be extra cautious if screening sensitive and confidential details.*

- *Check all equipment, including your computer, in advance. Don't rely on others—do it yourself. Be sure.*

- *Don't go overboard on the use of pointers. Laser lights are very popular at the moment and user-friendly. But ask yourself whether you really need to point. Isn't the visual material clear enough in the first place?*

- *Check the level of light. What is necessary to black out for successful AV use? Rehearse when and where it is planned. Talk to the person operating the lighting and make certain s/he understands your needs. No surprises.*

- *Do not to mix visual aids. Jumping from video to slides and flip-charts will cause confusion—a band-aid solution.*

- *If you are using video or film, make sure you are not speaking while it is showing. Do not ad-lib when introducing or showing clips. Let the operator know exactly what your word cue will be. For example, 'Let's go to the videotape.'*

- *Once you have finished making all of your visual aids, number them very carefully. Only begin when absolutely everything is in place. Do not number slides or images 3a, 3b, 3c, etc. This is a sure-fire way to stuff up 3, 4 and 5.*

Your visuals should be in harmony with what you are going to say. If you say one thing, especially with numbers, and the image states the facts differently, you will appear foolish, unprepared and unprofessional. Say what you mean to say and mean what you say. Support your figures.

Say what you mean to say and mean what you say.

Rehearsal is critical to success. It will ensure you relax, secure in the knowledge that all of your material is in the correct order to that master of all presentations—timing. Consequently, 'on the day' you will know merely by glancing at your watch how you are going for time—ahead or behind.

Leave nothing to chance, because when nothing is left to chance the performance and presentation of visual aids will go like clockwork.

Along with all of this precision, never underestimate the impact of surprise and emotion among the audience.

As patron of ROMAC (Rotary Overseas Medical Aid for Children) I was part of a closing 25-minute presentation at the national Congress of Rotarians at Darling Harbour Convention Centre in Sydney. First-up information and inspiration was delivered by the founder of ROMAC, Barrie Cooper from Bendigo. He spoke about his dream, the passion and reality of being able to help almost 150 young people since 1988 in urgent need of medical attention. Nearly fifty ROMAC patients have been treated in Australia.

I was allocated only 10 minutes to share my thoughts about

Barrie and the children we had been able to help. How could I share all that I wanted to in such a small window of time? Discipline and planning. Understanding what 10 minutes meant in terms of words (10 x 60 x 4 words/sec = 2400 words approx.) was the key.

I decided to talk about one child only—Jesse Ryder and her courage.

At the age of just four months this tiny baby was abandoned by her mother. Six years later, while living with her aunt, she was

horrifically burnt when her dress caught fire. The doctors said she was as good as dead. It took most of a day to get her from the remote Fijian village of Lekutu by rowboat and through the jungle to the nearest basic medical centre for rudimentary treatment.

With burns to 90 per cent of her body, Jesse's future looked grim. Scar tissue had welded her arms to her sides; her legs were joined by 7.5 cm of scar tissue, and her chin was attached to her chest.

When ROMAC located her, the youngster's distorted and scarred body had stretched to accommodate her growth. For fifteen months she had been kept hidden from the world. When Barrie Cooper and his wife Claribel were returning a mended child to Fiji, they glimpsed a look of hope in those big, brown eyes.

At Cliveden Hill Hospital in Melbourne, the brilliant reconstructive surgeon Dr Murray Stapleton freed Jesse's limbs and chin. In all, Jesse was operated on fourteen times. After being hospitalised for eighty days Jesse was finally able to lift her arms, walk at ease and smile naturally . . . things we all take for granted.

I posed the question. 'I wonder what Jesse is up to right now? Wouldn't it be great to see her again?' On that cue, Jesse quickly made her way from high in the back of the massive auditorium past rows of cheering people. 'Don't forget me . . . don't forget me!' The crowd of more than 1500 people stood as one to get a glimpse of this tiny girl—grinning.

Murray Stapleton's outstretched arms met Jesse's at the edge of the podium. If Jesse could be adopted, Murray would be first in line . . . me second. We asked her two or three questions. Her replies were timid and softly spoken; the smile lopsided but genuine. A beautiful little girl.

From stage to back row, glassy eyes gave way to sobs and tears.

ROMAC had 25 minutes to make their presentation—people, slides and Jesse. I dare say no one that stood in that hall that day will ever forget the impact of that close.

So far ROMAC have helped more than 150 children get a chance to live, as we would say, a normal life.

Titles of talks are very important to attract interest, sell a speaker and convince the client. Marine biologist Reg Lipson's first crack at a title was pretty bland: 'Underwater Exploration'. It would probably only appeal to groups of dedicated divers. Limiting! After chatting to Joan Saxton, they called it 'Exotica and Erotica of the Deep'. It gained him many engagements.

A good talk is like an Apollo space mission.

At the Best of Health 'From Bedroom to Boardroom' seminar in Sydney, Dr Ross Walker was brilliant with his provocative freshness on the subject of heart health and happiness. The leading cardiologist is the author of two fantastic titles—*If I Eat Another Carrot I'll go Crazy* and *What's Cooking, Doc?*

Doctor Rosie King was compelling listening. Rosie helps couples find balance when partners have differing sex drives. The experienced sex therapist and educator called her presentation 'Good Loving—Great Sex'. An absolute winner.

Father John Brosnan, former Pentridge gaol chaplain and Catholic priest speaks about 'Thirty Years in the Nick'.

Bill Green or WEG the master cartoonist, and a great friend of ours, appropriately titles his presentation 'Stretching Things a Little'. (Like my nose, teeth, moustache and chin. Thanks, Bill.)

It is ideal to have a few different titles. This will give the decision-making committee something to chew the cud over before saying 'yes'. I like to shape my talks to exactly what is needed at the function, then think of an interesting title. It works for me to have a briefing first then agree on a title. But this doesn't suit every situation. For example, printing may already be completed on a seminar program or a 'theme' agreed on for the event.

Consider the enormous numbers of charities, sporting clubs, schools, corporate conferences and seminars, institutes and technical associations there are in Australia. Each might generate three or four 'occasions' every year at which speeches will be needed. Tap into the possibilities. Believe in your ability to make a contribution—you can and will.

An invitation to speak to a meeting of Rotarians or other charity groups is a perfect environment to generate word-of-mouth reputation of your ability. Twenty years ago I had never given a motivational address—I had listened to many but never delivered.

Ronald Dale Barassi, the Australian Rules icon and super-coach, was unable at the time to keep his commitment to 'fire up' and inspire a small group of executives from Philips Industries.

The procedure to accept the job then work out how later was not foreign to me. Architects operate like this all the time—I've done it myself. Unsure of exactly how the building sits on the ground near the staircase and entrance, simply draw in a tree or two, add a few people and a couple of cars. Beautiful set of drawings—no problems. Sort out the detail later.

My first target in terms of research was Dr Dick Telford, now an administrator at the AIS Canberra. Back then he was the fitness coach for the Victorian cricket team. Even today I will go back to that speech skeleton for inspiration. I approached Dick first because I respected his opinions and he was accessible.

A good talk is like an Apollo space mission. Without a great launch you're going nowhere. You must engage the audience's attention right from the start. Turn them on first up. If you fail to, then making points understood later will be twice as difficult.

I really was a beginner that night, and I began: 'In business, sport or for that matter, life, it is your choice—to be a winner or a loser . . .' I was choosing to be a winner merely by turning up. The audience didn't know Barassi was not coming! Imagine their disappointment—no blood, fire and brimstone. Only the genial giant fast bowler from Bay 13 at the MCG.

It took me 5 or 6 minutes to state my case, justify being there . . . and gain credibility. I have never glanced back since. But I have continued to work at that original skeleton being current and relevant. Being sensitive and aware of my client's expectations is important.

Recently I found myself back in the same room at the RACV Club in Healesville. Even the U-shape of the table setting was similar. Only the colour of my hair and the corporation

> We knew it would be a tough night. No cars and no noise meant no people—maybe no pay envelope.

was different. This time it was Zurich Insurance Company—a wonderful bunch of guys and gals to spend an hour with. Question time was all-encompassing and challenging.

On debut two decades back, I tried to keep my core message simple and relevant. I think it worked. If you are a beginner, try to bring your personality to the performance. Maybe get one, two or three amusing, serious or fantastic ideas to talk about and talk to your audience in the most natural manner possible. Imagine you are around a campfire 'talking' to a few intimate friends. Share a secret, give a little of yourself. Hook them up and take your friends on a wonderful word picture journey.

Never introduce a story or anecdote by saying, 'That reminds me of . . .' or 'I heard a very good story . . .' This is bad. Let the story glide in of its own accord . . . 'as happened to the building surveyor I knew . . . there was a time when travel was different . . .'

I had driven on, for 20 minutes, past the venue, the Woori Yallock Hotel. Visibility in the low-hanging fog was 10 metres—like pea soup.

The sportsnight panel consisted of Peter Bakos the miniature jockey, myself and the great E. J. Whitten, Mr Football. By the time I found my way to the muddy, dim and deserted hotel car park it was 7.50 p.m. Ted pulled up beside my car.

We knew it would be a tough night. No cars and no noise meant no people—maybe no pay envelope. It unfolded into a remarkable evening. We pushed open the bar door to expose P. Bakos sitting on the counter, both hands blue from the cold, cupped around a whisky on the rocks. Dressed in a boy's suit.

'Where have you bastards been?' Peter asked. Ted chipped in, 'We're bloody early'. The realisation hit home—empty pub! Ted said, 'Geezzuz . . . what are we going to do? I can't fire unless there's 200 in the crowd.' Completing the knuckle-crunching handshake.

The sum total of attendees that frosty July night in the early 1980s was thirteen, including the hotel proprietor, his wife and son plus the three guests of honour (the panel). It was like the last supper. Long wooden bench laden with food and drink—too much. Nevertheless we contentedly sat and chatted. The more Ted drank, the better and bawdier the yarns.

The half dozen 'extras' who paid to be there that night will never forget it. That's what storytelling is all about. Don't think the publican didn't contribute to the night. He and Ted kept topping each other. The facts at no stage destroyed the elasticity of the stories. This was not a pompous telling of rather unimportant clusters of facts as many nights turn out, but a genuine, spontaneous interaction of people.

We all possess a collection of unforgettable incidents. And they will always work in the retelling, provided you match your material to the audience. A scoreboard of characters colour life in sport and business, and a few become mates. All are potential subjects to extract a laugh from. As Ted, Peter and I playfully described many well-known names, the name Keenan kept bobbing up. The ambience and crowd was ideal to recall yarns such as this after-match scenario centred around Mr Keenan.

Three huge drops of blood made an interesting abstract pattern as they splashed quietly into the bowl of cream-of-chicken soup. My team-mate, Peter 'Crackers' Keenan, had managed to get his nose broken earlier in the afternoon in a bitter brawling encounter between Melbourne and Essendon. Judging by the swelling and the exaggerated kink in his more than ample nose, Essendon not only won the match, but they also won the fight!

Crackers Keenan is not a pretty bloke at the best of times. In fact I'm sure his head was chiselled out of granite. And his recently busted beak didn't help. Nevertheless, our weekly after-match ritual of getting together was now well underway. Win, lose or draw—it was always good for the team spirit and morale.

Sitting opposite the huge, macho ruckman was the wife of one of Melbourne's most respected businessmen. Their blue Rolls Royce was parked outside the restaurant and she was dressed in splendour—blue rinse hairdo, bright red lipstick, enormous diamond sparklers hanging from each ear and several dead foxes draped across her pale shoulders. The beautifully manicured lady couldn't help but notice the three rapidly spreading blobs of blood in my mate's bowl.

Cool as an ice-cube, the big fella looked up, straight across the table, took a deep breath through his partly blocked nose—to stem the flow of blood without having to use his handkerchief—then confidently plunged his silver spoon deep into the heart of his soup.

At the same time the elegant lady's cheeks became ashen-grey. Yes, as she feared, Crackers was going to eat it—blood and all. How could he? All it took was a quick stir and raise of the eyebrows.

There he was, Peter Pius Paul Keenan, fresh from the famous Catholic college at Kilmore—Assumption—dressed in a 'closing-down sale' priced, purple polyester suit, pink shirt, wide Paisley tie matching his even wider lapels, white socks and an outrageous pair of black pointy-toed shoes. It was clear to see our man was right at the forefront of early 70s fashion, even though he was sitting on his taste buds.

Within seconds he'd swallowed the first spoonful of bloodstained soup, with much disgust all round—it really was a sickening sight. His 'friend' across the soup bowl waited only three more spoonfuls before leaving the party. Crackers said, 'Where's she gone, the night's only just begun!'

But so too had the meal . . . not much more was eaten by anybody after the starter from Crackers! A real showstopper.

> **Always be shorter than anyone dared hope. Leave them wanting more.**

Now, I admit this true story would not suit a corporate occasion, but with a glass in the hand, E.J. to back me up, and a captive audience—yes, a real pub story.

By way of comparison at a much more formal gathering:

George Bernard Shaw was once invited to speak at a dinner in England where the speeches had been far too many and far too long for the patience of the audience. They waited expectantly for the wordsmith who was to speak last. When the roar of applause had subsided, he said, 'Ladies and Gentlemen. The subject is not exhausted, but we are!' and then sat down.

Always be shorter than anyone dared hope. Leave them wanting more. Try to be topical, tactful and have a nice mix of seriousness and levity.

Begin with a chuckle or two and work up to the more serious message with an orderly arrangement of your subject matter. Work hard at being effective and pleasing in your delivery. Try listening to your tape-recorded voice or even better, study a video of your performance. Get a second opinion from somebody who cares.

Develop high and low, light and shade to maintain attention. Delivering your words in a monotone voice will make you a sleep-inducing loser. Also don't underestimate the effect of a longish pause—silence.

In constructing what you have to say, build a little undefinable extra into your presentation, for instance, a current news item, achievement or critical facts.

A good speech, especially after dinner, should sound relaxed, even impromptu. Believe me though, a lot of preparation is necessary to achieve this effect. If your speech is learned by heart and recited parrot fashion, it is in grave danger of sounding level or flat (no highs and lows in delivery) and unconvincing. Remember it is a talk and not a read!

The aim is to have made your audience amused and eager for you to continue speaking—a perfect time to finish.

Similar to the skill of writing well is the need to discover your own voice. This is the personal manner you bring to instinct. Trust your gut feeling and believe in your own ability. Then practise, practise, practise. It is the only way you will improve.

One cold and miserable evening in Bendigo, Ron Barassi stood up to speak. Initially you could hear a pin drop. The legend was in the prime of his coaching life—a man to sit on the edge of your seat and take notice of. An air of expectation gripped the local Mechanics Hall.

Totally out of character, Ron decided to try his hand at making people laugh. Normally they would cower into a corner at the sound of his booming voice. After 15 minutes the locals were restless and began chatting among themselves. The master coach tried to resurrect the window of opportunity by doing a total about-face and began to talk serious football politics.

Then the crowd got what they expected—flashpoint! A young woman enjoying the confidence of alcohol stood up and shouted from the belly of the room with Ron in mid-sentence: 'Shut up Barassi. You love the sound of your own voice too much. So sit down and give someone else a say!'

Ron's eyes focused on the loud woman like a wedge-tailed eagle about to strike. Then he started to verbally rip his poor unthinking prey to shreds.

'A lot of people have paid good money to come here tonight to listen to me speak. So if you don't like it then piss off! You see the door with the EXIT sign—go! (arm outstretched) The trouble with Australia right now is that there are too many people like you around—don't listen, don't want to believe what they hear. They sit on their bums criticising others for having a fair dinkum crack at the world. Now get out of here, or sit back down and let me get on with what I want to say!'

Ron was red in the face, pointing, pointing, index-finger moving up and down like a pistol about to be discharged. This was the

> **Develop high and low, light and shade to maintain attention. Delivering your words in a monotone voice will make you a sleep-inducing loser.**

real Ron Barassi. 'Give us more of this,' you could hear 'em thinking. The girl was a blubbering mess, with tears flowing like a dripping tap. She stayed seated . . . wounded!

Yours truly can have the opposite problem. If I remain too serious for too long—there is an expectation of humour. I need to blend my subject matter with my attitude and voice—a little mischief.

PERSONAL REPORT CARD

- *Was I interesting?*
- *Was I boring?*
- *Was my humour effective?*
- *Was my subject matter in keeping with the topic or theme?*
- *Was my energy level high or flat?*
- *Did I irritate?*
- *Did I answer the wants?*
- *Was I genuinely sincere?*
- *Was my closing statement effective?*
- *Did my start grab them early?*
- *Was my dress appropriate?*

Remember, some of the most memorable messages are couched in humorous stories, quips or incidents.

Don't be in too much of a hurry. It will take a few talks before you completely discover your proper voice and gain the confidence to use it. Persevere—the result will be satisfying.

> *Remember, some of the most memorable messages are couched in humorous stories, quips or incidents.*

Have someone you can trust to be an honest sounding board. Most people won't really know how to react to objective questions about your performance, and will be too shy to say where you might improve. My wife Kerry is perfect for me. It doesn't take me long to get over the criticism. Then I thank her for her perception and honesty. We all need feedback, no matter what our pursuits.

To experience the spontaneous applause after 'bringing the house down' will make you feel amply rewarded for any amount of preparation and rehearsal.

Every time I speak at a function, Saxton monitor my performance by asking the client to rate both me and the agency. This provides essential feedback and keeps my mind sharp. Not everyone can have a speaker's agency monitor their performances but we can all be honest with the person in the mirror. There is no value in telling lies to your image in the mirror.

When you do finish speaking take time out to reflect on how you performed. Ask yourself a few hard questions. Answer them honestly in your diary or journal. I have a special section at the back of my diary for speaking notes and thoughts. Let's call it the Personal Report Card.

Answer these questions positively and you're doing most things right. Make a habit of documenting each of your performances.

Mike and I have come to the conclusion that there are too many shows—breakfasts, lunches and dinners—to fit inside the cover of this book. Inside our collective heads is the sum total of our life experiences, the achievements, the tragedies, the lessons and the pitfalls. So many images and sounds keep jostling for recognition.

We trust our words are peeling off the pages to excite and to help you overcome the nerves and fear. We trust the read is giving you an insight into how it can work for you. Have confidence and trust yourself.

From here on in take it to the max—you're well equipped. Go to it and good luck. Make your next appearance at the microphone a memorable experience . . . FUN!

As I often say, the mind once stretched by a new idea will never return to its original shape. Dare to use your imaginary can opener to expose your mind to all the exciting possibilities of speaking in public. You'll forget the fear that used to be a lid on your potential. And smile . . . remember, a smile is an inexpensive way to improve your looks!

7

The Box, Radio and the Press

Think of cameras and microphones as a bunch of friendly people. Confide in them.

MAX WALKER

Words are, of course, the most powerful drug used by mankind.

RUDYARD KIPLING

In the first part of the twentieth century, a public speaker would address a gathering in the order of hundreds and gain an immediate reaction—a standing ovation, the odd boo or a murmur around the crowd. If the speaker was particularly good, the word might spread during the course of the following few days.

Much has changed since the development of a couple of communications miracles—radio and television. We are now able to watch war on television—live! Bombs exploding, people being killed, cities being devastated and an ever-present voice describing the images. The NATO bombing of Kosovo happened virtually in our lounge-rooms.

What a quantum leap from the concept of our friend and colleague, the late Alan McGilvray, who used to create the sound of bat on ball by tapping a pencil on a piece of timber in a tiny Sydney studio in the middle of the night. Pictures of foreign grandstands tacked to the soundproof walls aided his ball-by-ball descriptions of England versus Australia Test matches played in the UK. Australian listeners would huddle around their wireless in anticipation of Bradman and Ponsford, or another green-capped hero caressing endless boundaries to all parts of the ground.

McGilvray was merely using the theatre of his astute mind in 1938. With the help of a delayed telex he would imaginatively relay the scoring sequence of every over. The silky smooth doyen of the ABC was brilliant at using the art of word pictures to convey his passion for the game as well as a player's insight.

Television arrived in Melbourne in 1956, along with the Olympic Games. Can you believe that, back then, the TV rights for the Games were sold for the astronomical sum of £80? Today the Australian rights for the Sydney Olympics are tens of millions of dollars. And good public speakers are paid thousands of dollars. Yes, speaking in public has become a profession in much the same manner as amateur sports have evolved into professional businesses. The major players are handsomely paid.

How did a first-class cricketer, especially one qualified in the profession of architecture, become a member of the poison typewriter club? That is the name cricketers use to refer to the print media and several commentators. Using tone of voice and body language, the reference can be quite cutting and caustic! But generally, it's fun.

After retiring as a player I made my debut as a cricket commentator at Kardinia Park, Geelong, in January 1982. Drew Morphett and I covered the match between Victoria and South Australia for ABC radio. We worked from 10.59 a.m. on day one until 6 p.m. at the end of day four!

Several weeks later I progressed to describe a one-day international between Australia and the West Indies in front of a huge crowd at the MCG. I shared the commentary box with the very best of commentators, Alan McGilvray. In fact I was more nervous fronting up in the commentary box than I was before playing in my first Test match almost a decade before on the same ground. Before going to air,

> *Speaking in public has become a profession in much the same manner as amateur sports have evolved into professional businesses. Players are handsomely paid.*

Mac gave me some valuable advice. 'Son,' he said, 'if you imagine you are talking to a blind man when describing the game you will do all right—call it colour radio, use word pictures.'

I consistently use Mac's wisdom in combination with my own philosophy—it is invariably easier to be an armchair critic than being out in the middle doing all the hard work. Batting and bowling, being vulnerable.

Before each day's play commenced, I would write at the top of my notepaper positioned next to the microphone: 'Cricket played at this level is a very difficult game.'

It is too easy to become a coach at the microphone. Experience has taught me that both the game and the public want a fair, unbiased description of the action without too much advice from old players like myself.

> It is invariably easier to be an armchair critic than being out in the middle doing all the hard work.

These words helped me to get the contest into proper perspective. I was privileged and lucky enough to listen to and meet three of cricket's greatest voices—Alan McGilvray, England's John Arlott and South African Charles Fortune. These gentlemen were able to improvise and remain unflustered no matter what. Each man had the intuitive ability to get inside a player's head, to interpret the possible thought process. A kind of confidence which included the listener.

But let's be honest: there are occasional problems. I've had my share, which began to happen very early on in my career.

Let's begin with my first one-day international commentary stint. The ABC commentary box was a very small hothouse, positioned high beyond the sight screen at the rear of the cigar smokers' stand (for MCC members). The temperature on that unforgettable day was a boiling 45 degrees Celsius. Being an architect, I offered, free of charge, to redesign what was effectively a 2 metre by 3 metre split-level chook house without the wire mesh. The MCC declined.

In order to occupy my position behind the mike I had to climb over the shoulders of both Mac and our ever-reliable master of statistics, Jack Cameron. With a nickname like 'Tanglefoot' it was pretty obvious I was not going to achieve my objective without incident, especially in such a confined space. Tanglefoot off the short run.

The kneecap of my leading leg clipped the silver-haired legend plum on the back of his head. Cigarette at 45 degrees tilted towards the microphone hanging from the corner of his mouth. Binoculars pressed hard up against the thick heavy-rimmed glasses. Mac almost swallowed the glowing cigarette and couldn't hit the cough button in time. The binocs almost fractured the lenses of his glasses as they dropped onto the desk below. The old-timer didn't acknowledge what had hit him. Nevertheless I could sense imaginary smoke floating from his ears. He was not a happy man.

> No Unisys computer in those days, merely a couple of shoe boxes containing our statisticians' lifetime documentation of the game.

My second step landed on the corner of Jack's cardboard box. No Unisys computer in those days, merely a couple of shoe boxes containing our statistician's lifetime documentation of the game. Cards lovingly and accurately marked with red, black, blue and green felt pen. Averages and aggregates. Numbers likely to change were entered in pencil. Rubber in the pocket.

As my size 11 landed, the lid of his facts box yawned open like the upper jaw of a crocodile, sending cards spewing into the crowded members' enclosure like confetti. But no love lost here—he hated my guts . . . well, momentarily! His beloved books were safe, but the career stats were in a state of total disarray.

The old-fashioned headphones used by expert comments man Norman O'Neill were full of stale perspiration—last night's beer. The odour was disconcerting as the contents trickled to below my ear lobes and down my neck.

I finally sank into my seat. My nerves were shot. I knew I'd upset the other two. Soon they settled down and became sympathetic. Both men helped me through my nerves and the initial session of play, which lasted an hour. When it was time for me to climb out, a similar predicament occurred. Now, every article of my clothing was soaked in sweat! My new Pierre Cardin suit, especially obtained for the job, looked as if I had showered in it. Bad luck about the armpit odour and dark patches. Even Aerogard wouldn't work in those conditions! We became great friends . . . in time.

My work in the media has included many remarkable incidents—a lot funny and one or two quite moving. During the Adelaide Centenary Test, ABC colleague Jim Maxwell arrived in the commentary box with a box of Mars Bars. He offered one to me and then took his place at the mike, ripping the paper from the chocolate bar, apparently to take a bite.

I acknowledged him by taking a mouthful. Jim, who was just starting his roster, immediately asked a short sharp question. I had trouble for the next 35 seconds or so attempting to separate my tongue from the roof of my mouth, my upper teeth from my lower teeth in an attempt to answer the question. By this time, Jim had put his Mars Bar down and swayed away from the mike with his hanky over his mouth in uncontrollable laughter. Clean bowled!

Often, in Sydney during the night cricket, several kind souls will make cakes and send them up to the commentary box. As with the Mars Bars, the big decision remains just when and how to take a bite. And to those of us with a devious sense of humour, the objective or challenge is to see which one of the ball-by-ball commentary team can be caught out with a mouthful of cake.

There also have been a few sensitive and emotional moments. During the Fifth Test between Australia and the West Indies in Sydney in 1985, Alan McGilvray was calling his 219th Test—his last. The match neared the final stages of a memorable Australian victory, we'd already witnessed the emotional departure of the great Clive Lloyd. The much-celebrated captain lingered long on his walk from the ground as if to soak in the acknowledgment of the 25,000 spectators . . . one last time!

At the adjournment tea, with only two wickets intact, it was obvious this would be Mac's final session of Test commentary. It was a great honour to be rostered on with him. Alan Marks, the executive producer for ABC cricket, had asked Mac to be in the box five minutes early for special comments.

> *The much-celebrated captain lingered long on his walk from the ground as if to soak in the acknowledgment of the 25,000 spectators . . . one last time!*

The real reason was for him to listen to a special taped tribute from then Prime Minister, Bob Hawke. This was pre-recorded because no one could predetermine the conclusion of the Test match, or Alan's last shift at the microphone.

Mac settled into his chair. He heard his name boom out of the public address system. There was a mix-up. The high-tech electronic scoreboard had begun to broadcast the Prime Minister's tribute for all to hear—45 seconds earlier than ABC radio.

Once Mac recognised the PM's voice he took off his headphones and pulled the sliding glass windows open in order to hear more. Then we had drama as Alan Marks asked Mac to close the windows and trust him. Firstly he refused, and only agreed when he heard the same voice come through his headset.

What the PM had to say obviously moved the articulate commentator. Alan glanced in my direction and whispered, 'What a wonderful compliment.'

Then, just as the game was due to get under way for the final session of play, the diamond-vision screen of the huge electric scoreboard came to life in a kaleidoscope of colour with the words 'Thanks Mac, you are the greatest' etched into the 40,000 light globes that constituted the screen.

Simultaneously, the crowd stood with eyes cast high to Alan McGilvray in the commentary box at the rear of the Sir Donald Bradman stand. Hands clapping above their heads, they gave the man who belonged to the voice, who so many people have loved and respected for almost fifty years, a thunderous, standing ovation.

Two balls had been bowled in the middle as we both stood

before the crowd. Mac lifted his hands in acknowledgement, just as royalty would. Something very special was happening. Above the roar of the crowd he turned away from the microphone choked with emotion, and repeated softly, 'What have I done to deserve this? I'm just a cricket commentator. I do my job like everyone else.'

Alan McGilvray wasn't just another commentator. For almost half a century, from the 1938 synthetic Test match broadcasts, he was the undisputed voice of cricket in Australia.

He ended his innings with grace a few minutes later in the second over when he asked Alan Marks, 'Is it possible to have another commentator in the commentary booth please, I would now like to leave.'

> **'What have I done to deserve this? I'm just a cricket commentator. I do my job like everyone else.'**

He simply stood up, turned and walked away from Test cricket in Australia. Then, with his chair momentarily vacant, I was left with three options. The lump, the size of a tennis ball, formerly lodged in my throat, was now up around my ears. The atmosphere inside the enclosed com box was emotionally charged. Unforgettable. Poignant.

Firstly, I could do a ball-by-ball commentary, an exercise I hadn't attempted in the past. Secondly, I could give expert opinion on the last ten or so deliveries bowled (none of which I'd taken much notice of). Or finally, I could put in a few well-earned words of praise. I opted for the latter. Spoken from the heart . . . as a boy he lit the fire in my belly that made me want to be a Test cricketer.

It might have been difficult for the West Indies batsmen trying to cope with the spin of Bob Holland and Murray Bennett, but it was no less difficult for me, battling behind the mike. Feeling vulnerable and publicly hypersensitive. His empty chair on my left.

> *Alan McGilvray wasn't just another commentator.*

I was pleased when Dennis Cometti finally sat down next to me. He was also stunned and speechless for about 15 seconds. It seemed like eternity, but as we say in the box, the ball was in his court. He was the first commentator I've seen gold-fish . . . mouthing words but no sound!

In the early 1980s I was invited to become Channel 7's cricket expert on *World of Sport*. I was apprehensive at first because the show had been running for twenty-five years with many of the original people. Good luck, Maxie, I thought. I was to need some too!

At Dorcas Street South Melbourne, in a large barn-like warehouse, I was to experience first-hand the on-camera and behind-the-scenes pranks of Lou Richards and his cohorts.

My first day appearing on television was a pretty hair-raising experience. No instruction, no coaching, pick your own subject, and talk when the red light on the camera starts flashing.

Everyone else on the floor in that spartan old studio was joking, laughing and generally uninterested in what I was about to say. After all, District Cricket wasn't exactly the sort of television viewing that would make you put off going to make a cup of coffee.

During my inaugural piece to the camera, I sucked in a long, large nervous breath. But before I could make a second hard-hitting point, the director, the God Almighty stationed upstairs in the control room, had slipped in a commercial break. Finished before I even started.

There is a lot of difference between being asked questions in an interview situation and being the up-front person making the sensible comments. It sure can be tough asking the pertinent questions, particularly if the first two or three thought-provoking prodders manage only a blunt 'yes' or 'no' in response! So to perform articulately and at the same time make sense for three minutes is a very difficult assignment without notes or autocue.

Former GTV9 newsreader Brian Naylor used to speak at approximately five words per second. Yours truly is a fair degree slower at three per second. As you can imagine, sitting in front of camera as a terrified and new face for 180 seconds can seem like an energy-sapping 500-metre dash. It never ends . . . a sprint the entire distance.

So to perform articulately and at the same time make sense for three minutes is a very difficult assignment.

Segments don't always go quite as planned. That's when life really gets interesting. For example, during my second weekend at Dorcas Street, the totally unexpected happened, much to everyone's delight!

The culprit was one of Louie's best mates, mentioned in an earlier chapter. A pear-shaped, bespectacled man, tipping the scales at more than 20 stone . . . affectionately referred to as Uncle Doug or Unca, Doug Elliot was the bloke most likely to plug the products.

He would be Mr Patra orange juice, Mr Red Tulip Chocolates, cheese, meat—you name it, Unca would be flogging as hard as his firm jaw and shaking head would allow.

He had a sharp wit and penchant for poetry, which he often read on air. The big fella's appetite was legendary—it was rumoured that if they X-rayed Unca's stomach, they'd find three or four meat pies nestled comfortably inside without even a tooth mark on 'em! He wasn't a guts as several of his mates often suggested—merely a fussy connoisseur of all edible sponsor products.

> *From time to time things don't go quite as planned, and that's when life really gets interesting.*

Like all of the team, Unca loved a practical joke. I do too as long as I'm not the subject. Unfortunately, as the new boy on the show, my 'initiation' on the set was going to be much fun for everyone, except for Channel 7's brand new cricket expert.

After less than 30 seconds regurgitating several well-rehearsed comments on the leadership qualities of the blond-haired blue-eyed boy from the West, Kimberley Hughes, my friend with the thick-rimmed glasses, appeared alongside the camera. I couldn't believe my eyes.

Now I don't wish to sound rude and unattractive, but this was how it happened. Uncle Doug brazenly stood slightly left of my line of sight. Slowly he unbuckled the belt holding up his creased and baggy trousers. I was in a state of confusion. Should I ignore him and continue talking, try to make sense to a totally unaware audience? I persevered for a few more uncomfortable seconds.

Then, when his trousers slipped past his knobbly kneecaps into a crumpled pile around his ankles, it became too much. The laughter was hard to suppress. Remember, there was no seven-second delay. This was pure, live television. Without even thinking, I blurted out, 'I don't believe it. He's just dropped his daks!'

Unca's reaction was to about-face and touch his toes. He had the worst set of hamstrings I had seen in many years, completely devoid of muscle tone, and polar-bear white in colour.

Meanwhile, cameras were jockeying for position like dodgem cars to capture the mature gentleman dragging his trousers up above the plimsoll line. I've never seen a pair of trousers and fly-zip hoisted so quickly on the silver screen. It was an unforgettable second day at HSV7.

After my initiation, Uncle Doug wrapped his arm around my shoulder: 'That was great son. Spontaneity is what this caper is all about. The show thrives on it.'

How true. *World of Sport* was the only live television show I knew of that could be running 30 minutes behind schedule after only being on air for an hour. The madcap ad-lib and semi-organised 'chaos' was half the charm and attraction of this almost compulsory Sunday viewing in Victoria.

Day three turned out to be every bit as exciting. My motto should have been 'prepare for the unexpected'. This time Lou eased into the proceedings. Again yours truly was on the receiving end. Many people suggested Louie the Lip wouldn't be super helpful. After all, he barely knew which end of a cricket bat to pick up, but he had done a lot of miles in front of the camera. So when the chunky little ex-rover from Magpieland offered some advice, I thought, 'Don't be quick to judge, maybe he's genuine.' The straight face was too serious to believe—but gullible old me did. This rough-hewn, loudly spoken master of the ad-lib suggested I use an 'idiot sheet' like all the pros—Don Lane, Bert Newton and Mike Walsh.

> **My basic problem was not being able to say 'Goodbye' quickly.**

My basic problem appeared to be not being able to say 'Goodbye' quickly enough! In other words, they couldn't shut me up! Lou thought that if I was scripted, the problem wouldn't arise. Shoe is on the other foot these days at GTV9. My little mate is still having trouble distinguishing the difference between a 13-second chat and a 49-second conversation. He watches that familiar 'wind-up' hand movement delivered by the floor manager too often. We both like to have a chat!

At the completion of my District Cricket wrap-up, Louie stood next to the camera, legs slightly apart and arms held high, supporting a huge sheet of butcher's paper. In the corner of his mouth his cigarette began to glow a bright red as he inhaled quickly. His mischievous eyes were dancing left and right, seeking attention. He had all the encouragement he needed.

My architecture-school lecturer, Ron Centre, would have been proud of the lovely uppercase lettering on the beige-coloured paper. The graduate from Collingwood Tech had obviously sat down and neatly written my closing message. What a nice gesture, I thought, as I began to read, word for word: 'Well, that just about wraps up the District Cricket...'

I never did make it to the end of line two, because quick as a flash Lou had dug deep into his trouser pocket and produced a cigarette lighter. No ordinary lighter either—a Dunhill, thank you very much. A sure sign the boy from the back streets of Collingwood had a few bob to spend on himself. Well, he won't spend it on anyone else.

What do you think he did with the tiny gold flame thrower? You guessed it—he lit the bottom two corners of the paper. Everyone fell about laughing as I strained to concentrate for the next 19 seconds. The bottom half of the script was going up in smoke. Lou began to cough loudly. Unreal.

'Someone call the fire brigade—and avagoodweekend' was the best I could think of as a quick way out.

A lot of water has flowed down the gutters of Melbourne since then. Both Lou and myself crossed the tramlines to join Channel 9. I stayed almost fifteen years; Lou is still there.

After watching a troupe of female body-builders complete their routines for the world title one morning on *Wide World of Sports Sunday Edition*, I asked Lou a simple straightforward question: 'What did you think of Diane, the one in the orange bikini?' I knew he fancied her.

After one more squint at the TV monitor, Lou let loose with a rip-snorter of a reply: 'She'd be pretty handy on a half-back flank for Collingwood, wouldn't she?'

Needless to say, we received a hundred-plus letters about his tactless quip. But at the time Collingwood weren't winning too many games and he probably meant it. In fact they still aren't winning many games.

Another Sunday the little bugger poured a mug full of coffee over me during a commercial break. Everywhere—shirt, tie, jacket, trousers. He wouldn't stop apologising for making my underpants hot and sticky. It was very hard to keep a straight face as the floor manager counted 5, 4, 3, 2, 1 and his arm dropped! The light was ON, and away I went introducing the next story. A very tight-framing shot had to be used—throat to top of head, no collar or tie.

Then he dared me to introduce the following part of the show—trouserless—blazer and tie, and underpants. 'Go on' he said. 'You're gutless—Graham Kennedy did it once!'

It never ends. The chatter is constant. 'Did ya hear the one about the two hard-boiled eggs on their wedding night?' I'd heard that one 45 times, but if a new cameraman is on duty, he's worth a try. That's Lou's theory!

The business of talking to people for the benefit of television and radio audiences is not as easy and laid-back as it looks. Each confrontation between the interviewer and interviewee is punctuated with the 'unexpected'.

Maybe that's why I enjoy my occupation so much. It's like being a bowler. The strategy is to subtly play to the batsman's strength in order to find a weakness. And despite all the planning in the world, it is impossible to predetermine what a batsman will ultimately do.

Take for example Geoff Boycott, the former great English batsman. His biggest problem in life was whether or not to play a shot in the first hour or the second hour of a Test match—hardly charismatic, but very effective (151 first-class centuries). Trying to interview some players is a bit like bowling to the English opener's broad bat—very difficult to make much impact.

While I was working for Channel 7, it was my difficult task to have to chat to the assistant manager of a touring Sri Lankan cricket team, Mr W. Silva. In 1984 they had only just been granted full ICC status. Before we started talking, if you could call it that, we used 40 seconds of overlay graphic footage of Jeff Thomson and Dennis Lillee terrifying the living daylights out of them in the 1975 World Cup match at the Oval. Two of the Sri Lankan batsmen retired hurt, thanks to being hit by Tommo.

'Things have changed since 1975 haven't they?'

'Yes,' was his blunt reply.

Always be prepared to load up another question, just in case: 'You have now got some pretty good young batsmen in your line-up?' I probed.

> *The business of talking to people for the benefit of television and radio audiences is not as easy and laid-back as it looks.*

Again, 'Yes,' followed by an agonising pregnant pause and blank stare.

Sweat was present on his forehead. I suspected he was nervous, so I attempted to relax him with an easier question: 'Have you enjoyed the tour so far?'

While he uttered the monosyllabic 'Yes' once more, his team was struggling to score runs at the MCG against Victoria's pace attack.

'Well, what about the immediate future of Sri Lankan cricket?'

Another enlightening response: 'It looks good.'

Then I thought, Here's my chance—go for the kill. 'Why?' I asked.

But the sweaty-palmed assistant manager again did me like a dinner.

'Good players.' He still only half smiled. Talk about defensive! An economy of words.

At this stage, the floor manager was giving me the wind-up signal—index finger dragged across his throat.

> At this stage, the floor manager was giving me the wind-up signal—index finger dragged across his throat.

I quickly thanked the man for joining us on the show and Lou Richards sarcastically yet humorously congratulated him on his enlightening answers to some difficult in-depth questions, and then sent him packing with the usual champagne, carry bag, ham, chocolates and orange juice giveaways.

He looked mighty relieved when it was over, but not half as much as I was. I learned a lot during that harrowing 90 seconds on air—never ask questions that can be answered by 'yes' or 'no'.

Armed with this valuable experience I had ambition to become another Michael Parkinson. In fact, one of the best and most enjoyable interviews I've conducted was with him.

Michael was back in Australia to promote his book *Sporting Lives*. Saul Shtein was producing *Wide World of Sport* then. He was adamant that six minutes would be enough. The man's passion for people and sport was evident as he kicked goals from obscure angles with the help of a dunny door, cherished his choosing of each brand-new cricket bat, fired a dart or two at the bull's eye and talked of being ringside for a couple of the fights of the century. His ability to ask questions is matched only by his ability to answer questions.

The interview lasted 12 minutes before I was asked to wrap up. I could have listened to him sensitively and with humour create word pictures of great memories all afternoon.

By contrast, fast bowlers are an unpredictable lot, especially around the press. At Channel 7 during the 1984–85 cricket season, Rodney Hogg had bowled like a demon against Pakistan in Perth during the First Test. So he was the likely target for an interview during the Second Test at Brisbane. What do they say about fast bowlers—on a clear day you can see straight through one earhole and out the other? Lucky I was considered only a medium-pace bowler!

Now let's be honest about Rodney. He's never liked being interviewed, even today. But I thought being an ex-player and a mate, everything would be fine. Well, I was partly correct. I waited as any good reporter should for the 'customary' half hour after stumps while the boys have a drink. The sun sets very early in

Brisbane in November and the ground was quickly draped in darkness. Thus floodlights were needed for our chat to be captured on videotape.

Finally, Hoggie agreed to come to the microphone—not an ounce of sweat in sight. My introduction was imaginative and sprinkled with several appropriate adjectives to describe the fearsome strike bowler. It lasted about 25 seconds. I was happy. I smiled and turned—only to be greeted with the response: 'Jesus those lights are bloody bright, Tangles. Can't you do something about them?'

I never did get my introduction to Rodney Hogg quite as polished as the first one. But I did manage to get him to smile once on camera, which must have been a career first for the stony-faced 'quick'. He was a mean customer in full-cry—and very good. Ask Geoff Boycott—his bunny.

Then I pursued the world champion super-heavyweight weight-lifter from Bulgaria. Gee he was a strong man! I thought the bar holding the weights was going to break, he loaded so many on each end.

The huge problem with this outstanding athlete was how to make an interview via an interpreter look good on television. First I had to ask my question to the interpreter, who in turn repeated my words in Bulgarian to the man mountain, who then stumbled over a suitable answer in Bulgarian. It took a long time to extract a 'Yes'. Rivetting.

I knew there was no way John Sorell back at the GTV9 newsroom would use the interview. Then as we were leaving, the big fella started to talk to me in broken English. It turned out that he was a cricket fanatic and he suggested he'd love to have a hit on the MCG. Unfortunately time was against the strongman wielding a cricket bat in anger on the sacred turf, but just the thought of it conjures up fascinating images, doesn't it? Wish he'd have spoken to me in broken English at the beginning!

In 1986 it was my duty to cover the story of an exhibition game of Australian Rules football to be played in Japan after the Hawthorn–Carlton Grand Final. The late Jack Hamilton, then VFL president, was to present a genuine, real leather, made-in-Australia Match II football to the Deputy Mayor of Yokohama. The whole exercise turned out to be fun, with the Deputy Mayor and his non-English speaking party entering into the spirit of the occasion.

Again an interpreter was needed to explain what they had to say to each other as they exchanged gifts. The Deputy Mayor could speak a few words of English, so we got him to answer two simple questions with the aid of a bilingual idiot sheet. Well, this guy, proudly wearing a Richmond Football Club jumper over a shirt and tie, was a sensation. He made John Wayne look like an amateur when it came to reading lines.

I simply answered the questions for him, and he merely returned my words back to the camera . . . after only two takes! Brilliant!

Even the super-confident, eccentric Mark Jackson of football, weight loss, battery and media fame has had his difficulties with the interview, so I'm told. 'Jacko', as he is known to his masses of fans, refused to do a live radio interview once on the grounds that he was sick and tired of being misquoted by the press. It's a bit hard to get misquoted when you're answering questions live-to-air on radio. In fact, impossible, eh?

I was once badly misquoted in a newspaper article after my second Test match. I managed to take six wickets for 15 runs against Pakistan at the Sydney Cricket Ground. I ran through their batting line-up after the team endured a night out eating pork sandwiches! And we clinched an unlikely victory.

When asked what it was like out in the middle, I explained that it was easy, having a fast bowler like Dennis Lillee bowling at the other end. The newspaper headline the next day read 'Test Cricket Easy—Max Walker'. Try explaining that one to your mates at work without appearing to be an egomaniac.

In many ways, speaking to the press can be similar to a visit to

In many ways, speaking to the press can be similar to a visit to the dentist.

the dentist. You can hope it's not going to turn out to be a bad experience. Often we're wrong. Which rekindles memories of the little boy in the dentist's chair. The drill operator in white says, 'Just open wide, son, and relax. Trust me—it'll be all right!'

Just as the whirr of the drill commences, a tiny arm reaches out from under the protective apron and grabs the dentist firmly on the testicles with a confident reply, 'We're not going to hurt each other now, are we?'

It's a pity we can't grab the righteous columnists who sit in judgement and preach to the masses, without them having the right of reply. I've never forgotten this description of a critic: 'a person who knows the way but can't drive the car!'

When cricket writers travelled on the team bus and ate with players after matches in my playing days, we used to call them the 'Poison Typewriter Club'. They enjoyed our description and a drink or two. Attitudes have changed. Beware the TV or radio interviewer who has a separate agenda interviewing you. More than asking you questions, they want to impress everybody with their knowledge by filling the question with as much information as they can get. By the time the question has been asked, there is nothing left for the subject to say but 'Yes' or 'No'.

I timed a colleague whose best question lasted 51 seconds. The answer was, predictably, 'Yes!' It was actually very funny to watch.

Don Lane was interviewing controversial American author Hunter S. Thompson. The producers, knowing Thompson's reputation for colourful language, had arranged for the interview to be delayed by several seconds so that if the 'F' word was dropped, it gave the audio director sufficient time to 'bleep' it.

Don introduced the guest. Hunter's first comment to Don was, 'Do you mind if I take my coat off?' 'Sure,' said Don, and Thompson draped the coat around the back of his chair. Unfortunately it fell to the ground and Mr Thompson said, '#@!$ing Hell.'

The studio audience laughed and Don said to the viewers

'Sorry we can't share this moment with you as we've taken a certain precaution.' Don grinned. At that moment the floor manager was waving frantically at Don. There was a problem. The audio was not in delay and everyone heard it.

The important lesson here is that whenever you're interviewed, or appear on a show, always treat the microphone as live. Especially during commercial breaks. That way you'll always be prepared. Some sportsmen will never learn . . . even when they are in the business. Top score I'm aware of is three times—unacceptable!

A slice of bad luck occurred in Perth about six months before Kim Hughes and the other rebel cricketers toured South Africa for the first time in the early 1980s.

Ian Brayshaw of ABC radio and myself were to talk to South African administrator and power broker Ali Bacher (a former South African captain). The telephone hook-up was all set. Bacher picked up the phone in Johannesburg as planned and we were away—a national scoop.

> 'This yarn's got a fair way to run.'

No one else in Australia had been able to speak to Bacher, the man who had a major input into making the rebel tour happen. He was speaking about safety, insurances, money, sponsors, attitudes—everything we wanted was being talked about.

Unfortunately our studio technician or audio-tape operator had not pressed the 'record' button. Many doubted we had actually spoken to Ali Bacher . . . only our word.

Check, check and check again. It turned out to be a bad mistake and really there was no acceptable excuse.

The cast: Ray Martin, Max Senior, Max Junior
The venue: *Midday*, GTV 9 studio, Bendigo Street, Richmond, Victoria
The objective: General father/son chat

Ray Martin opens with a question to Big Max: 'Got any good stories like your son?'

Max answers, 'They're all my stories. In fact, I should get royalties on all those books.' He then started to tell his version of what I believe to

> **'Why don't we go and sit in the audience and enjoy the story. There's nothing for me to do up here.**

be one of the most loved sports night stories in the last thirty years. *Best of Mr Walker*, page 97—'Sunday Arvo'.

Big Max hadn't drawn breath in two minutes when I interjected, and at this stage he had the audience eating out of his hand. I said to Ray, 'This yarn's got a fair way to run.'

His reply was, 'Why don't we go and sit in the audience and enjoy the story. There's nothing for me to do staying up here.'

At the eight-minute mark, Ray and myself were sitting somewhere around deep mid-off in the studio crowd. Ray suggested, 'Okay, let's wind him up—we've run out of time!'

I said, 'Ray, that's your job. You're the host.' So we returned to our seats next to Big Max who hadn't missed a beat. He had several punch-lines still to come.

Archie, the floor manager, was desperately giving Ray the urgent 'throw to the break' sign. Ray was trying, but Big Max wasn't listening. Rather than wasting hand-printed words on the idiot sheets, Archie walked centre stage, arms outstretched in front of the camera like a sightscreen. The audience was having a ball, but Ray was about to have a bawl. And I was not shocked by proceedings at all. After all, he's my dad!

> *After 20 questions, our replies would have totalled 23 to 24 words.*

As we went to a commercial break, Big Max was peering around the huge piece of cardboard proclaiming that he still hadn't finished the story, and it wasn't fair. During the commercial break he even suggested to Ray that if he wasn't careful, he'd be doing his job next year. 'Live TV's pretty easy isn't it, Ray?' he grinned.

It's hard to believe anyone could talk more constantly than my old man, but Mark Spitz, the legendary swimmer from the USA, was being interviewed on *Wide World of Sports* because of his intention to make a comeback to Olympic swimming at the age of 42. I thought he was crazy and questioned him first up about his age and the reality of again being a success in the pool . . . at Atlanta in 1996 (you're right, this was the first and only question). Via satellite hooked up to our studio in LA, the answer lasted twelve and a half minutes, and prevented my sidekick, Ken Sutcliffe, from having any chance for his interrogation. Fortunately the interview was pre-recorded and was able to be cut in half to fit in the six-minute 'window' in the program.

Similarly, a live cross to the greatest soccer player the game has ever seen, Pele. This interview proved almost impossible. Pele was standing in front of a noisy soccer crowd while he tried to answer our questions. Given his limited use of English, coupled with the distracting noise from the crowd, and his desire to promote the power of prayer in pursuit of sporting glory, we found it very difficult to cut short Pele and God—some might say one and the same.

By contrast, the outrageously overpaid giant basketball megastar of the 1990s, Shaquile O'Neal, personified an economy of words. Ken Sutcliffe and I found ourselves with a very tough assignment when we invited him to be a Saturday afternoon guest.

His image filled a wall of twenty Sony monitors. Our questions barely gained one-word answers: 'Yes, No, Yes, No, Too hard, Maybe, No, Yes . . .' After twenty questions, our replies would have totalled 23 to 24 words. With three minutes remaining, I'd run out of questions. When I gestured to Ken to ask the next question, it was obvious he'd run out too. Not quite a pregnant pause followed, but those huge lips stayed motionless on the two-storey bank of monitors.

In our earpieces, from more than one source came the pleading 'Piss him off—Boring—Piss him off.'

Through clenched teeth, Ken attempted to thank him for his 'huge contribution' to the afternoon's sporting content. It's moments like these when you love a commercial break!

The cast: Kerri-Anne Kennerley, Max Walker Senior, Max Walker Junior

The venue: *Midday*, TCN9 studio, Sydney, NSW

The objective: Publicity tour for the book *Chip off the Old Block*

One of the first media stops was the bubbly Kerri-Anne Kennerley and her *Midday Show*. The program used to be one of the best vehicles for any author because of the massive purchasing power of its audience. Know your market. Women buy most of the books.

We were researched by the show's segment producer responsible for our 'spot'. We helped her in obtaining pictures and file footage. We even recommended the ideal anecdotes and stories from the book.

They briefed me. I briefed the old man. Seven minutes was the duration. I stressed to my dad, maybe three answers each would be all we'd get, and a bit of chit-chat with Kerri-Anne.

'WELCOME BACK . . .' KEN AND MAX ON SET.

It is perceived that one of the reasons for my story-telling ability came from witnessing Big Max in full cry across the bar at the Empire Hotel (the better and longer the story, the more beer would be sold). So, in promoting a theme for the Big Max, Little Max interview, TCN's set designers recreated the front bar of the Empire Hotel. Kerri-Anne playing barmaid and Big Max and I perched on stools.

To this day, one of the drinks I've found unforgettable from adolescence (it is still popular in Hobart) was beer with raspberry cordial. This brew was always going to look good on television. The fact that I'd not touched the stuff in thirty years added to the scenario.

> One of the drinks I've found unforgettable from adolescence (it is still popular in Hobart) was beer with raspberry cordial.

The segment begins, autocue intro, cut to Kerri-Anne pouring the first of the two 'raspberries'. The audience welcomes the pair of us and we acknowledge. The first question was fired at Big Max: 'This must bring back a few memories of the old Empire days . . .'

Only minutes before in the green room, with a plan to gain total maximum impact from our seven minutes on national TV, we agreed that under no circumstances would we get involved with the retelling of the 'after-hour raids' by the licensing squad on the pub. Well, it landed on deaf ears. As advice—absolutely useless! The excitement and adrenalin rush from being on television.

Seven minutes later, Kerri-Anne frantically began ringing the bell on the counter to signal 'time up'. I could easily have phoned my contribution in. All I did was nod and laugh where I could—I was never going to get a word in anyway. Nevertheless, a good story—one story only.

We still ran 90 seconds over time, with Kerri-Anne apologising that she really did have some good questions for me. By the way, I had some good answers for her.

I added, somewhat mischievously, 'Yes, it was a good book, I only wrote it.' Followed by a grin through clenched teeth.

At the time I was devastated, or maybe just disappointed. I thought we'd blown a huge opportunity. But in the weeks that followed it was amazing the number of times people came up to me in the street to impress on me what a wonderful guy my old man was: 'He sure can talk, can't he. Neither Kerri-Anne nor you could get a word in.' It only goes to prove that on TV, being natural always wins. My old man is a great guy.

Don't allow yourself to be interviewed because the interviewer can't 'get' someone else. Think of the ramifications before you agree. And if you haven't got something nice to say about someone, generally don't say anything.

Unlike the printed media, a good thing about radio if you're 'live to air' is that you can't be misquoted. But if you pre-record, you can be edited and cut. Same applies to TV.

When being interviewed, have four or five points that you want to make, and if necessary swing the conversation around to include them. 'Yes but . . .' is a good way to alter the direction of an interview. Use your best material. Anticipate the worst possible question and prepare your answer. It's bound to be asked.

> *When being interviewed, have four or five things that you want to say, and if necessary swing the conversation around to include them.*

How does the idea of travelling to Wellington, New Zealand, for a live radio debate on the subject of 'Kiwis Do It Better' sound? I was apprehensive at first, until the organisers of the event mentioned I would be captain of a three-man team, including

Tony Greig, the former England cricket captain, and former cricket commentator as well as Australian rugby union champion Roger Gould.

The attractive aspect of the trip was that our team would debate the negative side of the argument, which I must admit did sit rather comfortably with all three of us.

Our opponents were, as it turned out, three well-rehearsed and talented orators on the topic. A learned man named Jim Hopkins was leader of the opposition, and unfortunately he was brilliant. Batting No. 2 for New Zealand was a batsman used to the position, John Reid, whose main claim to fame is being a cousin to ultra-tall fast bowler Bruce Reid. Third was a grim, determined All Black named Andy Hayden, who definitely appeared over-dressed in a dinner suit, the attire mentioned on the invitation.

Obviously, some Kiwis don't take any notice, because Jim Hopkins was clad in anything but a 'dickie-bird' suit. His white crumpled cotton jacket and light-brown shirt would have been more at home on a university campus. And from the length of his greying hair and manner of speaking, he had obviously spent many a year on campus. Maybe even decades! A career academic.

Each speaker was given six minutes to verbally assault the topic through a microphone system that carried our verbal joust to 32 radio stations around New Zealand. I was of the opinion they only had two, and that they went off air at 9 p.m. when the lights went out.

After talking for five minutes, a huge gong would be belted, the loud message being simply, one minute to wrap! Tony Greig so correctly quipped, 'Five minutes is ample time to present the positive of "Kiwis Do It Better", but six minutes is not nearly enough time to tear the statement apart.'

When the crowd of 500 (497 Kiwis) stopped booing, the lanky blond all-rounder continued, 'We'd need about 45 minutes each!' More uproar.

The visiting trio seemed to be in for a hiding in front of a very parochial home crowd. Our 'three wise men' had been given absolutely no chance to recover from a torrid Air New Zealand landing into a stiff breeze on the extremely short runway at Wellington Airport (the driver must have been a taxi driver in his spare time). Windiest place on the planet.

Anyway, we decided not to go down without giving 'em heaps! And we did.

On the stroke of 8 p.m. Kiwi-time, the exaggerated Kiwi voice of the MC stated unashamedly that he'd tossed the coin, and Australia would speak first.

It was a lie, and I didn't want all of those New Zealanders who had tuned in their crystal sets for the night's entertainment to think we were wimps, so I jumped to the lectern and set the story straight. I took a 20-cent coin out of my trouser pocket and tossed it high in the air, where it sparkled like a jewel in the night against the bright television spotlights. I grabbed it as only a great fine-leg fieldsman could, and shouted 'Heads or tails?'.

Before I even got a semblance of an answer from the local boys, who by the way couldn't believe their eyes, I put the 20-cent piece back where it belonged in the pocket of my hired dinner suit and quietly stated, 'Bad luck fellas, we win—you talk first!'

By the time my tail hit the seat, 10–15 seconds of pregnant

silence had elapsed, and believe me that's a lot of silence on radio. So we caught 'em with their pants down, but I must admit, some six minutes later, we almost wished we hadn't pulled our brazen stunt. The eccentric John Hopkins landed several very low body blows which even hurt Tony Greig, who has come to his senses after leaving South Africa and England, to settle in Australia. A sort of Clayton's Aussie.

> *Nice of the Kiwis to take their plastic toy boat out of the bath and finally give it a go in some real water at Fremantle.*

It's common knowledge that the demographic centre of New Zealand is right plonk in the middle of Bondi Junction, a mere Aussie place-kick away from the Sydney Cricket Ground. While thousands of Kiwis are on the dole in our country and I don't think they should be allowed to get away with it, only 37 Australian-born persons, from whom I wish to disassociate myself, are registered on the dole in New Zealand. I can't understand this because even with the drop in the Aussie dollar they're still getting paid less.

Needless to say, dingoes, beer, cricket and the Olympic Games were heavily commented on by the home side. I bit the bullet and went for broke. I doubt if New Zealand radio will ever be the same again, and not purely because of our strine and Afrikaans accents. 'Australia is a country where men are men and sheep are nervous. On the other hand, New Zealand is a place where men are dubious and sheep are slow, and the sale of gumboots very high—not necessarily to stop tinea,' I said.

More boos, but I continued.

'What about your Prime Minister? At least our PM Bob Hawke can handle the Pritikin diet. The best your bloke can do is go on a "staple diet"! (The Kiwi PM had his stomach stapled.) And wait until the rust sets in—he'll freight real ordinary then.'

They didn't like it!

'How about "Piggy" Muldoon (no offence). Didn't he over-react a bit after the under-arm incident? He practically wanted to declare war on Australia . . . and now big American boats aren't allowed to park in Wellington Harbour. Whatever happened to the ANZUS pact?'

Deathly silence greeted that one. (Very sore point.)

When Tony Greig asked the women to take a long hard look at the fellas sitting next to them or opposite, there were more shouts of contempt.

'There must be some doubt about him, droopy moustache, longish hair and sideburns, pale face, pot belly, poor conversationalist. Does he really do it better? If there isn't a doubt, then you haven't tried the real thing!'

That one went down like a lead sinker, all the way to the bottom of the harbour, but I liked it!

Roger Gould gave 'em plenty on the rugby union scene. Coach Alan Jones and Australia were dominating the world at the time. The All Blacks no longer unbeatable! Today they are just shadows of past glories.

'I haven't forgotten about K-27 or "plastic fantastic",' I mentioned.

Unfortunately, it took a Belgian-born, Australian businessman to have the foresight to enter a challenge for the America's Cup on behalf of the Kiwis.

Do they do it better?

Nice of the Kiwis to take their plastic toy boat out of the bath and finally give it a go in some real water at Fremantle.

There's nothing to write home about in New Zealand either. They spat the dummy when a core sample from their yacht was mentioned. That story hardly made a ripple in Australian waters but was front page for three days in New Zealand, and even then the papers were a day late. How times have changed—they are now about to defend the America's Cup out of Auckland harbour.

The pilot said, 'Turn your watches on two hours when we arrive.' I reckon the clock should be turned back ten years.

> You won't be surprised to hear that I know many lovers of the liquid amber.

Sorry if I've offended any Kiwis, but it was a great debate. I'll admit we lost, but not by much.

Also I should mention the new DB Kiwi Lager. The reason for our gathering was to launch the new export lager. It's not a bad drop. I especially like the label colours, Australian green and gold.

C'mon Aussie, c'mon!

You won't be surprised to hear that I know many lovers of the liquid amber. His mates reckon he does his hair with a rolling pin, but thousands of fans will tell you that Channel 9's former *Wide World of Sports* co-host, Channel 10 and newspaper writer Mike Gibson had much more going for him than an undulating head of ginger-blond hair. And he really does love a beer, even on a cold day.

'Gibbo' as he was affectionately known to a cult following of lounge lizards on the other side of the silver screen and readers, is really everybody's mate. He's an earthy character with a relaxed chatty nature. It is easy to relate to him. He is very much in tune with what the man on the street thinks about sport's controversies and broader issues. He's a good read, too.

Gibbo never claims to be an 'expert', yet in many ways he is. As a journalist, one of the best in Australia, he has a vast track record of following the sports merry-go-round across many different playing fields. And he possesses a mischievous sense of humour, as I quickly found out.

In 1985 on a Saturday afternoon, the *Wide World of Sports* machine used to be a five-hour epic of live television, testing both concentration and intestinal fortitude. We drank a lot of tea, water and coffee during the program. Today, sadly after eighteen seasons, the program is dead! After several hours of fluid intake, one was in danger of overflowing, so to speak. The pressure becomes painful as nature takes its course.

I had only been co-hosting the show for about three weeks in Ian Chappell's absence. As subtly as I could suggest, I needed to leave my seat. There was a look of shock, horror and disbelief from the floor manager, Mike Moore, so I glanced across at Gibbo. I was hoping he was having a lend of me when he said 'That's just about impossible!'

With two hours of the program remaining, I quickly began to go blue in the face. Eventually the understanding floor manager agreed with Gibbo (who was really enjoying my discomfort) that I should be released. As I've said before, there are very few sensations in the world that even go close when you are under that sort of pressure! I had barely four minutes to get back. Relief, phew.

I was soon back in the chair smiling like Luna Park and ready to get on with the show. Then, just as I was about to introduce the next story, Gibbo leaned across to me with his hand over the microphone, and said cheekily, 'Maxie, your fly's undone!'

Well, what do you do? I summonsed all my will-power not to look down. I clenched my clipboard tightly to my tie at about navel height as a screen.

But sport and TV are great levellers, and though it was many months later, revenge was sweet. I arrived at TCN9 in Sydney early one Saturday morning to be greeted with a small item of local scandal—Gibbo's cat had had a bit of bad luck at his dinner party the night before. Great, I thought. Everyone agreed, we should mention it on the show. Mike didn't realise I'd heard about the unfortunate incident. Good.

Then the chance I had been waiting for. We'd just completed a taped segment covering the world equestrian championships. Neither Gibbo nor I really knew a great deal about equestrian events, so we decided to talk about anything other than horses.

'Gibbo, we both love animals a lot, and we discuss them a lot off the air, but is there any truth in the rumour that your cat had a bit of bad luck last night at the dinner party?'

He couldn't believe his ears. How did this scoundrel hear about it? His non-blinking eyes stood out like table-tennis balls. Still no comment forthcoming. Thinking . . .

THE BOX, RADIO AND THE PRESS

Against his better judgement he finally opened up, 'Yeah.'

'Well you can't leave everyone up in the air. Explain what happened!'

So off he went: 'All right, well it was like this—I was carrying the soup bowls back into the kitchen after the first course to put them in the dishwasher. My dishwasher has a lift-down front and a circular shaped window. All I could see were these two cat's eyes going round and round in circles. My cat must have hopped in earlier in the night to clean off some of the lunch plates!'

I asked 'What did you do?'

He replied, 'I opened up the front of the washer and out he plonked on the tile floor.'

'How was he?' I questioned.

'Oh,' he said, 'apart from two bloodshot eyes, very clean!'

> **Clean your plates off a little before placing them into the dishwasher, and keep the door shut!**

Now there's a message in that story. Clean your plates off a little before placing them into the dishwasher, and keep the door shut! Nothing's sacred any more.

Reading sports news for the first time on television for GTV9 in Melbourne would have to be one of the most nerve-wracking experiences . . . next to that first lecturette in Tasmania.

There I was, tucked neatly behind the news desk in the studio with barely a minute remaining in the commercial break. Anxiety plus tax. Finally, Bray, the floor manager counted me down with his fingers below the intimidating lens of camera No.

3: '5, 4, 3, 2, 1.' The red light on top of the camera lit up like an ambulance—it's now or never!

Seated next to me was the then king of newsreaders in Victoria, 'Brian told me' Naylor. He was immaculately dressed as always, with not a hair out of place, and appeared to not have a nerve in his body. Brian's personal hair-dresser used to groom him every night.

Brian had completed his world and local news read in a very professional manner. Then, with a brief introduction to my news reading career he said, 'and now for sport, here's Max Walker!' I was extremely self-conscious about the amount of hair spray in my own hair.

It's very difficult to put into words exactly how I felt at precisely that moment. My right hand had hold of my left in a vice-like grip for comfort, displaying eight white knuckles to the camera. The lump in my throat was now climbing around my ears. In fact, I thought for a moment I may have had the mumps!

Yes, I was certainly very nervous. It began earlier in the day as I discussed what topics were newsworthy with John Sorell the news director and my producer Rob Syme, a man of extensive journalistic experience and receding hair.

By the time Terry, Brian Naylor's make-up man, began to apply the 'pancake' to my face about 30 minutes before the news began, the butterflies in my stomach reached plague proportions. This was a tough introduction—make-up and 'on-air', all on the same night!

Now, it's not an unusual feeling before a performance to get butterflies in your stomach. The trick is to get them in a group formation and flying in a straight line. I can honestly say the variety of butterflies I had deep in my belly must have been ones with large wings—it felt like they were knocking the living daylights out of my stomach lining.

As I spoke, I actually wanted to say 'G'day', but opted to do the politically right thing and said 'Good evening'.

At that moment, my life and everything I had been told to do flashed before my eyes at an extraordinary pace. Here I was the end product of much behind-the-scenes expertise. In a way I was the hope of the side! Like being night-watchman. All that is needed is to occupy the crease for seven or eight minutes up until stumps. That's about the duration I had to remain behind the desk. All I had to do was to correctly read the sporting news, scrolling words reflected onto a glass lens by use of a mirror.

> *At that moment, my life and everything I had been told to do flashed before my eyes at an extraordinary pace.*

Anyone who's ever attempted either will realise that neither is an easy task. The attention of all and sundry is focused on the determination of the person to succeed without a mistake. They call it perfection, and it's very difficult to achieve!

Taking block in the middle of the MCG with only the narrow timber bat in your hands—eight minutes to go, and a crazy fast bowler charging towards the wicket—takes a lot of intestinal fortitude. In fact, the more I reflect upon my stint in front of the television camera as a rookie newsreader, the more parallels I find related to the nightwatchman theory.

Nevertheless, it was pleasing to read for the first time on home ground, Melbourne. And what a great feeling it was to be accepted into the team so readily. Generally in sport and business the best way to be accepted into a team is to perform. Don't talk about doing it, just do it. Actions will always speak louder than words.

When Australia was arguably the best cricket team in the world in the mid-1970s, our biggest single strength was our team spirit. There definitely was, back then, a similar spirit in the Nine newsroom. They continue to win all the important ratings. That means money!

Politicians love the '16 second grab'.

My job was to report sports stories as I interpreted them. I also had to introduce the videotape packages describing each event in the news. At one stage in my debut I felt my eyes must have taken on the glaze of a dead fish's. The glare of the lights and the huge television camera lens pointing straight at my nostrils wasn't comfortable. I could feel myself rushing. The first cricket story was easy. Then came football and I got my tongue stuck around one word. I can't remember which, but I thought, don't blow it now! Yes, I proved I was human, and it was 'live' but in television you're not supposed to stumble. With a nickname like Tanglefoot I guess it was going to happen sooner or later. Amazingly that was fifteen years ago—the experience makes me smile now.

Next I tried to relax as I approached the finish line—the daily double, Bert Bryant's tips, and finally the quadrella. Pronouncing some of the more flamboyant horse names over the years has been a challenge. Even Kenny Callendar has his moments with the totes, especially those names beginning with 'S'!

I did remain not out at stumps that night, thanks to everyone in the team. Like speaking to an audience, reading autocue became more familiar and comfortable but never easy. Read aloud to anyone in your family who will listen. Children are a great place to start.

I've fronted the camera for in excess of 3000 hours of live television and believe me, never take anything for granted. When you get your chance, you might like consider these points:

TELEVISION TIPS

- Don't worry about which camera, it's their job to find you.
- The moment you sit down in front of a TV camera you will appear to be 4 kg heavier than you really are. That's why skinny people look best on TV.
- Don't worry. Once make-up has finished with you, there is nothing you can do.
- People have a tendency to rush. Relax and slow down—consciously speak a little slower. Suck a mint before you go on . . . it'll clear your throat.
- Remember, the slightest move is exaggerated.
- Politicians love the '16-second grab'. Any longer and the network won't use it.
- Keep your hands still—together, clasped. Any gesture should be small, like a show of the open palm.
- As your interviewer researched you, you should do the same on them.
- When interviewed, don't try to convey too much information. Short answers are always more easily understood.
- Study the other people being interviewed, and practise every day. Watch presenters and learn from their strengths and weaknesses.
- When you think you're going to 'er' or 'ah', take a pause.
- Remember it's natural to blink—don't stare at the camera. It's unnatural.
- Always have a glass of water nearby. You may dry up.
- Coloured clothing will work better than white on camera.

Norman May at the best of times has always been a one-eyed Australian, and that's not because one eye is glass. He is so patriotic that even his glass eye weeps during the raising of the Australian flag and the singing of the National Anthem. At one point in Auckland during the 1990 Commonwealth Games, he turned to Ray Warren and asked, 'Do you mind if I sing "Advance Australia Fair" this time?'.

Norman is the only commentator I know who has had a triple orgasm 'on air' as he screamed, 'Aussie gold, gold, gold!' at the Los Angeles Olympics. It is now a legendary comment. To ease the nerves, a bottle or two of Bollinger champagne the previous night contributed to a networking of roadmap-like lines in his eyes. He occasionally has imbibed so much his artificial sphere was looking a bit bleary.

Every time I share a 'quencher' with the former ABC caller with whom I spent my early days of cricket commentary, I can't help but wonder whether his party trick is as captivating as the late Colin Milburn's. He was the former England opening batsman who lost an eye in a car accident in the prime of his career but continued playing at first-class level.

'Ollie' Milburn's practical joke was a classic and like Nugget, the bulbous Ollie was a fabulous raconteur. Give either an audience and a drink and a fascinating evening of anecdotes would naturally and skilfully follow. These guys made some of my school teachers appear second-rate when it came to communication of the necessary points. They had the ability to totally mesmerise their audience with amazing tales.

It was indeed a first-time experience in England when I was

invited to a little pub in Northampton to meet Colin Milburn, the charismatic cutter of a cricket ball. He hated running between wickets, so fours and sixes were his game.

The circle of listeners under his spell in the cocktail lounge that night consisted of a few young ladies and about eight lucky Australian cricketers, including yours truly. After swapping many stories and yarns, Ollie proclaimed, 'Jeezus, somebody's nicked off with my eye! Strewth, has anyone seen it?'

Sure enough, one eye was missing. The limp lid had dropped down over the empty cavity like a roller door with lashes. However, the working unit was alert and sparkled with a playful expectancy. A sense of devious fun was the best way to describe his manner.

He suspected all the players first, and one by one he blatantly 'quizzed' them. Doug Walters didn't have a comeback. He continued to drag on his cigarette and turn his glass of amber fluid towards the light to get a better view of the explosion of tiny bubbles as they headed for the white frothy blanket half-way up.

Finally, Ollie asked one of the women. The one sitting next to the infamous British joker stated categorically that she hadn't sighted it, despite the best possible view. He disagreed and swore in a most remarkable tone of voice that she'd actually pinched it. His remaining eyeball locked into an accusing gaze, which locked into a stare during the brief discussion about his missing 'marble' eye.

Eventually, everyone guessed what he was on about. Like a magician, he kept the gathering spellbound. We all waited for him to produce the marble from its special hiding place.

Then he did just that! Hey presto! There it is!

'Where?' enquired the young woman next to him as she had a tiny taste of her brandy and dry ginger ale. Ollie leaned across to his left, with his good eye covering all quadrants of the circle of friends for acknowledgment. Then he placed one hand around the clutching fingers of the girl's right hand to steady her drink and delved deep into the tumbler of ice-blocks and golden grog with his other hand. The shape of the woman's face dropped a few inches below the bottom jawline in horrible expectation . . . and total disbelief!

She realised that she had been sipping away on her drink, while all the time the missing eyeball that Ollie had now retrieved with his index finger and thumb had been rolling around in the bottom of her glass below the ice cubes. She wasn't sure whether she wanted to be physically sick or grin through clenched teeth in brave acceptance.

Ollie calmed her by suggesting there was no chance of catching germs from his coloured agate. It was always clean. And he proceeded to demonstrate.

'Look!' he said, as he popped it into his mouth. A quick suck or two to make sure he could 'see' out of it, up went the garage door—nobody home and the lights were out. Then he hesitated.

'Before I pop it back where it ought to be, would you like a taste?' he suggested to his squirming female companion, who had now separated the brandy glass from her taste buds by as far as her arms could reach. By now her mouth was pumping copious quantities of saliva from under tongue to flush away the lingering aftertaste of the eyeball.

Even with only one eyeball, Colin Milburn could see he may

have pushed his prank a little too far. She was the equal to this 'delivery', deemed it short of a good length and consequently hit it for six with the comment, 'It's not funny. I hate you!' She then got up and stormed out, a budding friendship nipped in the bud.

Norman May didn't have time to play tricks with his 'marble' on the opening day of the swimming. Nugget and Ray Warren were sharing their three operating eyes, scanning for more information about the kid from Papua New Guinea. And the information available on the kid was scant. Neither of our broadcasters had done much research on swimmers from that part of the world. And neither had ever called a race of any kind with only one participant. Ray may have called horse races with two or three, but only one was ridiculous! Airline problems had robbed the race of its two other swimmers. They failed to show up in time for the contest. Lucky for the kid who had drawn lane 4.

As the starter's gun punctured the air (what a waste of a bullet), both were well aware that the swimmer was going to take about 20 seconds longer than the world record holder, Adrian Morehouse, to complete the two laps, and that meant more air time to fill!

They were nonplussed. Both were not known to be short of a word, although not always the appropriate ones. I recall a classic comment from Ray a few days later when he was calling Glen Houseman in full flight: 'He's a swimmer!' Another time he said, 'He uses every available inch of time.'

Norman and Ray were going to exhaust all their best lines as Felipe took the limelight. Felipe hit the water as if it was a big final. There was a mighty roar from the crowd who appreciated Felipe having a go. The clear blue water, reflecting the colour from the tiles below, was now the domain of the young man from north of Cape York. By this time, his head had bobbed up and down a couple of times in the water, sucking in the air and dragging himself along. The geometric waves were rebounding off the edges of the pool.

All of a sudden the crowd became totally preoccupied with the lone breaststroker, cheering and roaring for the swimmer who knew in his heart he would not qualify for the final event even after a victorious swim in the heat. The New Zealanders in the gallery enjoyed the chance to barrack for a competitor without getting drowned out by shouts of 'C'mon Aussie, c'mon'.

There was a rumour doing the rounds that this was the first time the swimmer had experienced the joy of swimming in a 50-metre international standard pool.

It was said that back home he trained in the river, making sure not to cause too many ripples as they would disturb the crocodiles that floated on the surface asleep in the sun. The 'understanding' on the river was that the far bank belonged to the scaly monsters, and the closest water edge was human territory. Provided each stayed in their own muddy water, no one would end up a victim. At last count the score was: humans eaten seven, crocodiles eaten nil. In theory it worked, but in reality it depended on how hungry the crocodiles were and how desperate the swimmers were to train.

Ray and Norm chose their words carefully as usual, not wasting breath or adjectives. But there was a limited amount you can talk about in a one-horse race, and there was still a long way to go with the end of the first 50 coming up. How do you pump up the excitement in this case? Perhaps do a 'Richie Benaud'—remain silent and let the pictures and crowd reaction tell the story. It's a good philosophy—if there's nothing to say, don't utter a word. Silence sometimes is golden, but there was no silence outside the broadcasting area because the crowd was bringing the roof down, urging on young Felipe to produce his absolute best.

It wasn't the finest tumble-turn we were to see in the pool, but at least he was pointed in the direction of the finish end of the

if there's nothing to say, don't utter a word.

pool. His split was only about 42 seconds, but for Felipe the time was 'quickish'. He was now basically competing against himself, for his self-esteem and for the people who had helped him gain selection.

No need to look under an arm or over a shoulder—Felipe had his race absolutely shot to pieces. Ray and Norman knew it too—their call increased by about 25 decibels.

The touch of a hand against the pressure plate on the wall of the pool stopped the clock at 1:24:43—a career-best swim by our neighbour. He'd cut four seconds off his personal best time. A long way short of world record time.

The kid dashed straight for the victory dais, hopped up on the gold medal spot, and thrust one hand in the air in recognition of victory. It was only a heat, and he was never going to get near a medal, but then it was a personal-best time, and so far he was unbeaten in the games.

Adrian Morehouse went on to take the gold in the event, but Felipe epitomised what sport in the purest form is all about—better yourself first and then if you reach the dizzy heights of being a world or Olympic champion, well and good.

Felipe's performance was what the so-called 'friendly games' was all about. His effort proved that the major battle is between the ears and within the inner body. The number of successful experiences is up to the individual. Felipe was on the way. Felipe never knocked back his opportunity to perform and it paid off handsomely. The bigger challenge was how to call the race!

It was 'one of those weeks' in television. The regular host of the show was ill (Stuart Wagstaff had hepatitis), the executive producer was away in Hong Kong, and Mike was in charge. Ernie Sigley had hosted the show the week before, but he had commitments back in Adelaide. Who could be found as a replacement?

Rather than put a tried and true performer in, Mike decided to 'have a go', and managed to track Ted Whitten down 'somewhere in Gippsland' where he was working in his job with Adidas.

Question and answer in the media can be a minefield.

'You're joking,' said the boss at Channel 9.

'You're bloody joking,' Ted said when he replied to Mike's telegram.

Some big names had been booked for the show so after agreeing to do it Ted was pretty well 'hemmed in'. People like Brian Doyle, Kamahl, former VFL umpire Geoff Crouch sang a song, and the show was to be a good fun one.

After having lunch with Ted, Mike realised that Ted should only have 'a couple' on the day of the show, and placed a ban on him going anywhere near a watering hole, and he agreed. Nevertheless he still tried to 'make a break for it' occasionally.

> *Throw a television camera with a red light in front of most people and they will freak out.*

To his great credit, Ted did everything asked of him, and the show was an amazing success. Moments before he went into the studio he said. 'Mike, I've played footy in front of all kinds of crowds, in all sorts of games, but I've never felt like this in my life. I'm scared shitless!'

As to the unpredictability of TV, this show, which would have been wonderful to air around the time of Teddy's death, was somehow or other 'wiped'. There is no record of one of E.J.'s finest hundred minutes of entertainment!

Throw a television camera with a red light in front of most people and they will freak out. Take away the coloured light and cameraman and call it a radio studio and the circumstances change, but it is no less difficult to perform well. Both are different again from the traditional stand-up-and-deliver technique of an after-dinner speaker.

Question and answer in the media can be a minefield. Ask anyone who has been misquoted or written about out of context.

I use the word 'communicator' to describe what I do for a living. Imagine the engine has four different gears.

In radio it is a constant chat, no black spots—creating word pictures. As Alan McGilvray said, 'Imagine you are speaking to a whole bunch of blind people—keep them happy and you will be well on the way to success.'

In television the pictures are already there. I have heard it described as using the three Es: emotion, enthusiasm and education.

We have described the art of being on your feet in public. Here you have feedback from your audience, the ability to use body language, tone and eyeball contact, different methods of delivery and all the other skills we have discussed as well as audio-visual aids.

Writing is a different gear again, particularly storytelling. The written word is very different to the spoken word. In text the creator of the story has to explain in more detail the senses of taste, sound, touch and smell to bring two-dimensional words and paragraphs to life.

All four gears are satisfying to communicate in, but it is a good start to understand that each is different. Varying skills are required to use them effectively.

Become a student of language and people. Dare to be unpredictable. Never be dull or boring. Believe in your own ability. Back yourself. Practice will not make you perfect but the exercise will make you a whole lot better. Good luck!